Woman's Day
SIMPLY DELICIOUS
COLD DISHES

WOMAN'S DAY

by

Carol Truax

Simply Delicious Cold Dishes

Doubleday & Company, Inc.
GARDEN CITY, NEW YORK
1984

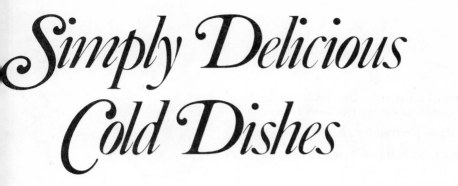

Copyright © 1984 by CBS Publications, the
Consumer Publishing Division of CBS Inc.

Printed in the United States of America

Library of Congress Cataloging in Publication Data

Truax, Carol.
    Woman's day simply delicious cold dishes.

    Includes index.
    1. Cookery (Cold dishes)   I. Title.
TX830.T77   1984   641.7′9   83-16612
ISBN 0-385-18537-5

Contents

Foreword

Food served cold can be tempting and delicious. Cold dishes are not only summer fare, but can be savored throughout the year.

This is a book devoted entirely to dishes that are served cold. You no longer have to search (often in vain) through countless cookbooks in order to find the recipes you want for one or two courses or for an entire cold meal.

Included are appealing salads and splendid desserts, as well as both traditional and unusual main dishes seldom found in cookbooks. There are also menus for simple luncheons and elaborate four-course dinners. Every aspect of cooking and serving cold meals for family or guests is considered.

Cold food is ideal for make-it-ahead entertaining. After the dishes are set out on the table, you can actually be a guest at your own party.

A cold buffet is always appealing—it helps solve the problem of late-comers and lets everyone eat at his or her own pace.

This cookbook is in praise of cold food, and we hope you enjoy every one of these simply delicious cold dishes.

Ovens are to be preheated.

Freshly ground pepper and coarse salt are recommended.

You may substitute margarine for butter if necessary.

For any item marked with an asterisk (*) in an ingredients list, consult the index for the recipe.

Appetizers

Appetizers include canapés as well as first courses served at the table. As a general rule, canapés are served with cocktails or an aperitif. They are usually finger food, and they offer a great many choices. Very popular is a platter of chilled, colorful, fresh, crisp vegetables with an interesting dip; or a platter of cheeses with crackers or sliced French bread or both. A little more trouble, but worth it, are pâtés, Deviled Eggs, Mussel Cocktail, and other tempting morsels to whet, but not satiate, the appetite.

Appetizers as a first course, served at the table, offer an enormous number of choices, from Mushrooms Marinated in Vermouth to Chicken Liver Pâté in Aspic. Antipasto Platter, Spinach Quiche, Soy Sausage Balls, and Guacamole are all good cold and make excellent appetizers. Nothing can get a meal off to a better start than to sit down at a table laden with tempting appetizers.

ANTIPASTO PLATTER

2 medium artichokes
Lettuce leaves
8 ounces thinly sliced salami, rolled up
8 ounces mozzarella cheese, cut in fingers
4 roasted peppers, cut in strips
20 ripe olives
Anchovy Dressing*

Wash the artichokes and trim them as directed in recipe for Boiled Artichokes*. Halve lengthwise, remove the chokes, and place the artichoke halves, cut side down, in a medium skillet. Add water to half cover. Bring to a boil, reduce heat, cover, and simmer 10 to 15 minutes, until the bases are tender when pierced with a fork. Remove with a slotted spoon, drain, and chill several hours or overnight. Line 4 chilled dinner plates with the lettuce. Arrange a half artichoke and a quarter of the salami, cheese, peppers, and olives on each plate. Serve with the dressing on the side. Serves 4.

BOILED ARTICHOKES

4 medium artichokes
2 tablespoons lemon juice
2 teaspoons salt
White Wine–Lemon Mayonnaise*, Vinaigrette with Herbs*, or sauce of
    your choice

Wash the artichokes. With a large, sharp stainless-steel knife, trim stems
at base; rub cut surfaces with cut edge of lemon to prevent discoloration.
Snap or cut off small discolored outer leaves at base. Cut off about 1
inch from top of each leaf. Stand the artichokes upright in a large deep
saucepan. Add 4 cups boiling water, the lemon juice, and the salt. Cover
and boil gently 35 to 45 minutes, or until a leaf pulls out easily. Remove
with a slotted spoon; drain well upside down and chill. Serve with the
sauce of your choice. Before serving, remove choke if you prefer. Serves 4.

HAM-AND-HERB-STUFFED ARTICHOKES

4 medium artichokes
2 tablespoons lemon juice
1 cup chopped onions
5 tablespoons oil, preferably olive
1 cup chopped cooked ham
½ cup fresh bread crumbs
⅓ cup minced parsley
½ teaspoon thyme
½ teaspoon salt
⅛ teaspoon pepper
3 carrots, chopped
½ cup dry white wine

Prepare the artichokes as in Boiled Artichokes*, but cook, uncovered,
in 4 cups boiling water and the lemon juice, only 10 minutes. Remove
with a slotted spoon and drain. Press each firmly, crown down, on a
board to spread the leaves. With a spoon, scoop out and discard small
inner leaves and fuzzy chokes; set the artichokes aside.
    Sauté ⅓ cup onions in 2 tablespoons oil just until tender but not brown.
Remove from heat; stir in the ham, bread crumbs, parsley, thyme, salt,
and pepper. Lightly stuff the ham mixture in center and between leaves

of artichokes. Place the artichokes upright in saucepan; surround with the remaining ⅔ cup onions, carrots, and remaining oil. Cook over medium heat until vegetables begin to brown. Add the wine and ½ cup water; cover and simmer 35 minutes, or until artichoke bases can be pierced easily with a fork. Remove artichokes with a slotted spoon; discard cooking mixture. Cool. Serve at room temperature. Serves 4.

ASPARAGUS VINAIGRETTE

1½ pounds fresh or 2 (10-ounce) packages frozen asparagus spears, cooked
    and drained
¼ cup wine vinegar
½ teaspoon salt
¼ teaspoon pepper
½ cup olive oil
3 tablespoons minced fresh or 2 teaspoons crumbled dried basil
2 tablespoons chopped almonds or pecans (optional)

Place the asparagus in a shallow dish and chill. Stir the vinegar with the salt and pepper until the salt dissolves. Stir in the oil and basil. Pour over the asparagus, cover, and chill at least 3 hours. Sprinkle with the nuts before serving. Serves 4 to 6.

BEETS STUFFED WITH HORSERADISH

8 very large cooked beets
½ teaspoon salt
¼ teaspoon sugar
1–2 tablespoons prepared horseradish
¼ cup heavy cream, whipped
Minced parsley (optional, for garnish)

Cut a slice from the stem end of each beet. Chill. Scoop out a large hole from each center. Fold the salt, sugar and horseradish into the whipped cream and fill the beets. Top with a little parsley if you wish. Serves 8.

CAULIFLOWERETS VINAIGRETTE

1 large or 2 small heads cauliflower
¼ cup minced parsley
1 tablespoon *fines herbes* or vegetable-herb blend
2 teaspoons Dijon-style mustard
½ cup Lemon French Dressing*

Break the cauliflower into flowerets. Cook in salted water or steam. Cook only until crisp-tender, about 10 minutes. Drain, cool, and place in a serving bowl. Add 2 tablespoons parsley, the herbs, and mustard to the dressing. Mix well and pour over the cauliflower. Toss. Sprinkle with the remaining parsley and chill. Serve as a first course. Serves 6 to 8.

SPICY CAULIFLOWER

½ cup oil
½ cup white vinegar
2 teaspoons salt
1 teaspoon sugar
¼ teaspoon hot pepper sauce
1 small head cauliflower (about 1 pound), separated into flowerets
½ (4-ounce) jar sliced pimientos, undrained

Mix the oil, vinegar, salt, sugar, and hot pepper sauce in a large bowl. Cut the cauliflowerets in half lengthwise. Add, with the pimientos and their liquid, to the oil mixture. Stir gently to coat. Cover and chill, stirring occasionally, several hours or overnight. Drain. Serve on toothpicks as an hors d'oeuvre with cocktails. Serves 6 to 8.

CELERY STUFFED WITH OLIVES AND NUTS

1 (3-ounce) package cream cheese, softened
¼ cup finely chopped salted peanuts
¼ cup finely chopped stuffed olives
6 large ribs celery (about 9 inches long)
Thinly sliced stuffed olives (for garnish)

Mix the cheese, peanuts, and olives well. Spread in the hollow of each celery rib. Cut into 1-inch pieces. Garnish each piece with an olive slice. Serve chilled. Yield: 54 pieces.

CHEESE TWISTS

1 recipe biscuit dough (from mix or home recipe)
Melted butter
1 cup shredded Cheddar cheese
½–1 teaspoon paprika
Chicken Salad I* or II* (optional)

Roll the dough to ¾ inch thick. Cut in 1-inch strips. Brush with a little melted butter. Roll in the cheese mixed with the paprika. Twist the ends in opposite directions to make a spiral. Place slightly apart on a foil-lined baking sheet. Bake at 400° F. until golden brown, 8 to 10 minutes. Watch to make sure they do not get too brown. Serve at room temperature, with Chicken Salad if you wish. Serves 10.

CREAM CHEESE AND BACON SANDWICHES

1 (4-ounce) container whipped cream cheese
3 slices cooked bacon, drained and chopped
2 tablespoons prepared horseradish
8 thin slices pumpernickel bread
1 large tomato, peeled and cut in 8 slices
8 spinach leaves, stems removed

Combine the cream cheese, bacon, and horseradish; spread on 4 slices bread. Top each with 2 tomato slices and 2 spinach leaves. Top with remaining bread and halve or quarter. Serves 4 to 6.

RICOTTA CHEESE WITH COFFEE

8 ounces ricotta cheese, at room temperature
¼ cup sugar
¼ cup freeze-dried or instant espresso coffee
¼ cup rum or brandy
Crackers or bread

Blend the cheese with the sugar. Mix the coffee with the rum, adding a little water if necessary. Stir the coffee paste into the cheese, blending thoroughly. Cover and chill for several hours. Serve with crackers or thin-sliced dark or French bread. Yield: about 1½ cups, or about 36 bite-size servings.

DUTCH CHEESE–HAM SPREAD

1¾ cups shredded Leyden, Edam, or Gouda cheese (about 8 ounces)
¼ cup Mayonnaise*
1 tablespoon grated onion
¼ cup deviled ham
2 teaspoons Dijon-style mustard
1 teaspoon prepared horseradish
¼ teaspoon pepper
Cocktail pumpernickel bread rounds or squares

Mix well the cheese, Mayonnaise, onion, ham, mustard, horseradish, and pepper. Spread on pumpernickel rounds. Yield: 1¼ cups, or about 36 canapés.

   Or put in small crock or ramekin, cover, and store in refrigerator until needed. Serve surrounded with toast or crackers.

SHERRIED CHEESE SPREAD

1 (8-ounce) package cream cheese, softened
⅓ cup dry sherry
1 teaspoon dry mustard
2 cups shredded Cheddar cheese (about 8 ounces)
Chopped parsley (for garnish)
Crackers

Beat the cream cheese with the sherry until blended. Mix the mustard with 1 teaspoon hot water and let stand 2 minutes to develop the flavor. Stir into the cream cheese mixture, along with the Cheddar. Turn into a small crock or bowl, cover, and chill until ready to serve. Garnish with parsley and serve with crackers. Yield: about 2 cups, or about 45 bite-size servings.

OVEN-FRIED CHICKEN WINGS

3 pounds broiler-fryer wings (about 24 wings)
⅓ cup butter or margarine, melted
5 cups corn flakes, crushed
½ teaspoon salt
Soy Dressing* (optional)

Cut the drumlet (meaty section) from the rest of the wing at the joint. Dip each drumlet in butter, then in a mixture of the corn flake crumbs and salt. Line a shallow baking pan with foil, lightly grease the foil, and arrange the chicken in a single layer in the pan. Bake at 400°F. 45 minutes. Serve at room temperature with Soy Dressing. Serves 8.

CHICKEN LIVER PÂTÉ IN ASPIC

1 envelope unflavored gelatin
½ cup chicken broth, plus more (optional)
½ cup dry red wine
½ teaspoon sugar
3 scallions, including tops, chopped
1 pound chicken livers
2 tablespoons butter
2 tablespoons chicken fat or olive oil
¼ cup heavy cream
2 hard-cooked eggs
1 tablespoon fresh or 1 teaspoon dried tarragon
1 teaspoon salt
¼ teaspoon pepper
Toast rounds or crackers

Soften the gelatin in ¼ cup cold water. Heat the ½ cup broth, wine, and sugar, add the gelatin, and heat and stir until the gelatin dissolves. Pour half the mixture into a mold or bowl and chill until set. Sauté the scallions and livers gently in the butter and chicken fat or oil until the livers are cooked but not browned, about 2 minutes. Put into a blender or processor with the cream, eggs, tarragon, salt, and pepper. Purée for 30 seconds or less, until blended but not too smooth. Add a little broth if using a blender. Stir in 2 tablespoons of the reserved gelatin mixture. Blend well and spoon on top of the set aspic. Pour the remaining aspic around the sides and, if there is any left, over the top. (You may have to heat the gelatin mixture slightly if it is set.) Cover and chill for several hours. When ready to serve, turn out onto a cold plate. Surround with toast rounds and/or crackers. Serves 6 to 8.

CHICKEN LIVER MOUSSE PÂTÉ

1 pound chicken livers
½ cup chicken broth
1 large onion, chopped
2 tablespoons butter
½ teaspoon salt
¼ teaspoon pepper
½ teaspoon oregano
2 teaspoons Worcestershire sauce
2 teaspoons minced parsley
2 hard-cooked eggs, grated
Toast rounds or crackers

Simmer the livers in the broth for about 5 minutes. Sauté the onions in the butter for a few minutes, until limp and pale golden. Put the livers, about ¼ cup broth, onions, and pan drippings in a blender or processor with the salt, pepper, and oregano. Process only until blended—it should not be too smooth. Gently stir in the Worcestershire, parsley, and grated eggs. Spoon into a crock or other dish in which it is to be served. Cover and chill until firm. Serve with toast rounds or crackers. Serves 6.

CHICK-PEA DIP

1 cup dried chick-peas
2 garlic cloves, minced
½ cup tahini (sesame paste)
2 tablespoons oil (any oil but olive)
½ teaspoon salt
2 tablespoons lemon juice
2 tablespoons chopped parsley
Paprika (for garnish)
Crackers and/or crudités

Soak the chick-peas overnight. Simmer until soft (follow directions on package). Cool and drain. Reserve a few chick-peas for garnish. Place the rest in a blender or processor, with the garlic, tahini, oil, and salt. Pour in the lemon juice and purée. Stir in the parsley. Turn into a serving bowl and sprinkle with the paprika and reserved chick-peas. Chill. Serve with crackers and/or crudités. Yield: about 2½ cups.

CUCUMBER BOATS WITH SALMON SALAD

2 large cucumbers, peeled, halved lengthwise, and seeded, to form boats
2 medium cucumbers, peeled, seeded, and diced fine
1 medium carrot, shredded
1 rib celery, chopped coarse
3 medium scallions, with tops, minced
½ cup Mayonnaise*
2 teaspoons lemon juice
1 teaspoon prepared mustard
¼ teaspoon salt
⅛ teaspoon pepper
1 (7¾-ounce) can salmon, drained
Watercress

Dry the cucumber boats with paper towels, then chill. In a bowl, mix well the diced cucumbers, carrot, celery, scallions, Mayonnaise, lemon juice, mustard, salt, and pepper. Gently stir in the salmon, breaking it up as little as possible. Cover and chill about 1 hour, or until cold. To serve, fill each cucumber boat with about ½ cup salad. Garnish with watercress, and serve on a bed of watercress. Serves 4.

NOTE: This is best served soon after preparation, to prevent the cucumbers from making the salad watery.

PICKLED EGGS AND ONION

1 tablespoon prepared mustard
1¼ cups cider vinegar
½ cup sugar
1 tablespoon salt
1 teaspoon whole pickling spice
1 medium onion, sliced and separated into rings
12 shelled hard-cooked eggs

In a small saucepan, blend the mustard with ¼ cup vinegar; add the remaining vinegar, ¾ cup water, and the remaining ingredients except the eggs. Simmer, uncovered, 5 minutes, or until sugar dissolves and onion is tender. Pour over the eggs. Cover and chill overnight. Can be refrigerated for up to 2 weeks. Serve the eggs with the onion. Serves 8 to 12.

DEVILED EGGS
(Basic)

8 hard-cooked eggs
1 teaspoon prepared mustard
2 teaspoons minced scallions or chives
3 tablespoons Mayonnaise*
½ teaspoon *fines herbes* or marjoram
½ teaspoon curry powder (optional)
Parsley sprigs or paprika (optional, for garnish)

Cut the eggs in half and remove the yolks to a bowl. Mash them with a fork. Combine the mustard, scallions or chives, Mayonnaise, herbs, and curry powder (if using). Mix well and add to the mashed yolks. Fill the egg whites with the mixture. Decorate the tops, if you wish, with a sprig of parsley or a dash of paprika. Serve chilled. Serves 6 to 8.

DEVILED EGG VARIATIONS (for 6–8 eggs)

With Anchovies: Add 8 anchovy fillets, chopped fine, to Deviled Eggs*.
With Avocado: Add the flesh of 1 small avocado, mashed with 1 teaspoon lemon juice, to Deviled Eggs*.
With Bacon: Add 3 slices bacon, cooked, dried, and crumbled, and 1 teaspoon bacon drippings to Deviled Eggs*.

GRAPEFRUIT-SHRIMP APPETIZER

2 grapefruit, halved crosswise
2 tablespoons olive oil
1 small clove garlic, crushed
¼ teaspoon salt
Dash pepper
12 medium shrimp, cooked for 5 minutes (no more), peeled, and halved lengthwise
Watercress sprigs (for garnish)

Cut cores from the grapefruit. Cut around each section, loosening fruit from membrane. Remove alternate sections (save for another use). Drain ¼ cup juice from the grapefruit into a small bowl; add the oil, garlic, salt, and pepper; mix well. Toss the shrimp with the dressing. Place a shrimp half in each empty grapefruit section. Chill. Place watercress sprig in center. Serves 4.

GRAPEFRUIT-AVOCADO APPETIZER

Lettuce leaves
2 large grapefruit, peeled and sectioned
1 large avocado, peeled and sliced
Lemon juice
½ pound small shrimp, cooked and shelled
½ cup Yogurt Mayonnaise* made with lemon juice

Line a platter with lettuce and arrange the fruit attractively on it. Sprinkle the avocado with a little lemon juice. Top with the shrimp and serve chilled, with the dressing on the side. Serves 4.

GUACAMOLE I

1 very large or 2 medium avocados, peeled
2–3 teaspoons lemon juice
½ teaspoon salt (or more)
½ clove garlic, crushed
Dash Worcestershire sauce
4 slices cooked bacon, crumbled (optional)
Tortilla or corn chips

Mash the avocado with a fork and add 2 teaspoons lemon juice at once. Stir in ½ teaspoon salt, the garlic, and the Worcestershire sauce. Add more lemon juice or salt to taste. Chill. You may add the bacon for a change. Serve with tortilla or corn chips. Serves 6 to 8.

GUACAMOLE II

1 large avocado, peeled
2 tablespoons lemon juice
1 large tomato, peeled, seeded, and chopped
2 tablespoons chopped canned chili peppers
1 clove garlic, crushed
1 tablespoon grated or minced onion
½ teaspoon salt
Corn chips or tacos (optional)

Mash the avocado with the lemon juice. Stir in the remaining ingredients. Taste for seasoning. Cover with plastic and chill. Good served with corn chips or tacos. Serves 6 to 8.

HAM-LEEK QUICHE

2 medium to large leeks, trimmed, well washed, and sliced thin (about 1
    cup)
1 large onion, sliced thin
3 tablespoons butter
1 tablespoon flour
½ teaspoon salt
⅛ teaspoon nutmeg
⅛ teaspoon pepper
1 cup milk
4 eggs, slightly beaten
1 cup finely diced cooked ham
1 unbaked 9-inch pastry shell

In a large skillet, sauté the leeks and onion in the butter until tender.
Over low heat, stir in the flour, salt, nutmeg, and pepper. Gradually
stir in the milk and cook until mixture thickens and just begins to boil.
Remove from heat. Stir some of the milk mixture into the eggs, then add
eggs to remaining milk mixture. Stir in the ham. Pour into the pastry
shell. Bake at 400° F. 30 minutes, or until a knife inserted in the center
comes out clean. Cut into wedges. Serve at room temperature. Serves
6 to 8.

STUFFED LETTUCE LEAVES

7 large or 14 small lettuce leaves
2 cups cooked rice
½ cup raisins, plumped
⅓ cup chopped walnuts
¼ cup chopped onion
3 tablespoons plain yogurt
½ teaspoon salt

In a large skillet, bring to a boil enough water just to cover the bottom.
Reduce heat; add the lettuce. Cover and steam a few minutes, until
pliable yet still crisp and opaque. Drain and cool. (This preparation is
not necessary when using tender lettuce such as Boston or Bibb.) Meanwhile, mix the remaining ingredients well. If necessary, remove tough
ribs from lettuce leaves; halve large leaves lengthwise (leaves should be
at least 6 × 4 inches). To stuff, place 2 rounded tablespoons rice mixture
in the center of each leaf. Fold one end over rice mixture, then fold sides
in; roll to enclose filling. If necessary, secure with a toothpick or skewer.
Chill. Serves 4 to 6.

MELON AND PROSCIUTTO

1 honeydew, casaba, or Spanish melon
⅓ pound thin-sliced prosciutto
Lemon or lime wedges

Chill the melon. Peel, remove seeds, and cut into about ½-inch slices.
Alternate with the prosciutto on 6 chilled plates. Serve with lemon or
lime wedges. Serves 6.

MUSHROOMS MARINATED IN VERMOUTH

⅓ cup white vinegar
1½ teaspoons Italian herb seasoning or *fines herbes*
1 teaspoon sugar
1 teaspoon salt
½ teaspoon pepper
4 cloves
¼ cup olive oil
⅔ cup dry vermouth
12–16 ounces small mushrooms, wiped clean

In a small nonaluminum saucepan heat the vinegar, 2 tablespoons water,
herbs, sugar, salt, pepper, and cloves to boiling point. Reduce heat and
simmer 5 minutes. Stir in the oil and vermouth, then the mushrooms.
Cover and chill several hours or overnight, stirring occasionally. Serve
the mushrooms with toothpicks. Serves about 8.

STUFFED MUSHROOMS

1 pound medium mushrooms
⅔ cup sour cream
2 tablespoons minced onion or scallions
2 tablespoons minced celery
1 teaspoon minced parsley
1 teaspoon Worcestershire sauce
½ teaspoon salt
¼ teaspoon pepper
1 teaspoon dried or 1 tablespoon fresh tarragon, oregano, or marjoram

Wipe the mushrooms and remove the stems. Reserve the caps. Chop
about one third of the stems fine. Combine the chopped stems with the
remaining ingredients. They may all be chopped in a processor; be careful
not to make too smooth a purée. Stuff the caps and chill. Serves 8.

MUSSEL COCKTAIL

5 pounds mussels
1 cup water or white wine
1 clove garlic, slivered
2 teaspoons lemon juice
½ cup Mayonnaise* made with lemon juice
Minced parsley (optional, for garnish)

Soak the mussels in cold water, wash thoroughly, and debeard. Place in a deep pot with the water or wine and garlic. Cover tightly and steam until the shells open, about 5 minutes. Take out the mussels and, when cool enough to handle, remove them from their shells, discarding any that have not opened. Place in a bowl. Reduce the liquid they were steamed in to about 1 cup. Cool and pour over the mussels, avoiding any sand at the bottom. Chill. Divide the mussels among 8 cocktail glasses. Add the lemon juice to the Mayonnaise and spoon a little in as you fill the glasses. Top with a little more Mayonnaise and garnish with parsley if you wish. Serves 8.

If you prefer, place the mussels on a chilled plate. Serve the Mayonnaise in a separate bowl and have toothpicks available. Serves 8.

ONION-ANCHOVY PIE
(*Pissaladière*)

1 envelope active dry yeast
2 tablespoons warm water
1¼ cups flour
1½ teaspoons salt
¼ cup butter, cut into small pieces
1 egg
6 cups thinly sliced onions (about 1½ pounds)
1 large clove garlic, unpeeled
1 bay leaf
¼ teaspoon pepper
¼ cup oil, preferably olive
1 (2-ounce) can anchovies, drained, halved lengthwise
8 ripe olives, pitted and halved

Dissolve the yeast in the water. In a large bowl, combine the flour and 1 teaspoon salt. With your fingertips, blend the butter with the flour mixture. Make a well in the center; drop in the egg and yeast mixture.

Knead until dough leaves sides of bowl. Cover; let rise in a warm, draft-free place about 1½ hours, or until doubled. Meanwhile, in a large covered skillet over low heat, cook the onions, garlic, bay leaf, the remaining ½ teaspoon salt, and the pepper in the oil 45 minutes, stirring occasionally, until the onions are tender but not brown. Discard the garlic and bay leaf. Set the onions aside.

Punch down dough. Knead 5 to 8 minutes, or until smooth and elastic. Pat evenly into a 9-inch pie plate. Spread onions over dough. Arrange anchovies in lattice patterns over onions. Place olive halves in lattice openings. Bake at 400° F. 20 to 25 minutes, or until crust is light brown. Serve at room temperature. Serves 10 to 12.

COUNTRY PÂTÉ
(*Pâté Maison*)

1 pound beef liver
1 cup minced onions
½ cup dry sherry
¾ pound pork sausage meat
½ pound ground beef
2 eggs
1–2 cloves garlic, crushed
1 teaspoon salt
½ teaspoon ground ginger
7 slices bacon
French bread

Chop the liver fine in a processor or blender or mince by hand; set aside. Cook the onions and sherry gently in a small saucepan, stirring occasionally to prevent burning, until the liquid has evaporated and the onions are tender. Combine the onions, liver, sausage, beef, eggs, garlic, salt, and ginger. The mixture will be loose. Line a 9 × 5 × 3-inch loaf pan with the bacon slices, placing them halfway across the bottom and up the sides so that a 1½-to-2-inch end extends over the pan edges. Spoon in the meat mixture and fold the bacon over the top. Place in a large pan with enough boiling water to come halfway up the sides of the loaf pan. Bake 375° F. 1½ hours, or until the juices run clear when loaf is pierced with a knife. Remove from oven. Cool in a water bath with a small pan or aluminum foil over the top weighted down with cans or other heavy objects. Chill. This will keep up to 1½ weeks in the refrigerator. Serve with French bread. Serves 8 to 10.

SAUSAGE ROLLS

1 small onion, minced
1 tablespoon butter
1 pound ground pork
½ pound ground beef
1 large potato (about ½ pound), cooked, cooled, peeled, and shredded fine
1 teaspoon salt
1 teaspoon crushed rosemary
½ teaspoon pepper
½ teaspoon ground allspice
1 cup milk

Brown the onion in the butter. Cool. Mix the onion, pork, beef, potato, salt, rosemary, pepper, and allspice with your hands until well blended. Gradually mix in the milk. Divide mixture in half and put each half on an 18 × 12-inch piece of foil. Dip hands in cold water and shape mixture into 8-inch-long firm, even rolls. Roll up tight in the foil. Twist ends in opposite directions to form firm rolls; tie ends with string. Place rolls on rack in roasting pan. With a knife point, prick foil along top of sausages at 1-inch intervals. Bake at 350° F. 1 hour, or until well browned and done. Cool and chill. Serve sliced thin, with toothpicks if you like. Serves 6 to 8.

SPINACH QUICHE

Pastry for 9-inch pie shell
4 eggs, beaten
1 cup milk
¾ teaspoon salt
¼ teaspoon pepper
¼ teaspoon nutmeg
1 (10-ounce) package frozen chopped spinach, thawed and drained well
1 cup shredded Swiss cheese

Roll out the pastry to fit a 9-inch pie plate. Flute the edges and prick the bottom. Bake at 425° F. 8 minutes. Mix well the eggs, milk, salt, pepper, and nutmeg. Layer the spinach and ½ cup cheese in the pie shell. Pour in the egg mixture and sprinkle with the remaining cheese. Bake at 425° F. 10 minutes, reduce heat to 325° F., and bake 25 minutes longer, or until a knife inserted in the center comes out clean. Cool and serve at room temperature. Serves 6 to 8.

SOY SAUSAGE BALLS

1 pound sausage meat
1½ cups fresh bread crumbs
¼ cup packed light brown sugar
½ teaspoon dry mustard
¼ cup soy sauce
2 cups pineapple chunks (optional)
1 green pepper, cut up (optional)
Sweet-Sour Apricot Sauce (recipe follows—optional)

Mix the sausage and bread crumbs well. Shape into 1-inch balls. Brown half at a time in a hot heavy skillet, remove, and set aside. Wipe the skillet clean. Mix the sugar and mustard well in the skillet, stir in the soy sauce and ⅓ cup water, and add the meatballs. Bring to a boil, reduce heat, cover, and simmer 5 minutes, or until the meatballs are cooked through. Serve at room temperature on toothpicks or place on skewers, alternating with pineapple and green pepper chunks. Strain the liquid and use as a dipping sauce, or serve with Sweet-Sour Apricot Sauce. Yield: about 24 balls.

SWEET-SOUR APRICOT SAUCE

1 (12-ounce) jar apricot preserves
1 (6-ounce) jar horseradish, drained

Mix the ingredients well. Yield: about 1½ cups.

SHRIMP-TUNA-PLUM SALAD

1 (7-ounce) can tuna, drained and broken in chunks
1 cup cooked and cleaned small shrimp
3 large plums, peeled and sliced
2 ribs celery, sliced thin
¾ cup Mayonnaise*
Dash hot red pepper
Crisp greens

In a bowl, combine the tuna, shrimp, plums, and celery. Add the Mayonnaise and red pepper; toss to mix. Serve at once, on greens. Serves 4.

TUNA DIP WITH ANCHOVIES AND OLIVES

1 (3½-ounce) can tuna, drained
2 (2-ounce) cans anchovies
½ pound pitted ripe olives
2 tablespoons chopped parsley
¼ cup brandy
2 tablespoons capers
1 teaspoon lemon juice
1 cup Mayonnaise*
Crackers, crudités, and/or dark bread

Break up the tuna and put into a processor or blender with the anchovies and their liquid, olives, parsley, and brandy. Blend, using the on-off technique, until chopped and well mixed but not too smooth a purée. Add the capers. Stir the lemon juice into the Mayonnaise and stir into the mixture. Cover and chill. Serve with crackers, crudités, and/or dark bread. Yield: about 2½ cups.

TUNA PÂTÉ

1 (6½-ounce) can tuna, drained
1 tablespoon chopped pimiento
3 drops hot pepper sauce
½ teaspoon dry mustard
½ cup heavy cream
Minced parsley
Melba toast or crackers

Combine all the ingredients except the parsley and toast in a blender or processor. Purée until smooth. Scrape into a crock or serving dish and chill for several hours. Sprinkle with parsley. Serve with toast or crackers. Serves 4.

YOGURT DIP

1 cup plain yogurt
½ teaspoon salt
¼ teaspoon pepper
½ cup Mayonnaise*
1 tablespoon minced parsley
2 teaspoons fresh or 1 teaspoon dried dillweed
½ teaspoon grated lemon peel
Crudités

Combine all of the ingredients, mix thoroughly, and chill. Serve with crudités. Yield: about 1½ cups.

Soups

TIME WAS when cold soups were never served unless the weather was torrid, and then they were limited to jellied consommés. These are still deservedly popular and quite attractive when garnished with slices of lime or lemon and a sprinkling of parsley or chives.

Gradually we added new cold soups to the menus: first, French vichyssoise and Spanish gazpacho, the latter sometimes accompanied by dishes of chopped raw vegetables. Next we added dozens of others—cream soups, vegetable, fish, meat, and fruit soups, many of them tastier cold than hot. Some fruit soups you may care to serve as a dessert.

All cold soups need not be served straight from the refrigerator; some are at their best at room temperature. Others should be very cold; gazpacho, for example, is often served with an ice cube in each bowl.

A handsome covered soup tureen, flanked by a ladle, is one of the most inviting sights that can greet one's guests as they seat themselves about the table.

Cold soups are perfect for make-it-ahead entertaining—a convenient and refreshing way to begin any meal.

ALMOND CREAM SOUP

½ pound almonds
5 cups chicken broth
½ teaspoon salt
2 cups light cream or half-and-half

Blanch the almonds. Set ¼ cup aside. Put the rest in a blender or processor for 1 minute to grind. Do not grind too fine. If using a blender, add 2 cups of the broth to the almonds. Simmer the almonds in the broth for 10 minutes. Cool. Add the salt and cream. Chill. Chop the remaining almonds by hand until quite fine. Add to the soup. Serves 8.

APPLE SOUP

3 pounds apples
2 tablespoons sugar
½ cup red wine
Sour or whipped cream (optional, for garnish)

Wash and core the apples. Do not peel them. Cut up all but 2 and simmer in 6 cups water for 15 to 20 minutes, until soft. Purée in a processor or blender with a little of the water they were cooked in. Add the sugar and wine. Chill. Serve topped with sour or whipped cream, if you wish. Garnish each bowl with a few thin apple slices from the reserved apples. Serves 8.

BEET SOUP

2 leeks, trimmed, well washed, and cut up
2 carrots, cut up
½ cup chopped celery
1 large onion, chopped
3 tablespoons chopped parsley
¼ cup butter
3 (10½-ounce) cans beef broth, not condensed
3 cups chopped cooked beets
1 teaspoon salt
½ teaspoon pepper
3–4 tablespoons lemon juice
Sour cream (for garnish)

Sauté the leeks, carrots, celery, onion, and parsley gently in the butter for a few minutes, stirring. Add the broth and beets. Simmer 2 minutes. Pour into a blender or processor and purée. You may have to do this in two lots. Pour into a bowl; add the salt and pepper and the lemon juice to taste. Chill for several hours. Serve with a little sour cream on top if you wish. Serves 8 to 10.

EASY BEET SOUP

Substitute 2 (16-ounce) cans beets for the raw beets in Beet Soup*. Purée them and add to the beef broth. Add the salt, pepper, and lemon juice. Chill and garnish with sour cream if desired. Serves 8 to 10.

BLUEBERRY-ORANGE SOUP

2 tablespoons cornstarch
½ cup sugar
2 cups blueberries
Cinnamon stick
1 (6-ounce) can frozen orange-juice concentrate
Lemon slices or sour cream

In a saucepan mix the cornstarch and sugar and 2½ cups water. Bring
to a boil over medium heat, stirring. Simmer until thickened and smooth,
about 2 minutes. Add the blueberries and cinnamon stick; bring to a brief
boil. Remove from the heat. Add the orange juice; stir until thawed.
Cover and chill. Before serving, remove the cinnamon stick. Serve in
bowls; top each with a lemon slice or dab of sour cream. Serves 6.

FRESH DILLED CARROT SOUP

2 cups thinly sliced carrots
1 medium onion, sliced thin
2–3 cups chicken broth
1 teaspoon salt
¼ teaspoon pepper
2 tablespoons chopped fresh dillweed
1 scallion, white part only, minced
½ cup sour cream (optional)

Place the carrots, onion, and chicken broth in a large saucepan, bring
to a boil, and simmer, covered, about 15 minutes, until vegetables are
tender. Whirl half the vegetables at a time in a blender with half of the
broth each time until smooth. Cool; add the salt, pepper, and dillweed.
Chill at least 2 hours. Serve in individual bowls with a sprinkling of
scallion and with a dollop of sour cream, if you wish. Serves 4 to 6.

CHICKEN-CLAM BROTH

4 cups chicken broth
3 cups clam broth
½ cup sour cream or whipped cream

Combine the chicken and clam broths. Chill. You may stir in the sour
cream or put it on top of the broth, just before serving. If using whipped
cream, put a spoonful on top just before serving. Serves 8.

SCANDINAVIAN CHERRY SOUP

½ cup sugar
2 tablespoons cornstarch
¼ teaspoon salt
1 cup orange juice
1 (2-inch) cinnamon stick
1¼ pounds dark sweet cherries, pitted (about 4 cups)

Stir together the sugar, cornstarch, salt, 1¼ cups water, and the orange juice in a large heavy saucepan. Add the cinnamon stick and stir over medium heat until thickened and smooth. Stir in the cherries and cook 2 minutes. Pour into a serving bowl, cover, and chill. Discard the cinnamon stick. Serves 4.

CITRUS SOUP

2 tablespoons butter
3 tablespoons flour
Grated peel of 1 orange
Grated peel and juice of 1 lemon
⅓ cup sugar
¼ teaspoon salt
1 egg yolk
¼ cup half-and-half or heavy cream
1 cup orange juice

In a heavy saucepan over medium heat, melt the butter. Blend in the flour; gradually stir in 3 cups hot water. Cook and stir until slightly thickened and smooth. Add the orange and lemon peels, sugar, and salt. Cover and simmer 5 minutes. Beat the egg yolk with the half-and-half until blended. Beat in about ½ cup hot mixture; return to saucepan; heat just to simmering. Stir in the lemon and orange juices; heat gently. Cool, then cover and chill. Serves 4 to 6.

Cut the sugar slightly if using as an appetizer soup rather than a dessert soup.

CHICKEN SOUP WITH AVOCADO AND LIME

½ cup finely chopped onion
1 clove garlic, minced
2 tablespoons oil
6 cups well-seasoned chicken broth
1½ cups chunked cooked chicken
⅓ cup canned mild enchilada sauce
½ avocado, peeled, cut in ½-inch cubes
1 lime, cut in wedges
Corn chips (optional)

In a large pot, sauté the onion and garlic in the oil 5 minutes, or until onion is tender. Add the broth, chicken, and enchilada sauce. Simmer 20 minutes. Cool, then chill. Turn into a large bowl and add the avocado cubes. Serve with lime wedges and, if desired, corn chips. Serves 8.

ICED CLAM-TOMATO SOUP

1 medium cucumber, peeled, seeded, and finely chopped
⅓ cup minced scallions, with tops
1 clove garlic, minced
3 cups clam-tomato juice
1 (16-ounce) can peeled tomatoes
2 tablespoons cider vinegar
1 tablespoon instant chicken broth

Combine all the ingredients in a blender or processor, and whirl until smooth. Chill well before serving. Serves 6 to 8.

JELLIED CONSOMMÉ WITH CAVIAR

3 (16-ounce) cans jellied consommé
6 tablespoons red or black caviar
6–8 lemon wedges

Chill the consommé overnight. When ready to serve, spoon it into individual chilled soup bowls. Top with the caviar and add a wedge of lemon to each bowl. Serves 6 to 8.

JELLIED CHICKEN CONSOMMÉ

2 envelopes unflavored gelatin
4 cups chicken broth
3 tablespoons dry sherry
½ teaspoon salt
¼ teaspoon pepper
Chopped watercress or minced chives (for garnish)
Lemon wedges

Soften the gelatin in ¼ cup cold water. Heat the chicken broth; add the gelatin. Stir and heat until the gelatin is dissolved. Add the sherry, salt, and pepper and chill several hours, until firm. Serve garnished with cress or chives and add a lemon wedge to each serving. Serves 6.

JELLIED TOMATO-CHICKEN CONSOMMÉ

2 envelopes unflavored gelatin
2 (14-ounce) cans chicken broth
1 (18-ounce) can tomato juice
½ teaspoon sugar
½ teaspoon salt
1 tablespoon minced cooked chicken, scallions, or chives (for garnish)

Soften the gelatin in ¼ cup of the cold broth. Add the remaining broth; heat and stir until dissolved. Stir in the tomato juice, sugar, and salt. Chill several hours or overnight. Break up the soup with a fork as you spoon it into serving cups. Sprinkle on your choice of garnish. Serves 6 to 8.

JELLIED CONSOMMÉ WITH CREAM CHEESE

3 (10-ounce) cans jellied consommé
1 (8-ounce) package cream cheese, at room temperature
2 tablespoons chutney (any kind)
2 teaspoons curry powder
2 tablespoons cream
2 tablespoons minced chicken or chives

Heat the consommé just till it becomes liquid and put into a processor or blender with the cheese, chutney, and curry powder. Purée. Remove to a cold bowl and stir in the cream. Chill several hours, until firm. Serve topped with minced chicken or chives. Serves 8.

CURRIED CREAM OF CORN SOUP

1 (17-ounce) can cream-style corn
1 teaspoon minced onion or scallions
1 teaspoon Worcestershire sauce
½ teaspoon salt
¼ teaspoon white pepper
1–2 teaspoons curry powder
1 cup milk or half-and-half
⅓ cup heavy cream
Fresh basil (optional)

In a processor or blender, whirl all the ingredients except the basil. Chill. Serve in cups, with a basil leaf on top. Serves 4.

GAZPACHO FROM MADRID

4 large or 6 medium ripe tomatoes, cut up, or 1 (14-ounce) can peeled
      Italian tomatoes
1 medium cucumber, peeled and cut up
1 medium green pepper, cut up
1 tablespoon olive oil
1 tablespoon wine vinegar or dry red wine
1 teaspoon salt
½ teaspoon pepper
1 teaspoon sugar
Chicken broth (optional)
4 slices French bread, soaked in water
1 cup light cream (optional)
Croutons

In a processor or blender, purée all of the ingredients except the bread, cream, and croutons. If using a blender, you may have to add a little chicken broth or water. Crumble the bread, and stir with its soaking liquid until smooth. Stir in. Add the cream and beat until smooth. Chill. Reseason to taste. Pass the croutons. Serves 6.

YOGURT-CUCUMBER-WALNUT SOUP

4 cups plain yogurt
½ cup chopped walnuts
2 cups diced peeled cucumbers
1 teaspoon salt
¼ teaspoon pepper
2 cloves garlic, crushed
4 tablespoons minced fresh or frozen dillweed

Beat the yogurt until smooth. Combine the remaining ingredients, add to the yogurt, and mix well. Thin with water if desired. Chill. Serves 4 to 6.

CUCUMBER-YOGURT SOUP

1 cup plain yogurt
1 cup chicken broth
1 medium cucumber, peeled, seeded, and chopped
1 clove garlic, crushed
½ teaspoon salt
⅛ teaspoon hot pepper sauce
Thin unpeeled cucumber slices (for garnish)
Minced chives or scallion tops (for garnish)

In a blender or processor, purée all the ingredients except the cucumber slices and chives. Cover and chill. Serve in chilled glasses or bowls. Garnish with the cucumber slices and chives. Serves 4.

CREAM OF CUCUMBER SOUP

2 medium cucumbers, peeled and cut up
1 large onion, chopped
1 (14-ounce) can chicken broth
2 cups light cream or half-and-half
1 cup mashed potatoes
Salt
Pepper
½ cup dry white wine
Minced dillweed or parsley (for garnish)

Simmer the cucumbers and onion in the broth for 15 minutes. In a blender or processor, purée with the cream. Heat, add the mashed potatoes, and stir until completely smooth. Cool. Add the wine and season to taste with salt and pepper. If the soup is thicker than you want it, thin with a little broth, cream, or wine to taste. Garnish with dillweed or parsley. Serve chilled. Serves 6 to 8.

CREAM OF MUSHROOM SOUP I

1 pound mushrooms, chopped fine
3 cups beef broth or consommé
2 cups heavy cream or half-and-half
Minced parsley (for garnish)

Combine the mushrooms with the broth and simmer for 3 minutes. Remove half the mixture to a blender and whirl with the cream. Return this cream mixture to the pot and heat. Adjust the seasoning. Chill. Sprinkle with parsley. Serves 6 to 8.

CREAM OF MUSHROOM SOUP II

1½ pounds mushrooms, cut up
1 medium onion, chopped
3 tablespoons butter
1 teaspoon salt
¼ teaspoon pepper
1 cup beef broth or consommé
1 cup dry white wine
2 cups heavy cream (or part half-and-half)
2 tablespoons minced parsley

Sauté the mushrooms and onion in the butter for 2 minutes, stirring. Add ½ cup water and simmer for 5 minutes. Add the salt and pepper and purée in a blender or processor. Pour into a pot with the broth, wine, and cream. Heat 2 minutes. Do not boil. Add the parsley. Chill. Serves 6 to 8.

MUSSEL SOUP

4 pounds mussels
2 cups dry white wine
1 medium onion, chopped
¼ cup chopped parsley
½ cup chopped celery
1 cup light cream

Soak the mussels for at least an hour in water to cover. Scrub and debeard them. Put into a deep pot with the remaining ingredients, except the cream. Cover and steam for 3 to 5 minutes, only until the mussels open. Take out the mussels and, when cool enough to handle, remove from their shells. Discard any that do not open. Cut off the soft portions and set aside with a little broth. (If the mussels were large, cut them up.) Put the hard parts of the mussels in a blender or processor with a cup of broth. Purée; remove and reserve. Strain the remaining broth and put the vegetables and ½ cup of broth in the blender or processor. Purée. Cool the remaining broth slightly to avoid curdling and mix in with the cream, being careful not to pour in any of the sand that may be in the bottom of the pot. Add to the purées and stir in the soft parts of the mussels. Chill. Serves 6.

BILLI-BI

Proceed as for Mussel Soup*, substituting 1 cup of water for 1 cup of the broth. After removing the mussels from their shells, cut up, return to the broth, and cook for 5 minutes to reduce the liquid. Strain through cheesecloth into a bowl. Stir in the cream and adjust seasoning. You do not use the mussels in the soup. It may be thickened, if you wish, by simmering 2 beaten egg yolks in a cup of the broth until thickened. Return to the soup, stir, and chill. Serves 4 to 6.

PEACH-PLUM-CRANBERRY SOUP

½ cup sugar
3 tablespoons cornstarch
1 teaspoon cinnamon
⅛ teaspoon ground cloves
4 cups cranberry juice
4 peaches or nectarines, pitted and sliced thin
4 plums, pitted and sliced
1 lemon, sliced thin

In a large saucepan, mix the sugar, cornstarch, cinnamon, cloves, and cranberry juice. Bring to a boil, stirring; boil 1 minute. Reduce heat. Add the peaches, plums, and lemon; cover and simmer 10 minutes, or until fruit is just tender. Chill. Serves 8.

PEAR SOUP

6 pears, peeled, cored, and cut up
2 small or 1 large scallion, with tops, cut up
1 stalk celery, cut up
½ teaspoon salt
1 teaspoon curry powder
2 cups chicken broth
2 cups half-and-half
Nutmeg or cinnamon (for garnish)

Put all the ingredients except the half-and-half and garnish in a processor or blender and chop. Simmer for 5 minutes, return to the processor, and purée. Pour into a bowl, stir in the half-and-half, and chill. Serve topped with a little nutmeg or cinnamon. Serves 6.

PIMIENTO SOUP

½ cup well-drained, cut-up roasted red peppers or pimientos
¼ cup sliced scallions (white part only)
1½ cups chilled chicken broth
1½ cups milk
½ teaspoon salt
Dash hot pepper sauce
Thin strips or slices red pepper (for garnish)

In a blender, whirl all the ingredients except the garnish until smooth. Chill. Serve in bowls garnished with red pepper strips. Serves 4 to 6.

SENEGALESE SOUP

4 medium onions, chopped
2 tablespoons butter
3 apples, peeled, cored, and cut up
¼ cup flour
2 tablespoons curry powder
1 quart chicken broth
2 cups half-and-half
Salt
Minced cooked chicken, chives, or parsley (for garnish)

Sauté the onions gently in the butter until transparent; do not brown.
Stir in the apples and cook for 2 minutes. Combine the flour and curry
powder and stir in. Pour in the broth slowly while stirring. Cook and
stir a few minutes, until slightly thickened. Purée in a blender or processor
for 1 minute. Chill. Stir in the half-and-half and taste for salt before
adding it. (The amount depends upon the seasoning of the chicken broth.)
Sprinkle each cup with minced chicken and/or chives or parsley. Serves
6 to 8.

TOMATO SOUP WITH DILL

3 pounds ripe tomatoes or 3 (14-ounce) cans peeled Italian tomatoes
2 onions, chopped
3 tablespoons olive oil
½ (6-ounce) can tomato paste
1 teaspoon salt
¼ teaspoon pepper
1 teaspoon sugar
¼ cup flour
1 tablespoon chopped fresh or 1 teaspoon dried dillweed
Cream (optional, for garnish)

If using fresh tomatoes, peel, seed, and chop them. Sauté the onions very
gently in the oil for about 5 minutes. Do not brown. Add the tomatoes,
tomato paste, salt, pepper, and sugar. Blend the flour with 2 cups water
and stir into the tomato mixture. Simmer several minutes. Cool. Process
in a blender or processor. You will have to do this in two or three batches.
Add the dillweed. Fresh dillweed is much better than dried; if using fresh,
save a little for garnish. Chill. Top, if you wish, with a little plain or
whipped cream. If you use cream, sprinkle the reserved dillweed on top
of the cream. Serves 8.

SPINACH SOUP

2 pounds fresh spinach
3 cups chicken broth
1 clove garlic, crushed
½ teaspoon salt
¼ teaspoon pepper
2 cups half-and-half

Pick over the spinach, removing any tough stems. Wash thoroughly.
Cook, covered, in 1 cup broth for a few minutes, until spinach is wilted.
Whirl in a blender or processor with the cooking liquid, garlic, salt, and
pepper. Stir in the remaining broth and half-and-half. Adjust seasoning,
chill, and serve in 6 cool bowls or a tureen. Serves 6.

TOMATO-CHICKEN CONSOMMÉ

3 cups tomato juice
4 cups chicken broth
½ cup dry red wine
1 teaspoon lemon juice
1 teaspoon sugar
Salt
Minced chives or parsley

Combine the tomato juice with the chicken broth, wine, lemon juice,
and sugar. Stir and taste for seasoning. You may need a little salt. Chill.
Serve in individual cups and garnish with chives or parsley. Serves 6 to 8.

TOMATO SOUP WITH SHRIMP

1 (10-ounce) can tomato juice
1 (10-ounce) can condensed beef consommé
1 teaspoon thyme
¾ cup finely chopped cooked shrimp
1 cup sour cream
3 tablespoons minced chives (for garnish)

Combine the tomato juice, consommé, and thyme. Simmer 5 minutes
and cool. Chill. Just before serving, add the cold shrimp and sour cream.
Stir to blend. Garnish with minced chives. Serves 4 to 6.

TOMATO CREAM SOUP

4 (10¾-ounce) cans condensed tomato soup
2 cups milk
½ teaspoon salt
¼ teaspoon pepper
2 teaspoons sugar
1 teaspoon dry or 1 tablespoon fresh chopped basil, tarragon, or oregano
Whipped cream, sour cream, or yogurt (for garnish)
Chopped chives or parsley (for garnish)

Heat the soup and milk together. Add the salt, pepper, sugar, and herb of your choice. Chill. Serve topped with cream or yogurt and/or chives or parsley. Serves 8 to 10.

VEGETABLE SOUP

1 (10-ounce) package frozen or 1 (12-ounce) can whole-kernel corn
1 (10-ounce) package frozen green peas
1 (10-ounce) package frozen diced or sliced carrots
2 (13¾-ounce) cans beef broth or consommé
1 teaspoon grated onion
2 tablespoons minced celery

Cook the frozen vegetables according to the package directions. Drain, set aside, and cool. Heat the broth, add the onion and celery, and chill. Add all the vegetables and mix thoroughly. Chill. Serves 8.

TOMATO AND GREEN PEPPER SOUP

4 medium tomatoes, peeled, seeded, and diced
2 medium green peppers, peeled and slivered
1 medium leek, trimmed, well washed, and sliced thin
5 cups chicken broth
2 tablespoons cornstarch
1 teaspoon salt
¼ teaspoon pepper
¼ teaspoon sugar
½ teaspoon thyme
3 tablespoons minced parsley (for garnish)
3 tablespoons minced chives (for garnish)

Combine the tomatoes, green peppers, leek, and chicken broth in a saucepan and bring to a boil. Reduce heat and simmer 15 minutes. Thicken with the cornstarch blended with a small amount of cold water. Bring to a boil, stirring, and simmer a few minutes, adding the salt, pepper, sugar, and thyme. Cool, taste for seasoning, and chill. Garnish with parsley and chives. Serves 8.

VICHYSSOISE

8 medium leeks, trimmed, well washed, and sliced
3 tablespoons butter
1 quart chicken broth
3 potatoes, boiled, peeled, and sliced
1 tablespoon curry powder
2 cups heavy cream
Salt
Minced chives (for garnish)

Sauté the leeks in the butter, using the white parts and a little of the green. Cook until soft, but do not let brown. Add 2 cups broth and simmer a few minutes. Purée in a blender or processor along with the potatoes. Add the remaining broth and the curry powder. Chill. Add the cream and taste for salt—the amount will depend upon the seasoning in the broth. Chill. Serve topped with chives. Serves 8.

CAULIFLOWER VICHYSSOISE

3 large leeks
1 medium head cauliflower, broken into flowerets
Salt
1 cup half-and-half
¼ cup heavy cream
Minced chives or parsley

Trim, wash well, and slice the leeks, using the white parts and part of the green. Boil with the cauliflower in salted water until tender. Drain the vegetables, reserving the liquid. Combine the leeks and cauliflower in a processor or blender with ½ cup water from the leeks. Stir in the half-and-half and chill. When ready to serve, add the cream and stir. Taste for salt. If too thick, add a little more water from the leeks. Chill and serve topped with minced chives or parsley. Serves 6.

GREEN VICHYSSOISE

2 cups peeled, diced potatoes
¼ cup chopped scallions, with tops
2 tablespoons chopped parsley
2 cups chicken broth
½ teaspoon salt
¼ teaspoon pepper
2 cups fresh or 1 (10-ounce) package frozen green peas
1 cup heavy cream
Minced chives or scallion tops (for garnish)

Cook the potatoes, scallions, and parsley in ½ cup water and 1 cup chicken broth, with the salt and pepper, about 15 minutes, or until tender. Cook the peas in ½ cup water about 5 minutes. Drain. If using frozen peas, follow package directions. Combine all in a processor or blender and purée. You may have to do this in two lots. Stir in the remaining broth and the cream. Chill until ready to serve. Garnish with the chives. Serves 6 to 8.

WATERCRESS-YOGURT SOUP

1 large bunch watercress
4 medium leeks, trimmed, well washed, and chopped
¼ cup butter
¼ cup flour
2 (14-ounce) cans chicken broth
½ to 1 teaspoon salt
¼ teaspoon pepper
¼ teaspoon rosemary
1 cup water or milk (or more)
2 cups yogurt

Remove the tough stems from the watercress and chop coarsely, setting a few sprigs aside for garnish. Sauté with the leeks in the butter until soft but not brown. Stir in the flour and pour in the broth slowly, stirring. Heat 3 minutes. Add the salt, pepper, rosemary, and 1 cup water or milk. Purée in a blender or processor. You may need to do this in two lots. Pour into a bowl, stir in the yogurt, and chill for several hours. If the soup is thicker than you want, add a little more broth or water. Top with a little watercress. Serves 8.

WALNUT-BUTTERMILK SOUP

¼ cup chopped walnuts
1 small onion, cut up
½ cup chicken broth or water
1 tablespoon olive oil
1 teaspoon salt
¼ teaspoon pepper
4 cups buttermilk
¼ cup minced parsley

Purée the walnuts, onion, broth, oil, salt, and pepper in a blender or processor. Stir in the buttermilk and parsley. Mix thoroughly and chill. Serves 6.

Main Courses

Fish and other seafood can be spectacular served cold—for example, a whole salmon, bass, or other large fish in aspic; smaller fish or fillets with a choice of sauces; or a ring mold of shrimp and salmon. Or it could be something as simple as tuna made into a delicious pâté. The possibilities are almost endless, from the familiar to the surprising.

Poultry doesn't have to mean fried chicken. It can be served in many imaginative ways, from a favorite chicken salad to such famous international delights as Pollo Tonnato or Duck and Onion Salad. It's low in calories, low in fats—what more can you ask for?

Meats range from the hearty to the elegant, with Baked Ham with Cloves, Tongue in Aspic, French Beef Salad, and much more.

And there are some new favorites: delicious pasta salads and vegetable salads that are nutritious and hearty enough to serve as the main attraction—Tortellini-Mushroom Salad, Ratatouille, or Vegetarian Chef's Salad, to name only a few.

AVOCADOS WITH HAM-MUSHROOM SALAD

1 cup diced boiled ham
4 radishes, sliced thin
⅓ cup water chestnuts, sliced thin
7 or 8 fresh mushrooms, sliced
⅓ cup Mayonnaise*
3 avocados
Lemon juice
Lettuce (optional)
Watercress (optional)

Mix the first 5 ingredients. Peel the avocados, cut in half lengthwise, and sprinkle a little lemon juice over each half. Fill with ham mixture and serve on lettuce and watercress if desired. Serves 6.

ECUADORIAN STUFFED AVOCADOS

3 avocados, halved lengthwise
1 teaspoon lemon juice
⅓ cup Mayonnaise*
1 small clove garlic, crushed
2 tablespoons tomato paste
½ teaspoon salt
⅛ teaspoon pepper
1 cup chopped cooked meat (chicken, pork, and/or ham)
½ cup cooked diced carrots
½ cup cooked cut green beans
Lettuce (optional)

Rub the cut surfaces of the avocados with the lemon juice to prevent discoloration; set aside. In a medium bowl, blend the Mayonnaise, garlic, tomato paste, salt, and pepper. Stir in the meat, carrots, and beans. Spoon into avocado halves. Serve on platter or individual plates, lettuce-lined if you wish. Serves 6.

BEEF SALAD

3–4 cups cut-up or thin-sliced cooked beef
1 large sweet onion, sliced very thin
2 ribs celery, diced
½ cup Mayonnaise*
½ cup sour cream
2 teaspoons lemon juice
2 teaspoons Dijon-style mustard
½ teaspoon salt
Greens (optional)

Combine the beef, onion, and celery. Mix the Mayonnaise with the sour cream, lemon juice, mustard, and salt. Stir the dressing into the beef. Serve on shredded greens if you wish. Watercress is good with this salad. Serves 6 to 8.

THREE BEAN–MEAT SALAD

1 large clove garlic, minced
1 teaspoon salt
½ teaspoon dried or 1 tablespoon fresh basil
½ teaspoon pepper
⅓ cup oil
¼ cup red wine vinegar
1 (16-ounce) can red kidney beans, rinsed and drained
1½ cups cooked cut green beans
1 (10½-ounce) can chick-peas, rinsed and drained
1½ cups julienned salami or pepperoni
1 large tomato, peeled, seeded, and chopped
1 cup chopped onion (about 1 large onion)
2 tablespoons chopped canned green chilies (optional)
Lettuce

In a large bowl, stir together the garlic, salt, basil, pepper, oil, and
vinegar until well blended. Add the remaining ingredients except the
lettuce and mix gently. Chill. Serve on lettuce. Serves 4 to 6.

BROWN RICE AND BEEF SALAD WITH WALNUTS

2 cups cold roast beef, cut in thin strips
2 cups cooked brown rice
3 tablespoons chopped walnuts
3 scallions, with tops, minced
2 tablespoons minced green pepper
1½ cups Chive Sauce*
Lettuce
Ripe olives (for garnish)
Parsley sprigs (for garnish)

Combine the beef, rice, walnuts, scallions, green pepper, and Chive
Sauce*. Toss gently. Chill at least 1 hour. Serve on lettuce; garnish with
the olives and parsley. Serves 6.

FRENCH BEEF SALAD

1 pound mushrooms, sliced
2 tablespoons oil
2½ pounds sirloin steak or cooked roast beef
¼ teaspoon thyme
6 tablespoons Lemon French Dressing*
Boston lettuce leaves
2 tablespoons minced chives or parsley
1 box cherry tomatoes

Sauté the mushrooms in the oil for 2 to 3 minutes, stirring gently. Remove and cool. Broil the steak (if using) until medium done. Cut the steak or roast beef into thin strips and combine with the mushrooms, thyme, and dressing. Toss to coat with the dressing. Cool and arrange on a platter on lettuce leaves. Sprinkle with the chives or parsley. Garnish the platter with the cherry tomatoes. Serves 8.

ITALIAN BEEF ROLLS

¼ pound ground beef
½ cup chopped hard salami
½ cup grated Parmesan cheese
¼ cup fine dry bread crumbs
¼ cup minced parsley
2 hard-cooked eggs, chopped coarsely
3 cloves garlic, crushed
½ teaspoon oregano
1 (10½-ounce) can condensed beef broth, diluted
1 pound (about 3 pieces) sirloin or round steak, ¼ inch thick, pounded very
    thin
2 tablespoons oil, preferably olive
¼ cup dry red wine (optional)
Tomato Mayonnaise*

In a large bowl, combine the beef, salami, Parmesan, bread crumbs, parsley, eggs, garlic, oregano, and enough broth (about 1 cup) to make a soft mixture. Divide mixture among the steak pieces and spread evenly. Roll up each piece jelly-roll fashion, tucking in the ends as much as possible. Tie each roll at both ends with kitchen twine. In a medium skillet over medium heat, sauté the beef rolls and brown quickly on all sides. When browned, pour in the remaining broth and the wine, if using. Cover and simmer gently about 20 minutes, or until rolls are fork-tender. Lift out and cool. When ready to serve, remove strings and slice beef thin. Serve with Tomato Mayonnaise*. Serves 6.

JELLIED BEEF

1 tablespoon oil
1 large garlic clove, slivered
1 (3–3½-pound) beef rump roast or other cut for lean pot roast
2 large onions, sliced
1 teaspoon salt
½ teaspoon pepper
½ teaspoon thyme
1 bay leaf, crumbled
1 cup dry white wine
2 pounds meat bones
1 envelope unflavored gelatin
1–2 tablespoons brandy
Chopped parsley (for garnish)

Heat the oil in a Dutch oven or heavy pot; add the garlic and meat and brown meat well on all sides. Add the onions, salt, pepper, thyme, and bay leaf. Add 1 cup hot water, the wine, and the meat bones. Cover and simmer until meat is tender, about 3 hours. Cool. Discard bones and strain broth through a fine sieve. Return broth to the pot and reduce to 2 cups over high heat. Chill. Lift off all fat. Trim beef of excess fat, slice thin, and arrange slices, slightly overlapping, on a serving platter. Cover tightly and chill.

Soften the gelatin in ¼ cup cold water. Bring the defatted broth to a boil. Add the brandy and check for salt. Pour the broth over the gelatin and stir until dissolved. Chill to the consistency of unbeaten egg white. Spoon over meat to glaze. Chill. Garnish with the parsley. Serves 6 to 8.

MARINATED STEAK AND VEGETABLES

1 (2-pound) flank steak, broiled rare and cut in thin strips
1 large tomato, peeled and sliced thin
1 large onion, sliced thin
1 (9-ounce) package frozen French-cut green beans, cooked and drained
½ cup olive oil
¼ cup dry red wine
2 tablespoons red wine vinegar
½ teaspoon dry mustard
¼ teaspoon salt
Dash pepper

Place the steak, tomato, onion, and green beans in a large shallow dish. Mix all the other ingredients and pour over. Cover and chill at least 3 hours or overnight, turning occasionally. Serves 4 to 6.

RAW BEEF SALAD

2½ pounds lean beef, such as sirloin
6–8 scallions, with tops, cut into thin strips about 2 inches long
1 cup French Dressing*
2 tablespoons prepared horseradish or mustard

Trim any fat from the beef and slice it into very thin julienne strips. Combine with the scallions. Mix the dressing with the horseradish or mustard, pour over the beef, and toss. Chill for 1 to 2 hours. Serves 6.

ROAST BEEF WITH GREEN SAUCE

1 (5-pound) rump or sirloin roast, not overcooked, chilled
1 cup Mayonnaise*
1 cup packed spinach leaves
1 cup packed parsley leaves
1 medium dill pickle
⅓ cup sliced scallions, with tops
¼ teaspoon salt

Slice the roast beef thin. Whirl all the other ingredients in a blender and pour over. Chill. Serves 8.

ROAST BEEF SALAD PLATE

2 large tomatoes, peeled and sliced
½ teaspoon sugar
1 pound cooked roast beef, sliced thin
1 bunch watercress, stems trimmed
⅓ cup French Dressing*
2 scallions, with tops, sliced

Arrange a quarter of the tomato slices, overlapping slightly, on each of 4 chilled dinner plates. Sprinkle with the sugar. Arrange the beef and watercress next to the tomatoes. Spoon the dressing over the tomatoes and beef. Sprinkle the scallions over the tomatoes. Serves 4.

TOSTADA SALAD

2 large tomatoes, peeled and diced
¼ cup chopped green pepper
1 small red onion, chopped
1½ tablespoons green chilies, chopped
¼ teaspoon salt
4 cups torn lettuce
1 pound lean ground beef
1 (16-ounce) can red kidney beans, rinsed and drained
1¼ cups cubed Cheddar cheese (about 6 ounces)
Corn chips (optional)

In a small bowl, mix the tomatoes, green pepper, onion, chilies, and salt; set aside. Place the lettuce in a large salad bowl; set aside. In a large skillet, cook the meat, breaking it up with a wooden spoon, until brown and crumbly. Drain off excess fat; cool. Add the meat to the lettuce, then add the beans, cheese, and tomato mixture; toss to blend. Serve with corn chips, if you wish. Serves 4 to 6.

COTTAGE CHEESE–SPINACH PIE

½ cup minced onion
2 tablespoons butter
¾–1 cup chopped cooked spinach
¼ cup milk
1½ teaspoons salt
¼ teaspoon pepper
⅛ teaspoon nutmeg
4 eggs, slightly beaten
1 cup small-curd cottage cheese
½ cup grated Parmesan cheese
1 baked 9-inch pie shell
2 large or 3 medium tomatoes, seeded and sliced
1 teaspoon sugar

Sauté the onion gently in the butter for 2 to 3 minutes, until softened but not brown. Add the spinach and heat the mixture. Stir in the milk, 1 teaspoon salt, pepper, and nutmeg. Put the eggs in a bowl with the cottage cheese and Parmesan cheese. Stir and fold in the spinach mixture; blend well. Pour into the pie shell. Arrange the tomato slices around the top and sprinkle them with a mixture of sugar and the remaining ½ teaspoon salt. Bake at 375° F. about 25 minutes, until set. Chill. Serves 6 to 8.

CHEF'S SALAD I
(Basic)

1 head lettuce, preferably soft
Assorted greens
2 large tomatoes, peeled and cubed
1 large cucumber, peeled, seeded, and cubed
4 scallions, with tops, minced
½ pound cooked chicken or turkey, cut in thin strips
½ pound ham, cut in thin strips
½ pound Swiss cheese, cut in thin strips
½–¾ cup French Dressing*

Tear up the lettuce and a few other greens such as watercress, young spinach, or endive. Put into a large salad bowl and place the other ingredients except the dressing on top. Arrange them attractively. Chill. Pour the dressing over and toss at table. Serves about 8.

Almost anything goes in Chef's Salad—add such vegetables as chopped celery or artichoke hearts; use other cheeses instead of Swiss, or other meats, such as bits of beef, smoked tongue, or, for a change of flavor, anchovies. Instead of French Dressing, try Blue Cheese Dressing with Parsley*, Mayonnaise*, or Thousand Island Dressing*.

CHEF'S SALAD II

3 cups torn greens
2 cups cooked whole small green beans
½ pound cooked ham, cut in thin strips
½ pound Swiss cheese, cut in thin strips
½ cup sliced radishes
¼ cup sliced scallions, with tops
2 large tomatoes, peeled and cut in wedges
1 medium cucumber, peeled and sliced
⅓ cup French Dressing*

Place the greens in a large salad bowl. Arrange the remaining ingredients, except the dressing, on the greens. Add the dressing just before serving. Toss at table. Serves 6.

VEGETARIAN CHEF'S SALAD

1 head soft lettuce, torn up
2 cups cut-up spinach and/or watercress
2 cups shredded iceberg lettuce
4 medium tomatoes, peeled and cut up
1 medium green pepper, seeded and cut into thin strips
1 large cucumber, peeled and sliced
3 medium carrots, sliced thin or diced
1 cup diced celery
4 scallions, with tops, chopped
1 (7- or 7¾-ounce) can tuna or salmon (optional)
¼ pound cheese, sliced or diced (optional)
½–¾ cup French Dressing*

You need a lot of greens and several of the vegetables. Use fish and/or cheese if you wish. The exact amounts depend upon the number of items included and the number of guests. Place the ingredients in separate piles on top of a bed of greens in a large salad bowl. Pour the dressing over and toss at table. Serves 6 to 10.

CHICKEN AND HAM WITH TARRAGON

4 boned chicken breasts or 8 thighs or a combination
½ teaspoon salt
¼ teaspoon pepper
2 tablespoons oil
½ cup Lemon French Dressing*
1 tablespoon chopped fresh or 1 teaspoon dried tarragon
½ teaspoon sugar
2 tablespoons Mayonnaise*
8 slices cooked ham
Lettuce

If using chicken thighs, bone them. Pound the chicken until about ⅓ inch thick. Sprinkle with the salt and pepper. Sauté gently in the oil, turning to brown evenly. Cook 15 to 20 minutes, until tender. Remove, drain on paper towels, and chill. Combine the dressing with the tarragon, sugar, and Mayonnaise. Mix thoroughly. Place the ham on lettuce (either soft leaves or shredded firm lettuce) on a cold platter. Put a piece of chicken on each slice of ham and pour the dressing over. Chill. Serves 8.

CHICKEN SALAD I

6 cups bite-size pieces cooked chicken
1½ cups diced celery
½ cup Mayonnaise*
2 tablespoons chicken stock (optional)
Lettuce
3 hard-cooked eggs (optional)

Combine the chicken and celery. Pour the Mayonnaise over and toss gently. If you have any leftover strong chicken stock, mix 2 tablespoons into the Mayonnaise. Chill. Serve on lettuce. Garnish with quartered or sliced hard-cooked eggs, if you wish. Serves 6 to 8.

CHICKEN SALAD II

4 cups cubed cooked chicken
2 cups diced celery
2 cups white seedless grapes, halved if large
¾ cup Mayonnaise* made with lemon juice
¼ cup sour cream
2 teaspoons curry powder
1–2 tablespoons strong chicken broth (if available)
Salt

Combine the chicken, celery, and grapes. Mix the Mayonnaise with the sour cream, curry powder, and the broth, if you have some left over. Taste for salt. Pour over the salad and toss gently until thoroughly mixed. Chill. Serves 6 to 8.

GARDEN CHICKEN SALAD

3 cups diced cooked chicken, chilled
1 (10-ounce) package fresh spinach, washed, drained, and torn into small
    pieces
¾ cup chopped walnuts
2 medium apples, cored and chopped
1 cup Vinaigrette with Herbs*

Combine all the ingredients and toss lightly. Serve immediately. Serves 6.

CHICKEN WITH APRICOT MAYONNAISE
(English Coronation Chicken)

1 (4½–5-pound) roasting chicken
1 cup Mayonnaise*
¼ cup apricot preserves (or more)
1 tablespoon curry powder
3 cups cold cooked rice

Poach or steam the chicken until tender, about 1½ hours. Cool, remove skin, and slice the meat onto a platter. Combine the Mayonnaise with the ¼ cup apricot preserves and the curry powder. Adjust seasoning to taste, adding more preserves if you wish. Spoon the sauce over the chicken. Chill or serve at room temperature, with the rice. Serves 6.

CHICKEN BREASTS IN ASPIC

3 pounds chicken breasts, skinned, split, and boned (reserve bones)
1 orange, sliced thin (with peel)
1 clove garlic, crushed
1 onion, chopped
3 sprigs parsley
1 teaspoon salt
3 tablespoons curaçao or other orange-flavored liqueur
½ cup liver pâté
2 tablespoons butter, softened
4 scallions, including tops, minced
2 tablespoons finely chopped water chestnuts
1 envelope unflavored gelatin
1 cup Mayonnaise*
3 tablespoons minced parsley

Place the chicken breasts in a skillet; cover with the orange slices; add the garlic, onion, parsley sprigs, salt, liqueur, and 1½ cups water. Simmer, uncovered, 15 minutes. Discard the orange slices and remove the chicken breasts to cool. Strain the broth and reduce to ½ cup over high heat; keep warm. Combine the pâté, butter, scallions, and water chestnuts. Spread over the cooled chicken breasts and chill until the pâté mixture is firm. Meanwhile, soften the gelatin in 2 tablespoons cold water and stir into the hot broth until dissolved. Stir in the Mayonnaise. Spoon half the gelatin mixture over the chilled chicken breasts. Chill until firm, keeping the remaining gelatin mixture soft over hot water. When the chilled chicken breasts are firm, turn them over and spoon the remaining gelatin mixture over the other side. Chill. Just before serving, garnish with the minced parsley. Serves 6.

BROWN RICE SALAD WITH CHICKEN

4 cups slivered cooked chicken
3 cups cooked brown rice
6 scallions, with tops, chopped
2 tablespoons capers, drained
3 pimientos, cut in julienne strips
1 green pepper, cut in julienne strips
1 tablespoon chopped fresh or 1 teaspoon dried tarragon
½–⅔ cup French Dressing*

In a large bowl, combine the chicken with the rice, scallions, capers, pimientos, and green pepper. Add the tarragon to the dressing. Add ½ cup to the salad. If the salad is not moist enough, add a little more dressing (salad should not be too wet). Chill or serve at room temperature. Serves 8.

STUFFED CHICKEN ROLLS

2 hard-cooked eggs, chopped fine
¼ cup minced parsley
¼ cup fine dry bread crumbs
1 clove garlic, crushed
½ teaspoon basil
½ teaspoon thyme
¼ teaspoon pepper
2 whole large chicken breasts, skinned and boned (about 1¼ pounds)
½ teaspoon salt
2 tablespoons butter
¼ cup chicken broth or water
Greens (optional)
Green Sauce* or other sauce

Stir together the eggs, parsley, bread crumbs, garlic, basil, thyme, and pepper; set aside. Pound the chicken breasts, smooth side down, between sheets of waxed paper until about ¼ inch thick. Season with the salt. Divide filling between breasts and spread to within ½ inch of edges. Roll up tight and tie with string. In a heavy skillet, brown in the butter over medium heat until golden. Add the broth; cover and simmer 15 minutes, or until tender. Remove chicken to dish. Pour pan juices over chicken; cover and chill overnight. Remove strings and slice thin. Good on greens; pass Green Sauce or other sauce of your choice. Serves 4.

CHICKEN CURRY MOLD

2 Bermuda or large red onions
½ cup butter
2 (4-pound) roasting chickens, cut up
1 teaspoon salt
¼ teaspoon pepper
1–2 tablespoons curry powder
1 envelope unflavored gelatin
1 cup heavy cream (or more)
Chutney

Slice the onions thin and sauté gently in the butter in a large skillet. Add the chickens and cook until lightly browned. Transfer to a heavy pot or Dutch oven. Sprinkle with the salt, pepper, and 1 tablespoon curry powder. Add 1 cup water to the skillet, scrape up the brown bits, and transfer to the chicken. Cover and simmer about 1 hour, or until chicken is tender. Add a little more water if necessary. Cool; take chicken from pot. Remove the skin and bones, discard, and cut flesh into bite-size pieces. Transfer to a bowl, dish, or casserole. Soften the gelatin in ¼ cup cold water; add to liquid in pot; heat and stir until dissolved. Stir in 1 cup cream and pour over the chicken. The chicken should be covered with liquid. Add a little more cream or water if needed. Add more salt and curry powder to taste. Chill for several hours or overnight. Unmold onto a cold platter. Serves 8.

CURRIED CHICKEN-RICE SALAD

1½ cups Mayonnaise*
1½ tablespoons curry powder
3 cups cold cooked rice
3 cups diced cooked chicken
1 medium green pepper, chopped
1 medium red pepper, chopped
5 scallions, including tops, minced
Salt
Pepper
Lettuce cups
Cherry tomatoes (garnish)

In a large bowl, blend the Mayonnaise and curry powder. Add the rice, chicken, peppers, and scallions. Toss lightly. Add salt and pepper to taste. Chill. Serve in lettuce cups; garnish with cherry tomatoes. Serves 6.

CREAMY CHICKEN SALAD WITH NECTARINES

3 cups diced cooked chicken
1½–2 pounds nectarines, diced (about 3 cups)
1 scallion, with top, minced
4 ribs celery, sliced thin
Juice of 1 medium orange (about ⅓ cup)
½ teaspoon salt
⅛ teaspoon pepper
½ cup heavy cream, whipped stiff
½ cup Mayonnaise*
Crisp greens
¼ cup finely chopped walnuts (for garnish)

In a large bowl, combine the chicken, nectarines, scallion, celery, orange juice, salt, and pepper; set aside. Lightly combine the whipped cream and Mayonnaise; fold into chicken mixture just to coat. Spoon into a serving bowl lined with greens. Garnish with the walnuts. Chill. Serves 4 to 6.

CHICKEN MOUSSE

1 envelope unflavored gelatin
2 tablespoons butter
1 tablespoon flour
2 teaspoons curry powder
½ teaspoon salt
¼ teaspoon pepper
1 cup milk
4 cups minced cooked chicken
½ cup Mayonnaise*
½ cup heavy cream, whipped
Watercress or parsley sprigs (for garnish)

Soften the gelatin in ¼ cup cold water. Melt the butter; stir in the flour, curry powder, salt, and pepper. Add the milk slowly, stirring. Cook 2 minutes, until smooth and slightly thickened. Add the gelatin and heat and stir until gelatin is dissolved. Cool; stir in the chicken and Mayonnaise. Blend well and fold in the whipped cream. Taste for seasoning and pour into a mold or bowl. Chill for several hours, until set. Turn out onto a cold platter and garnish with cress or parsley. Serves 8.

CHICKEN MOUSSE LOAF

1 (5-pound) chicken, broiled, steamed, or roasted
3½ cups chicken broth
1 onion, cut into quarters
3 ribs celery, cut into several pieces
4 sprigs parsley
4 slices white bread, crusts removed, crumbled
2 tablespoons lemon juice
Paprika, watercress, black olives, and lemon wedges (for garnish)

When the chicken is cool enough to handle, remove the skin and bones and cut the flesh into small bite-size pieces. Add the skin and bones to the broth, with the onion, celery, and parsley. (If you have used a boiled chicken, substitute 3½ cups of its liquid for the chicken broth.) Simmer, covered, for 1 hour. In a blender or processor, purée 2 cups broth with the vegetables and add any scraps of chicken. Remove into a bowl. Meanwhile, mix the bread with ½ cup broth until smooth. Combine the purée with the bread mixture and lemon juice. Add enough broth to make it the consistency of thin cake frosting. Taste for seasoning. Mix the chicken with half of the sauce and pile on an oval platter. Form into an oval mound, flat on top. Spread the sides and top with the remaining sauce. Chill overnight. An hour before serving, sprinkle with the paprika. Decorate the platter with the watercress, olives, and lemon wedges. Serves 8.

CHICKEN WITH VEGETABLES VINAIGRETTE

1 (3½-pound) broiler-fryer, cut up
½ teaspoon salt
½ teaspoon paprika
½ cup milk
Dried bread crumbs
2 (10-ounce) packages frozen mixed vegetables
¼ cup French Dressing*

Sprinkle the chicken with the salt and paprika. Dip in the milk and then turn in the crumbs. Place skin side down in a baking dish and bake at 425° F. about 50 minutes, until done, turning the chicken once. Cool. Cook the vegetables according to the package directions, omitting the butter. Drain the vegetables and pour the dressing over. Chill. When ready to serve, divide the cold chicken among 4 plates and surround with the vegetables. Serve at room temperature. Serves 4.

CHICKEN-MUSHROOM-RICE SALAD

1 cup rice
1⅓ teaspoons salt
1 pound mushrooms
¼ cup olive oil
3 tablespoons lemon juice
2 tablespoons chopped fresh or 2 teaspoons dried oregano
3 tablespoons minced onion or scallions
¾ cup diced or slivered celery
1½ cups diced or slivered cooked chicken

Put the rice in 2 cups cold water with 1 teaspoon salt and cook 20 minutes. Drain and cool. Wipe the mushrooms and slice. Put the mushrooms in a bowl with a mixture of the oil, lemon juice, remaining ⅓ teaspoon salt, and oregano. Stir in the onion and celery. Let stand for 1 to 2 hours. Rake in the rice, using a fork instead of a spoon. Fold in the chicken and toss gently. Taste for seasoning. Chill if you wish. Serves 6.

CHICKEN WITH WALNUT SAUCE

2 medium carrots, halved lengthwise
1 medium onion
1 rib celery, with leaves on
3 sprigs parsley
1 teaspoon salt
¼ teaspoon pepper
1 (4–5-pound) roasting chicken
3 slices white bread, crusts removed
2 cups walnuts
1 clove garlic, crushed
1 teaspoon grated lemon peel
1 teaspoon lemon juice
1 tablespoon paprika
1 tablespoon minced parsley

Bring about 5 quarts water to a boil in a large pot. Add the carrots, onion, celery, parsley sprigs, salt, and pepper. Carefully lower the chicken, breast side up, into the water. Bring again to a boil, cover, and cook over medium heat 30 minutes. Remove from heat and refrigerate at once (do not lift cover). Allow the chicken to cool in the broth about 3 hours, or until sides of pot are cool to touch. Remove chicken and strain broth, reserving ½ cup for the sauce. Discard skin and slice breast meat thin;

cut off remaining meat in chunks. Arrange all on a platter, cover, and set aside.

Tear the bread in pieces into a blender. Pour in the reserved broth and blend at high speed until well mixed. Add the walnuts ½ cup at a time, blending at high speed until well mixed. Add the garlic, lemon peel, and lemon juice and blend again (sauce will be the consistency of mayonnaise). Pour sauce over chicken and sprinkle with the paprika and minced parsley. Chill. Serves 6.

SOY-SESAME CHICKEN WITH PINEAPPLE

4 cooked chicken legs
¼ cup sugar
¼ cup soy sauce
1 tablespoon sesame seeds, toasted until golden
1 (8-ounce) can pineapple rings

Place the chicken legs in a shallow pan. Mix the sugar and soy sauce and pour over, turning chicken to coat. Marinate in refrigerator, turning occasionally, at least 4 hours or overnight. Sprinkle evenly with the sesame seeds. Garnish with the pineapple rings. Serve chilled or at room temperature. Serves 4.

TOMATO ASPIC RING WITH CHICKEN SALAD

2 envelopes unflavored gelatin
1½ cups tomato juice
2 cups orange juice
¼ cup lemon juice
¼ teaspoon salt
½ teaspoon Worcestershire sauce
3–4 cups Chicken Salad I* or II*
White grapes (optional, for garnish)

Sprinkle the gelatin over ½ cup tomato juice in a saucepan; stir over low heat until gelatin dissolves, about 3 minutes. Remove from heat and stir in the remaining tomato juice, orange and lemon juices, salt, and Worcestershire. Pour into a 4-cup ring mold that has been rinsed in cold water; chill until firm. Unmold onto a serving plate. Spoon the chicken salad into the center (garnish with any remaining chicken salad); garnish with grapes if desired. Serves 6.

CHICKEN WITH YOGURT

1 (3-pound) broiler-fryer, cut up
2 cups plain yogurt
1 large clove garlic, crushed
1 tablespoon lime juice
1 tablespoon butter, melted
1 teaspoon chili powder
½ teaspoon coriander
⅛ teaspoon powdered ginger
⅛ teaspoon cardamom seeds, crushed

Remove the skin from the chicken pieces except the wings. Cut small slits in several places on each piece. In a large shallow baking dish, stir together the remaining ingredients. Add the chicken and spoon sauce over it. Cover and marinate in refrigerator several hours or overnight. Transfer chicken, with any marinade that clings to it, to rack in broiler pan. Broil about 6 inches from heat source, 20 minutes on each side, or until chicken is tender and juices run clear when meat is pierced with fork. Chill or serve at room temperature. Serves 4.

CORNISH GAME HENS

4 large Cornish game hens
1 teaspoon salt
¼ teaspoon pepper
3 tablespoons butter, melted
3 tablespoons chicken broth

Cut the hens in half and rub with the salt and pepper. Place skin side down in a pan and bake at 350° F. for 20 minutes. Baste with a mixture of the butter and broth. Cook 10 minutes; baste again, and turn over and baste. Bake 30 minutes, basting several times. Cool and serve at room temperature or chilled. Serves 8.

DUCK AND ONION SALAD

Lettuce leaves
2 large Bermuda, Spanish, or red onions, sliced thin
3 cups diced or slivered cooked duck
¼ cup French Dressing*
2 tablespoons Mayonnaise*
2 tablespoons orange juice
Grated peel of 1 orange
Minced parsley (for garnish)

Line a salad bowl with lettuce. Put half the onions on the lettuce, add half the duck, and repeat. Combine the French Dressing, Mayonnaise, and orange juice and peel and mix thoroughly. Pour over the salad. Garnish with the parsley. Serve at room temperature. Serves 6.

HAM-CHUTNEY-RICE SALAD WITH PLUMS

1 cup Mayonnaise*
½ cup chutney, chopped
½ teaspoon salt
4 cups cooked rice
1½ pounds cooked ham, julienne-cut
1 (10-ounce) package frozen peas, cooked and drained
4 large plums, pitted and cut up
Lettuce

In a large bowl, mix well the Mayonnaise, chutney, and salt. Add the rice, ham, peas, and plums; toss until well coated. Chill. Serve on lettuce. Serves 4 to 6.

HAM SALAD WITH HAZELNUTS

2½–3 cups cooked ham, cut in small cubes
2 cups cooked rice
1 medium head lettuce, torn
1¼ cups toasted hazelnuts, coarsely chopped
1–1½ cups Sour Cream Sauce*
Parsley sprigs (for garnish)

Toss the ham, rice, lettuce, and hazelnuts with the sauce. Chill. Place on platter or individual plates and garnish with parsley. Serves 4 to 6.

BAKED HAM WITH CLOVES

1 (3-pound) can cooked ham
½ cup light brown sugar
2 tablespoons strong tea
12 cloves

Remove the ham from its can. Scrape off the gelatin and set aside. Put the ham in a roasting pan and score crosswise. Combine 2 tablespoons gelatin from the ham with the sugar and tea, and spread over the ham. Stick the cloves into the top, following the scoring lines. Bake at 325° F. 45 minutes, basting once or twice. Let cool before slicing and serve at room temperture. Serves 8.

The tea gives good color and interesting flavor to the dish.

HAM WITH HONEY-MUSTARD GLAZE

1 (5-pound) canned ham
½ cup honey
1 tablespoon prepared mustard
½ teaspoon cinnamon
2 medium oranges, peeled and sliced crosswise (for garnish)
Watercress (for garnish)

Slice the ham ⅛ inch thick and tie in the original shape. Bake in a 12 × 8 × 2-inch baking dish at 325° F. about 30 minutes. Blend the honey, mustard, and cinnamon. Brush some over the ham and bake about 30 minutes longer, brushing on more honey mixture and drippings occasionally. Place ham on a platter and cool. Carefully cut and remove the string, fanning out the ham slices slightly. Garnish with the orange slices and watercress. Serve at room temperature. Serves 12.

JELLIED HAM MOLD

2 envelopes unflavored gelatin
3 beef bouillon cubes
1 teaspoon thyme
Dash hot pepper sauce
2 tablespoons minced parsley
2 cups julienne-cut cooked ham
1 large carrot, coarsely shredded
Watercress sprigs (for garnish)

In a mixing bowl, soften the gelatin in ½ cup cold water. In a saucepan, combine 2½ cups water and the bouillon cubes and thyme. Bring to a boil and stir to dissolve cubes. Pour the boiling liquid over the gelatin mixture and stir until gelatin is completely dissolved. Add the hot pepper sauce and parsley; chill to the consistency of unbeaten egg white. Fold in the ham and carrot. Turn into a 5-cup mold. Chill until firm. Unmold onto a platter and garnish with watercress. Serves 4 to 6.

CURRY LAMB LOAF

1½ pounds ground lamb
1 medium onion, chopped fine
1¼ teaspoons salt
1 tablespoon curry powder
¼ cup chopped chutney with syrup
¼ cup slivered almonds
⅓ cup chopped tart apple
1 cup soft stale-bread crumbs
½ cup milk
1 egg, slightly beaten

Combine all the ingredients and mix well. Pack into a 9 × 5 × 3-inch loaf pan. Bake at 350° F. 1 hour. Cool, then chill. Slice thin to serve. Serves 4 to 6.

LUNCHEON PLATTER

Lettuce, shredded
2 (4⅜-ounce) cans sardines
8 thin slices baked or boiled ham
8 thin slices cooked chicken or turkey
8 hard-cooked eggs or Deviled Eggs*
4 tomatoes, peeled and sliced
⅓ pound Swiss or feta cheese, cut up
½ cup French Dressing*
Watercress sprigs

Line a platter with lettuce. Pile the ingredients on the platter, arranging them attractively, alternating colors. If using hard-cooked eggs, cut in halves. Tuck the watercress in around the edges and pour the dressing over all. Serves 8.

SALADE NIÇOISE

2 tablespoons dry white wine
2 tablespoons wine vinegar
1 teaspoon salt
½ teaspoon pepper
½ cup olive oil
2 tablespoons minced scallions
1 tablespoon minced parsley
8 medium potatoes, cooked, then peeled, sliced, and kept warm
1 small head Boston lettuce
¾ pound green beans, trimmed, cooked crisp-tender, and cut into 1½-inch
    pieces
1 (6½-ounce) can tuna, drained and broken up
4–6 hard-cooked eggs, halved or quartered
8 anchovy fillets
½ cup pitted ripe olives

Stir the wine, vinegar, salt, and pepper in a large bowl until the salt dissolves. Add the olive oil. Reserve ¼ cup dressing. To the remaining dressing add the scallions and parsley. Stir to mix. Add the potatoes and toss gently until each slice is well coated with dressing. Cover and refrigerate 2 hours. Line a platter with lettuce leaves and arrange the potato salad, beans, tuna, and eggs on the lettuce. Crisscross anchovies on the salad and dot with olives. Pour the reserved dressing over all. Serve immediately. Serves 4.

PASTA SALAD WITH CHICK-PEAS

½ cup French Dressing*
1 teaspoon oregano
½ pound pasta (shells or bows) cooked and drained
1 (16-ounce) can chick-peas, rinsed and drained
1 pint box cherry tomatoes, halved
¼ pound mozzarella cheese, cut in thin strips
1 green pepper, seeded and cut in thin strips
½ cup pitted ripe olives
2 tablespoons minced parsley

Combine the French Dressing with oregano, add the remaining ingredients, and toss thoroughly. Place in a salad bowl and chill. Serves 6 as a luncheon dish.

PASTA WITH CHICKEN

1 pound thin pasta: thin linguine, vermicelli, or spaghettini
2 teaspoons salt
¾ cup French Dressing*
½ cup Mayonnaise*
4 cups cubed cooked chicken
16 cherry tomatoes or 6 medium tomatoes, peeled and quartered
3 scallions, with tops, chopped
16 tiny cooked or canned beets
1 medium avocado, peeled and cut into small wedges
1 teaspoon lemon juice
1 large red or green pepper, slivered

Cook the pasta in deep water with the salt 4 or 5 minutes. Vermicelli cooks very quickly—do not overcook. Drain and cool slightly. Mix the French Dressing and Mayonnaise. Pour half of it over the pasta and toss. Add the chicken, tomatoes, and scallions and toss gently. Chill. Pile the pasta in the center of a cold serving dish and surround with the beets, avocado sprinkled with lemon juice, and pepper. Pass the remaining dressing. Serves 8 to 10.

PASTA SALAD WITH VEGETABLES

5 small zucchini, sliced ½ inch thick
1 medium green or red pepper, cut in ½-inch chunks
2 large cloves garlic, crushed
¼ cup oil
1 pound spaghetti, cooked and drained
1½ cups cooked green peas
1 teaspoon salt
⅛ teaspoon crushed red pepper
⅓ cup grated Parmesan cheese
¼ cup minced parsley
10 cherry tomatoes, halved

In a large skillet over medium heat, stir the zucchini, green pepper, and garlic in the oil 3 minutes, or until crisp-tender. Add to the hot spaghetti with the peas, salt, and crushed red pepper. Toss to blend. Cool to room temperature. Just before serving, add the Parmesan, parsley, and tomatoes. Toss well. Serves 4.

WHOLE WHEAT PASTA WITH HAM

1 pound whole wheat pasta: macaroni, spaghetti, or Chinese noodles
2 teaspoons salt
⅓ cup Lemon French Dressing*
1 teaspoon oregano
½ pound cooked ham, cubed
1 (10-ounce) package frozen peas, cooked and drained
3 scallions, with tops, finely chopped, or 2 tablespoons minced chives
2 tablespoons chopped flat-leaf parsley or fresh coriander

Cook the pasta in deep water with the salt about 8 minutes. Drain and cool. Place in a salad bowl. Add the remaining ingredients, toss, and chill. Reseason and toss again just before serving. Serves 6.

PASTA WITH YOGURT-ANCHOVY SAUCE

1 pound pasta (linguine, fettucini, spaghettini, or small shells)
2 cups plain yogurt
¼ cup minced chives or finely chopped scallions, with tops
1 (2-ounce) can anchovies, cut up
1 clove garlic, crushed (optional)

Cook the pasta of your choice in a generous amount of salted water for a few minutes, 3 minutes for thin pasta, 5 for heavier. Do not overcook. Meanwhile, combine the yogurt with the remaining ingredients. Toss with the drained hot pasta and let rest at room temperature for several hours. Serves 4.

PESTO PRIMAVERA SALAD

1½ pounds pasta (vermicelli, linguine, or spaghettini), cooked, drained, and
    cooled slightly
1 cup broccoli flowerets
1 cup thinly sliced zucchini
1 cup asparagus, cut into 1-inch pieces
½ pound small mushrooms, sliced
½ cup chopped scallions, including tops
2 cups cherry tomatoes, halved
1 tablespoon olive oil
1 cup Pesto*

Place the pasta in a large serving bowl. Blanch the broccoli, zucchini, and asparagus in boiling water 1 minute. Refresh under cold water, drain, and add to the pasta. Add the mushrooms, scallions, and tomatoes to the pasta and mix gently. Add the olive oil and 2 tablespoons warm water to the Pesto; stir together and pour over the pasta and vegetables. Toss lightly to coat. Chill. Serves 6 to 8.

TORTELLINI-MUSHROOM SALAD

1 pound tortellini
1 teaspoon salt
½ cup light cream or half-and-half
¼ cup ricotta cheese
¼ pound coarsely chopped prosciutto or other ham
½ pound small mushrooms, sliced
2 tablespoons minced flat-leaf parsley
½ teaspoon salt
¼ teaspoon pepper
1 teaspoon oregano

Cook the tortellini in deep water with the 1 teaspoon salt 3 or 4 minutes. Drain. Place in a salad bowl. Mix the cream and ricotta until smooth. Pour over the pasta and toss. Add the ham, mushrooms, parsley, ½ teaspoon salt, pepper, and oregano. Toss thoroughly. Chill. Serves 6 to 8.

BRAISED PORK SHOULDER

1 (2–3-pound) boneless smoked pork shoulder, casing removed
12 cloves
1 (6-ounce) can frozen concentrated apple juice, thawed
1 teaspoon cinnamon

Put the pork in a deep skillet or kettle just large enough to hold it. Add ¾ cup cold water and simmer, uncovered, until water has evaporated and pork is browned well on all sides. Remove from skillet and stud with the cloves. Pour off fat from skillet. Add apple juice and cinnamon to skillet and blend together. Return pork to skillet. Cover and simmer 30 minutes per pound, or until pork is tender, basting occasionally, adding ¼ cup hot water at a time if necessary. Cover airtight and chill. When ready to serve, lift off fat, slice pork thin, and arrange on a serving platter. Brush slices very lightly with pan liquid, if you wish. Serves 4 to 6.

CHINESE PORK ROAST

1 (3–4-pound) pork loin, boned and rolled
½ cup soy sauce
¼ cup dry sherry
3 tablespoons sugar
1 large clove garlic, crushed
1 teaspoon ground ginger
Watercress sprigs and kumquats (optional)
Apricot Sauce (recipe follows)

Place the pork in a large heavy plastic bag or foil. Stir together the soy sauce, sherry, sugar, garlic, and ginger. Pour over the pork. Seal bag and place in shallow dish. Marinate in the refrigerator, turning occasionally, at least 4 hours, or overnight. Before cooking, bring meat to room temperature. Place on rack in shallow pan. Add water almost to top of rack but not touching meat. Steam-roast at 400° F. 2 hours, or until meat thermometer reads 170° F. Chill. Slice thin; garnish with watercress sprigs and kumquats if you wish. Serve with Apricot Sauce on the side. Serves 10.

This is excellent with Peach-Rice Salad*.

APRICOT SAUCE

½ cup apricot preserves
2 tablespoons cider vinegar

Mix well. Yield: about ⅔ cup.

HERBED PORK CHOPS

4 pork chops, cut ½ inch thick (about 1¼ pounds)
2 tablespoons butter
1 teaspoon salt
1 teaspoon Italian herb seasoning
⅛ teaspoon pepper

In a large heavy skillet, brown the chops in the butter. Sprinkle both sides with the salt, seasoning, and pepper. Cover and cook over low heat, turning once, 15 to 20 minutes, or until tender. Chill. Serves 4.

ONION-CHEESE QUICHE

1 (9-inch) pie shell with high, fluted rim
1 large onion, chopped
1 tablespoon butter
3 eggs
1½ cups milk
1 tablespoon flour
1 teaspoon salt
¼ teaspoon pepper
1½ cups shredded Swiss cheese (about ½ pound)

Prick the bottom of the pie shell and bake at 425° F. 10 minutes, or until light gold. Cool completely. Sauté the onion in the butter until tender; set aside. Separate 1 egg, then brush egg white on pie shell. Pour excess white into a large bowl. Add the yolk, remaining eggs, milk, flour, salt, and pepper; beat until smooth. Stir in the cheese and onion. Turn into pie shell. Bake at 325° F. 40 to 45 minutes, or until a knife inserted in the center comes out clean. Cool. Serve at room temperature. Serves 6.

RATATOUILLE

1 large sweet onion, sliced thin or chopped
2 cloves garlic, crushed or minced
¼ cup olive oil
1 large green pepper, chopped
4 small zucchini, sliced thin (not peeled)
1 medium cucumber, peeled and chopped
1 small eggplant, cut in ½-inch cubes
1 cup chicken or vegetable broth
½ (6-ounce) can tomato paste
3 medium tomatoes, peeled and cut into eighths
½ cup French Dressing*

Sauté the onion and garlic gently in the oil 5 minutes, until limp. Do not brown. Add the green pepper, zucchini, cucumber, and eggplant. Toss to coat with oil. Add the broth mixed with the tomato paste. Cover and simmer 3 or 4 minutes, until the vegetables are tender but not mushy. Stir in the tomatoes and cool. Add the dressing, toss, and chill. Serves 6 as a luncheon dish with garlic bread or toast.

ITALIAN SAUSAGE ROLL

1 loaf frozen bread dough
1 pound sweet Italian sausages, casings removed
1 medium green pepper, chopped fine
1 medium onion, chopped fine
1 clove garlic, crushed
½ teaspoon salt
⅛ teaspoon crushed red pepper (optional)
1 (6-ounce) can tomato paste
1 egg yolk, beaten

In a warm, draft-free place, thaw the dough in a bowl until soft and pliable, about 2 hours. In a medium skillet, break up and brown the sausage meat. Add the green pepper, onion, garlic, salt, and red pepper. Stir over medium heat until the pepper and onion are tender. Stir in the tomato paste and cook, uncovered, until most of the liquid has evaporated, about 10 minutes over medium-high heat. Cool. Roll out the dough on a 24 × 12-inch piece of waxed paper to form an 18 × 12-inch rectangle; brush lightly with some egg yolk. Spread meat mixture on dough. Roll tightly, jelly-roll fashion, tuck ends under, and pinch to seal. Lift roll with waxed paper to an ungreased cookie sheet. Discard paper. Brush roll with remaining egg yolk. Bake at 425° F. 25 to 30 minutes, or until top is well browned and a toothpick inserted deep in the center comes out clean. Cool completely before slicing thin. Serves 6 to 8.

AVOCADO-SEAFOOD PLATTER

2 chilled avocados, halved
1 (12½-ounce) can tuna, drained
12 cooked, peeled medium shrimp
1 bunch broccoli, trimmed, cut in short flowerets, blanched, and chilled, or
    1 (10-ounce) package frozen, cooked, drained, and chilled
12 radishes, sliced or cut decoratively
½ cup Mayonnaise* made with lemon juice

Fill each avocado half with a quarter of the tuna and top with 3 shrimp, a quarter of the broccoli, and 3 radishes. Spoon the dressing over and serve on chilled dinner plates. Serve at once. Serves 4.

BROOK TROUT IN ASPIC

1–2 pounds fish scraps and bones (no heads)
3 cups water
3 cups dry white wine
1 large onion, cut up
1 clove garlic, split
2 sprigs parsley
2 ribs celery, cut into several pieces
1 bay leaf
1 teaspoon salt
½ teaspoon pepper
8 (½–¾-pound) brook trout
2 envelopes unflavored gelatin
Lemon wedges
Mayonnaise* made with lemon juice

To make the broth, combine the first 10 ingredients in a large pot. Cover and simmer 1½ hours. Strain. Poach the trout in the broth 15 minutes. Remove trout carefully to a large deep platter, cool, and refrigerate. Boil the broth to reduce to about 3 cups. Soften the gelatin in ½ cup cold water. Add to the broth and heat and stir until dissolved. Cool until slightly thickened and syrupy. Pour over the trout. Cover thoroughly and chill until set. Cut away any aspic that has spread out around the trout, chop it, and spread around the platter. Decorate with lemon wedges. Serve with the Mayonnaise. Serves 8.

CRAB SALAD

2 (12-ounce) packages frozen crab meat, thawed and drained, or 1 pound cooked fresh crab meat
4 ribs celery, sliced thin
1 cup Mayonnaise* made with lemon juice
½ teaspoon dillseed
3 tablespoons minced parsley
Lettuce
Sliced tomatoes (for garnish)
Sliced green pepper rings or ripe olives (for garnish)

Combine the crab, celery, Mayonnaise, and herbs. Chill. Serve on lettuce. Garnish with tomatoes and pepper or olives. Serves 4.

FISH SALAD LORENZO

2 pounds cooked fish, cooled, flaked, and boned
1 tablespoon lemon juice
1 medium red onion, sliced thin and separated into rings
1½ cups chopped celery
⅛ teaspoon pepper
1 teaspoon fennel seed
¾ cup Lorenzo Dressing*
Lettuce cups

Sprinkle the fish with the lemon juice and chill. Flake fish and toss lightly with the remaining ingredients except the lettuce. Serve in lettuce cups. Serves 6.

MARINATED FISH, SPANISH STYLE
(*Escabeche*)

1½–2 pounds mackerel fillets, bass fillets, or boned kingfish steaks
1½ teaspoons salt
3 tablespoons flour
¾ cup olive oil
1 large red onion, chopped fine
½ cup sliced stuffed olives
¼ cup chopped parsley
½ cup white vinegar
1–2 large unpeeled cloves garlic, crushed (optional)
2 teaspoons paprika
¼ teaspoon cayenne pepper

Cut the fish in 1-inch pieces. Sprinkle with 1 teaspoon salt; coat with the flour. Heat ¼ cup oil in a skillet. Fry fish over medium-high heat until browned on both sides. Place fish, overlapping slightly, in a dish about 12 × 8 inches. Sprinkle with the onion, olives, parsley, and vinegar. Heat the remaining ½ cup oil in the skillet. Add the garlic and sauté until golden. Remove skillet from heat; stir in the paprika, remaining ½ teaspoon salt, and cayenne. Pour while hot over fish. Cover; chill 24 hours. Bring to room temperature before serving. Will keep, refrigerated, up to 5 days. Serves 4 to 6.

SCANDINAVIAN FISH MOUSSE

1 pound haddock, halibut, cod, or pike fillets, cut up
2 tablespoons butter, softened
1 egg
1 tablespoon flour
1 cup half-and-half or heavy cream
1 teaspoon salt
Dash hot pepper sauce
1 cup cooked crab meat, lobster, or shrimp (optional)
½ cup pitted ripe olives (for garnish)
Dill, parsley, or watercress sprigs (for garnish)
Lemon wedges (for garnish)
Cucumber Sauce* or Mayonnaise* made with lemon juice

Process the fish with the butter in a processor or blender until smooth.
Beat together the egg, flour, half-and-half, salt, and hot pepper sauce.
Gradually add the fish until smooth and fluffy. Spoon into a well-greased,
lightly floured 3-cup mold. Cover tightly with foil. Place mold on rack
in deep saucepan. Add hot water halfway up sides of mold. Cover; steam
30 to 40 minutes, or until mousse is firm to the touch. Remove from
water; cool on rack 5 minutes. Loosen around edges with the tip of a
knife; unmold. Cool, then wrap and chill. Cut in ½-inch slices; decorate
the platter with the seafood if you wish. Garnish with the olives, dill,
and lemon. Serve topped with Cucumber Sauce or Mayonnaise. Serves 4.

FISH-POTATO SALAD

4 medium potatoes, cooked, peeled, and sliced
1½ pounds cooked fish, cooled, flaked, and boned
2 tablespoons lemon juice
1 cup thinly sliced celery
1–1½ cups Green Goddess Dressing*
2 medium tomatoes, peeled and cut in wedges (for garnish)
Watercress (for garnish)

Layer the potatoes on a serving platter. Cover with the fish; sprinkle
with the lemon juice and then the celery. Pour some dressing over and
serve the rest of the dressing on the side. Arrange the tomato wedges and
watercress around edge of platter. Serve at room temperature. Serves 4.

MEDITERRANEAN FISH-RICE SALAD

2 cups cooked fish, flaked, boned, and chilled
1 medium onion, minced
2 medium tomatoes, peeled and chopped
3 tablespoons minced parsley
1 tablespoon minced fresh or 1½ teaspoons dried basil
½ cup chopped ripe olives
3 cups cold cooked rice
1 cup French Dressing*
Spinach leaves
Cherry tomatoes or tomato wedges (for garnish)

Combine the fish, onion, tomatoes, parsley, basil, olives, and rice; toss gently. Pour the dressing over, mix, and chill. Serve on spinach leaves and garnish with tomatoes. Serves 6 to 8.

SALMON PÂTÉ LOAF

2 eggs
½ cup milk
2 cups soft bread crumbs
1 medium onion, cut in chunks
1 cup loosely packed parsley
2 tablespoons lemon juice
½ teaspoon salt
½ teaspoon dry mustard
½ teaspoon dried or 2 tablespoons fresh dillweed
¼ teaspoon pepper
2 (16-ounce) cans salmon, drained
Parsley sprigs (for garnish)
Cucumber slices (for garnish)

Whirl the eggs, milk, and bread crumbs in a processor or blender; let stand 5 minutes. Add the onion, parsley, lemon juice, salt, mustard, dillweed, and pepper. Process until smooth. Add the salmon; whirl until smooth. Turn into a greased 7 × 3 × 2-inch loaf pan. Bake at 375° F. 45 minutes, or until top feels firm when pressed lightly with finger. Cool in pan 10 minutes. Turn out on rack, then invert onto serving platter. Chill. Slice thin and garnish with parsley and cucumber. Serves 6.

NOTE: An 8 × 5 loaf pan may be used. Check the pâté after 30 minutes for doneness.

FISH SALAD IN TOMATO ASPIC

2 pounds cooked fish, cooled, flaked, and boned
1 envelope unflavored gelatin
1½ cups tomato juice
2 teaspoons lemon juice
1 tablespoon minced or grated onion
2 tablespoons minced celery
2 tablespoons minced red or green pepper
Lettuce

Put the fish in a bowl. Soften the gelatin in ¼ cup cold water and heat in the tomato juice, stirring until the gelatin is dissolved. Add the lemon juice. Cool and add the onion, celery, and pepper. Combine with the fish. Stir and pour into an oiled mold. Chill several hours, until firm. Line a cold plate or platter with lettuce and unmold the fish onto it. Serves 8 as a luncheon dish.

POACHED SALMON

3 cups dry white wine
3 cups water
1 teaspoon salt
1 onion
1 rib celery
1 medium carrot, cut up
½ teaspoon thyme
2 bay leaves
1 teaspoon tarragon
6 peppercorns, slightly crushed
1 (6-pound) salmon
Watercress, parsley or dill sprigs, and lemon slices (for garnish)
3 tablespoons chopped fresh dillweed
Mayonnaise* or Sour Cream Sauce*

Place all the ingredients except the salmon, sauce, and garnishes in a large pot and boil 10 minutes or more. Gently place salmon in pot and reduce heat to a simmer. Simmer 20 minutes. Remove pan from heat and allow salmon to cool in the liquid. Chill. To serve, remove salmon from liquid and place on a platter. Garnish with watercress leaves, small sprigs of parsley or dill, and lemon slices. Add the fresh chopped dillweed to the Mayonnaise or Sour Cream Sauce. Serve on the side. Serves 8.

SALMON-SHRIMP MOLD

2 envelopes unflavored gelatin
¼ cup lemon juice
1 teaspoon salt
⅛ teaspoon hot pepper sauce
1 cup Mayonnaise*
12 ounces cleaned, cooked shrimp
1 (1-pound) can salmon, drained, bones and skin removed
½ cup finely chopped celery
¼ cup finely chopped scallions, with tops
¼ cup finely chopped pimiento
Celery leaves (for garnish)
Pimiento strips (for garnish)

Sprinkle the gelatin over 1 cup cold water in a large bowl and let stand
3 minutes to soften. Add 1 cup boiling water and stir until the gelatin
is dissolved. Stir in the lemon juice, salt, hot pepper sauce, and Mayonnaise until well blended. Set aside half the shrimp for garnish (select the
most attractive) and chop the rest. Stir the salmon, chopped shrimp,
celery, scallions, and pimiento into the gelatin mixture until blended.
Turn into a 6-cup mold and chill at least 4 hours, until firm. Unmold.
Garnish with the reserved shrimp, celery leaves, and pimiento strips.
Serves 8 to 10.

SHRIMP SALAD WITH CAULIFLOWER

1 large head cauliflower
1 pound medium shrimp
2 tablespoons ketchup
½ cup Mayonnaise*
¼ cup sour cream
1 tablespoon chopped fresh or ½ teaspoon dried dillweed

Cook the cauliflower in salted water or steam it only until crisp-tender.
Put the shrimp in boiling water to cover and cook for 4 minutes after
the water returns to a boil. Cool and peel the shrimp. Devein if necessary.
Trim the stem off the cauliflower so it will sit steady in a bowl. Spread
the slightly cooled flowerets apart and insert the shrimp in the spaces,
reserving some for garnish. Chill. Combine the remaining ingredients.
If using fresh dillweed, save some of it for garnish. Blend thoroughly.
Pour over the salad and top with the remaining shrimp and fresh
dillweed. Serves 6.

SHRIMP SALAD

1½ pounds cooked medium shrimp, peeled and deveined
2 tablespoons minced scallions, with tops, or 1 tablespoon minced chives
1½ cups diced celery
6 anchovies, cut up, or 1 teaspoon anchovy paste (optional)
Lettuce cups or aspic ring (optional)
½ cup Mayonnaise*
2 tablespoons heavy or sour cream
2 teaspoons lemon juice

Combine the shrimp, scallions, celery, and anchovies. Mix gently. Serve in lettuce cups, if you wish, or in an aspic ring, or just on cold plates. Combine the Mayonnaise with the cream and lemon juice and pour over the salad. Serves 6.

SHRIMP-FRUIT SALAD IN CANTALOUPE

1 pound cooked, peeled shrimp
1 medium grapefruit, sectioned
2 medium oranges, sectioned
1 cup seedless grapes
1 large banana, sliced or diced
1 teaspoon lemon juice
¾ cup Mayonnaise made with lemon juice or Yogurt Mayonnaise*
3 cantaloupes, cut in half

Devein the shrimp if necessary and cut them into 2 or 4 pieces, depending on their size. Place in a bowl and add the grapefruit, oranges, and grapes. Sprinkle the banana with the lemon juice and add to the salad. Add half the mayonnaise and toss gently. Fill the cantaloupes, and top with a dab of the dressing; pass the rest. Chill. Serves 6.

SUNSET SALAD WITH LORENZO DRESSING

1½ cups shredded young white cabbage
1½ cups julienne strips smoked cooked tongue
1½ cups cooked chicken, cut in strips
½ cup Lorenzo Dressing*

Combine all of the ingredients. There should be about the same amount of cabbage and meats. Do not use lettuce; the crispness of the cabbage is important. Serves 4.

This is always a popular luncheon dish.

TUNA-CLAM PLATTER

4 cups torn lettuce
1 (7-ounce) can tuna, drained and broken up (or substitute 2 cups cold
    cooked fish, flaked and deboned)
1 (6½-ounce) can minced clams, drained
1 large clove garlic, crushed
1 teaspoon prepared horseradish
1 tablespoon cider vinegar
½ teaspoon salt
¼ teaspoon pepper
1 cup Mayonnaise*
Paprika (optional)
2 hard-cooked eggs, cut in wedges (for garnish)
4 small dill pickles, quartered lengthwise (for garnish)
Cherry tomatoes (for garnish)

Place the lettuce on a deep serving platter. Top with the tuna and clams.
Stir together the garlic, horseradish, vinegar, salt, pepper, and Mayonnaise. Pour over the tuna and clams. Sprinkle with the paprika, if desired.
Chill at least ½ hour. Garnish with the eggs, pickles, and tomatoes before
serving. Serves 4.

TOFU SALAD
(Soybean Curd)

1 cup plain yogurt
2 tablespoons lemon juice
1 teaspoon salt
¼ teaspoon pepper
3 tablespoons chopped coriander leaves or flat-leaf parsley
½ pound tofu (soybean curd) cut in ½-inch cubes
2 tablespoons oil
1 large tomato, peeled and cubed
1 medium cucumber, peeled, seeded, and diced
4 scallions, with tops, chopped
¼ pound mushrooms, sliced thin
Lettuce

Combine the yogurt, lemon juice, salt, pepper, and coriander (or parsley)
and mix thoroughly. Sauté the tofu in the oil only until light brown. Drain
on paper towels. Cool. Toss the tofu very gently in a large bowl with
the yogurt mixture and the vegetables except the lettuce. Chill. Line a
deep platter or shallow salad bowl with lettuce and spoon the salad onto
the lettuce. Serves 4 to 6.

ITALIAN TUNA PIE

2 tablespoons oil
½ cup chopped onion
3 medium carrots, sliced thin
½ large green pepper, diced
1 clove garlic, minced
½ cup tomato sauce
½ teaspoon oregano
½ teaspoon basil
¼ teaspoon pepper
⅓ cup sliced ripe olives
2 (7-ounce) cans water-packed solid tuna, drained and flaked
1 (9-inch) pie shell, pricked and prebaked 5 minutes in 425° F. oven
2 large tomatoes, peeled, cored, and sliced thick, or 1 (14½-ounce) can
    sliced tomatoes, drained
¾ cup Mayonnaise*
¼ cup grated Parmesan cheese (preferably freshly grated)

Heat the oil in a large skillet. Add the onion, carrots, green pepper, and garlic. Cook over medium heat, stirring occasionally, about 15 minutes, or until carrots are crisp-tender. Add the tomato sauce, oregano, basil, and pepper. Cook and stir until thickened. Remove from heat and gently stir in the olives and tuna. Spoon into the pie shell. Bake 25 minutes at 400° F. Remove from oven and arrange the tomato slices, slightly overlapping, on top. Carefully spread a mixture of the Mayonnaise and Parmesan over the tomato slices, sealing the pie crust edges completely. Bake another 10 minutes. Serve at room temperature. Serves 6.

MACARONI-TUNA SALAD

1 pound elbow macaroni or small shells
2 (7-ounce) cans tuna, drained
3 scallions, with tops, or 1 medium onion, chopped fine
1 medium cucumber, peeled, seeded, and chopped fine
2 large or 3 medium tomatoes, peeled and coarsely chopped
½ teaspoon salt
2 tablespoons ketchup
½ cup Mayonnaise*

Cook the macaroni in deep salted water for 5 minutes. Drain and cool under running cold water. Drain. Break up the tuna with a fork and combine with the macaroni. Stir in the vegetables and salt. Mix the ketchup with the Mayonnaise and fold in. Chill. Serves 6 to 8.

TONGUE IN ASPIC

1 smoked tongue (about 5 pounds)
A few peppercorns
1 teaspoon salt
1 onion, cut up
1 bay leaf
2 envelopes unflavored gelatin
½ cup dry white wine
1 cup chicken broth

Put the tongue in a deep pot with the peppercorns, salt, onion, and bay leaf, with water to cover. Cover, bring to a boil, reduce heat, and simmer until tender, 2 to 3 hours. When cool enough to handle, peel the tongue; the skin should pull off easily from the warm tongue. Trim the root end, removing any small bones and gristle. Meanwhile, soften the gelatin in ¼ cup cold white wine. Strain 1 cup broth from the tongue, heat and stir in the gelatin and the remaining wine, and heat and stir until the gelatin is dissolved. Cool. Pour a third onto a deep platter or mold. Chill until set. Slice the tongue thin and arrange the slices on the aspic. Pour the remaining aspic over, being sure all slices are covered. Chill until firm. Unmold or serve on the platter. This is good served with Sour Cream Sauce* or Green Sauce* or Mayonnaise* to which 2 teaspoons prepared mustard have been added. Serves 8.

SMOKED TONGUE WITH SAUCE

1 smoked beef tongue (about 4 pounds)
1 medium onion, stuck with 4 cloves
2 bay leaves
1 teaspoon peppercorns
2 ribs celery, sliced
1 sprig parsley
1 slice lemon
1½ cups Sour Cream Sauce* or prepared horseradish

Wash the tongue, place in a Dutch oven or large heavy pot, and cover with water. Add the onion, bay leaves, peppercorns, celery, parsley, and lemon slice. Bring to a boil, cover, reduce heat, and simmer 3 hours, or until tender. Remove from liquid. Cool, remove skin and root from tongue, and chill. Slice thin and serve with the Sour Cream Sauce or horseradish on the side. Serves 6.

LENTIL-STUFFED TOMATOES

8 to 10 medium tomatoes
Salt
1 pound lentils, cooked and drained
½ cup finely chopped parsley
1 large red onion, minced
1 cup Lemon French Dressing*
Lettuce
10 ripe olives, chopped (for garnish)

Slice the tops off the tomatoes, scoop out the pulp, and sprinkle with salt. Turn tomato shells upside down and drain for at least ½ hour. Combine the lentils, parsley, onion, and dressing. Add a little tomato flesh. marinate at least ½ hour. Fill the tomatoes with the lentil mixture. Serve on lettuce and garnish with the chopped olives. Serves 8 to 10.

CUBED TURKEY SALAD WITH VEGETABLES

3 cups cubed cooked turkey
1 cup cubed sharp Cheddar cheese
1 (10-ounce) package frozen baby lima beans, cooked and drained
1 cup cooked elbow macaroni
2 ribs celery, chopped fine
1 small onion, chopped fine
½ medium red pepper, chopped fine
⅓ cup Mayonnaise*
¼ cup sour cream
1 teaspoon chopped fresh or ¼ teaspoon dried tarragon
½ teaspoon salt
¼ teaspoon pepper
Lettuce leaves
2 medium tomatoes, quartered (for garnish)

In a large bowl, toss lightly the turkey, cheese, beans, macaroni, celery, onion, and red pepper; set aside. Mix well the Mayonnaise, sour cream, tarragon, salt, and pepper. Combine with the turkey mixture. Cover and chill at least 1 hour. Just before serving, line a serving platter with lettuce. Pile the salad on the lettuce and arrange the tomato wedges around the edges. Serves 6.

TURKEY TONNATO
(Turkey with Tuna Sauce)

1 (6–8-pound) turkey
1 onion, cut up
3 ribs celery, with leaves, cut up
1 (2-ounce) can anchovies
2 cloves garlic, split
1 teaspoon salt
¼ teaspoon pepper
2 cups dry white wine
Chicken broth or water to cover

Sauce

1½ cups Mayonnaise*
2 teaspoons lemon juice
1 (7-ounce) can tuna
2 tablespoons capers, drained

Put the turkey in a large pot with the onion, celery, anchovies, garlic, salt, and pepper. Add the wine and enough broth or water barely to cover the bird. Bring to a boil and simmer, uncovered, until the turkey is tender, but not too soft, about 1½ hours. Remove from pot and cool. Remove anchovies and set aside. Strain and reduce the liquid to about 1½ cups. Skin, bone, and slice the turkey into good-size pieces and place on a plate. Pour a little of the reduced broth over to keep it moist. Cool. To make the sauce, combine the Mayonnaise, lemon juice, tuna, and capers. Add the reserved anchovies. Purée in a processor or blender. If too thick, thin with a little of the reduced broth. Arrange the turkey in slightly overlapping slices on a large cold platter and pour the sauce over. Serves 6 to 8.

POLLO TONNATO

Follow the directions for Turkey Tonnato*, substituting 2 (2–3 pound) chicken for the turkey (you will need about 3 pounds meat). Simmer the chicken for 1 to 1¼ hours.

TURKEY-PINEAPPLE KEBABS

1 (8-ounce) can pineapple chunks
2 tablespoons vinegar
2 tablespoons ketchup
1 teaspoon Worcestershire sauce
1 teaspoon salt
¼ teaspoon pepper
2 cups cooked turkey, cut into 1-inch cubes

Drain the pineapple and put the juice in a bowl. Add the vinegar, ketchup, Worcestershire sauce, salt, and pepper. Stir and add the turkey. Cover and leave in the refrigerator several hours or overnight. An hour or two before ready to serve, add the pineapple to the marinade. Alternate turkey and pineapple chunks on 4 long skewers. The turkey will be quite moist. Serves 4.

This can also be made with cooked chicken.

ZUCCHINI-PEPPER PIE

1 (9-inch) pastry pie shell
3 medium zucchini
2 scallions, with tops, sliced thin
1 large clove garlic, minced
2 tablespoons oil
1 medium tomato, peeled and chopped
1 medium green pepper, chopped
¾ teaspoon salt
½ teaspoon basil
¼ teaspoon pepper
3 eggs
½ cup heavy cream
¼ cup Parmesan cheese, grated

Prick the bottom of the pie shell and bake at 450° F. 8 minutes, or until lightly browned. Cool. Sauté the zucchini, scallions, and garlic in the oil about 5 minutes, stirring occasionally. Stir in the tomato, green pepper, salt, basil, and pepper. Cook over low heat, stirring occasionally, until vegetables are tender and liquid has evaporated, about 10 minutes. Spread vegetables evenly in shell. Beat the eggs and cream until mixed; pour over vegetables. Sprinkle with the Parmesan. Bake at 350° F. 30 minutes, or until set. Cool. Serve at room temperature. Serves 6.

Salads and Dressings

THE CUSTOM of serving a salad at the beginning of the meal probably originated in California, the salad center of the world. It has rapidly become popular in all parts of the country, and especially with people who are watching their weight, because it takes the edge off the appetite for the higher-calorie dishes that follow. In France, however, salad still follows the main course, a tradition with its roots in the French theory that it should not be eaten with the wines accompanying the entrees.

In this country, salad is welcome at any part of the meal—as an appetizer; as an accompaniment to flesh, fish, or fowl; as a main dish; or as a dessert, served with or without cheese.

The salads here include tasty, up-to-date versions of familiar favorites, as well as unusual combinations and ingredients. For a change of pace, try the pasta or brown rice salads. The many delicious salad dressings offer suggestions for varying old salads and creating new ones, according to your taste and ingenuity.

Salads

APPLE-CARROT SLAW

2 cups shredded cabbage
1 cup shredded carrots
1 medium apple, cored and cubed
½ cup Mayonnaise*
1 teaspoon sugar
½ teaspoon salt
¼ teaspoon ground ginger (optional)
Dash cinnamon

In a medium bowl, toss the cabbage, carrots, apple, and Mayonnaise until well blended. Add the sugar, salt, ginger, and cinnamon. Mix well. Cover and chill 1 hour, or until ready to serve. Serves 4.

APPLE-BEET SALAD

½ cup Mayonnaise*
1 cup chopped pickled beets, drained (reserve 3 tablespoons juice)
1 teaspoon prepared horseradish
½ teaspoon salt
¼ teaspoon pepper
2 unpeeled medium red apples, cored and shredded
2 cups shredded green cabbage
Minced parsley (for garnish)

In a salad bowl, mix well the Mayonnaise, beet juice, horseradish, salt, and pepper. Add the apples, cabbage, and beets; blend thoroughly. Chill 30 minutes. Sprinkle with parsley. Serves 4 to 6.

APPLE-CHEESE SALAD

2 medium apples, cored and cubed
¾ pound Muenster cheese, cubed
⅓ cup coarsely chopped walnuts (optional)
½ cup sour cream
1 tablespoon lemon juice
Dash sugar
10–12 large radishes, coarsely shredded (for garnish)
⅓ cup crumbled blue cheese

Combine the apples, Muenster cheese, and walnuts. Blend the sour cream, lemon juice, and sugar; pour over apple-cheese mixture and toss. Place in serving dish; garnish edges with the radishes and sprinkle the blue cheese in center. Chill. Serves 4.

APPLE, KUMQUAT, AND CHINESE CABBAGE SALAD

3 cups packed shredded Chinese cabbage
2 unpeeled medium red apples, cored and cut in thin wedges
6 preserved kumquats, sliced, or 1 orange, peeled, pith removed, sectioned
Soy Dressing*
2 tablespoons minced parsley (optional)

In a salad bowl, combine the cabbage, apples, and kumquats. Chill. Add the dressing; toss. Sprinkle with the parsley. Serve at once. Serves 4 to 6.

APPLE SLAW WITH SOUR CREAM DRESSING

¾ cup sour cream
1 tablespoon packed light brown sugar
3 tablespoons cider vinegar
1–2 tablespoons prepared mustard
½ teaspoon salt
¼ teaspoon onion salt
¼ teaspoon pepper
2 unpeeled medium red apples, cut into bite-size pieces
3 cups shredded green cabbage
⅓ cup chopped pitted dates (for garnish)

In a salad bowl, mix thoroughly the sour cream, sugar, vinegar, mustard to taste, salt, onion salt, and pepper. Add the apples and cabbage; mix well. Chill at least 1 hour before serving. Sprinkle with the dates. Serves 4 to 6.

ASPARAGUS SALAD

3 pounds asparagus
Salt
½ cup French Dressing*
Salad greens (optional)

Break off the tough ends of the asparagus and scrape the scales from the lower ends of the stalks. (The stalks may be left whole.) Cut diagonally into pieces about 1½ inches long. Boil 2 to 3 minutes in salted water; drain and rinse in cold water. Pour two thirds of the dressing over; toss and chill. Serve on greens if you wish. Pour remaining dressing over. Serves 6..

ASPARAGUS AND PASTA

1 pound asparagus, cut into 1-inch pieces, cooked and drained (do not
    overcook)
¾ pound pasta (linguine or spaghettini)
½ cup Soy Dressing*

Add the asparagus to the cooled pasta and pour the dressing over. Chill. Serves 4 to 6.

BANANA-ORANGE-RADISH SALAD

3 cups packed torn romaine lettuce
2 medium oranges, peeled, pith removed, sectioned
2 medium bananas, sliced
½ cup sliced radishes
½ cup Mustard Dressing*
⅓ cup slivered almonds, garnish

In a salad bowl, combine the romaine, oranges, bananas, and radishes.
Add the dressing; toss lightly. Sprinkle with the almonds. Serve at once.
Serves 4 to 6.

BARLEY SALAD EASTERN STYLE

1½ cups pearl barley
1 pint broth (any kind)
½ teaspoon salt
1 cup diced celery
1 large onion, diced
2 large carrots, diced
1 medium green or red pepper, diced
1 tablespoon minced fresh coriander leaves
⅓ cup coarsely chopped pistachios or toasted walnuts
½ cup French Dressing*

In a large covered pot, simmer the barley with 1 quart water and the
broth and salt 30 minutes. Add the vegetables and cook 20 minutes. Drain
and cool. Most of the liquid will have been absorbed. Add the coriander
and nuts. Toss with the dressing and chill. Serves 6 to 8.

BARLEY SALAD WITH GREEN PEPPERS

2 cups pearl barley
1 tablespoon plus 1 teaspoon salt
1 medium onion, chopped
3 medium green peppers, coarsely chopped
3 tablespoons oil (at least partly olive)
¼ teaspoon pepper
1 tablespoon minced parsley
1 tablespoon vinegar

Cook the barley in 2 quarts water with 1 teaspoon salt until tender but not mushy, about 50 minutes. Drain. Meanwhile, sauté the onion and peppers gently in 2 tablespoons oil 2 minutes. Do not brown. Cool and toss into the barley with the remaining 1 tablespoon salt and the pepper and parsley. Pour the vinegar over with the remaining 1 tablespoon oil. Toss and cool. Serve at room temperature. Serves 6 to 8.

BARLEY SALAD WITH VEGETABLES

1½ cups quick-cooking pearl barley
1½ teaspoons salt
½ cup chopped celery
3 medium carrots, slivered
4 scallions, with tops, coarsely chopped
1 medium green or red pepper, slivered
½ cup French Dressing* or Green French Dressing*
Lettuce (optional)

Boil the barley in 1 quart water with the salt 12 minutes. Drain and cool. Stir in the remaining ingredients except the lettuce. Toss and chill. Serve on lettuce if you wish. Serves 6 to 8.

MIDDLE EASTERN BEAN SALAD

2 large cloves garlic, crushed
1 teaspoon salt
3 tablespoons cider vinegar
⅓ cup oil, preferably olive
1 teaspoon cumin seeds, lightly crushed
¼ teaspoon pepper
1 (20-ounce) can red kidney beans, rinsed and drained
1 (20-ounce) can chick-peas, rinsed and drained
1 medium onion, sliced thin
⅓ cup minced parsley

In a bowl, mix the garlic, salt, and vinegar. Stir in the oil, cumin seeds, and pepper. Fold in the beans, chick-peas, onion, and parsley. Cover and marinate in the refrigerator at least 30 minutes, or overnight. Serve chilled or at room temperature. Serves 6.

GREEN BEANS

1 pound young green beans
¼ cup Lemon French Dressing*
Lemon wedges (for garnish)

Snip the ends from the beans and steam about 4 minutes, until crisp-tender. You may also cook them in boiling water, timing after the water boils with the beans in. Cool under running cold water. Chill. Arrange the beans in one direction in a serving dish and pour the dressing over. Garnish with the lemon wedges. Serves 4.

PINTO BEAN AND AVOCADO SALAD

½ cup oil
¼ cup cider vinegar
¼ cup chili sauce
1½ teaspoons prepared mustard
1 large avocado, peeled and diced
2 (10½-ounce) cans pinto beans, rinsed and drained
1 medium red onion, sliced thin
4 hard-cooked eggs, chopped

Stir the oil, vinegar, chili sauce, and mustard together until blended. Stir in the avocado. Place the remaining ingredients in a bowl, pour the dressing over, and mix gently. Chill. Serves 4 to 6.

WHITE BEANS

1½ cups small dried white beans
½ cup olive oil
2 cloves garlic, split
1 bay leaf
1 teaspoon salt
3 tablespoons chopped parsley
1 teaspon basil
1 teaspoon oregano

Wash the beans and soak them overnight in 2 cups water with the oil, garlic, bay leaf, and salt. Simmer until tender, about 1½ hours. The beans should be tender, not mushy. Remove the bay leaf and garlic. Add the parsley, basil, and oregano. Chill overnight. Serve in the marinade or partly drained. Serves 6.

ARMENIAN GREEN BEANS

¾ teaspoon salt
1 pound green beans, trimmed and cut into 1½-inch pieces
1 large onion, sliced thin
1 large clove garlic, crushed
3 tablespoons oil, preferably olive
2 medium tomatoes, peeled and diced (2 cups)
½ cup minced parsley
½ teaspoon pepper
5 thin slices lemon, quartered
Lemon slices (optional, for garnish)
Parsley (for garnish)

Bring ½ cup water and the salt to a boil. Add the green beans. Cover and cook over moderate heat 5 minutes, stirring occasionally. Drain. Sauté the onion and garlic in the oil until tender, about 5 minutes. Do not brown. Stir in the green beans, tomatoes, ½ cup parsley, and pepper. Cover and simmer about 15 minutes, or until beans are crisp-tender, stirring occasionally. Add the quartered lemon slices. Cool. Serve at room temperature or chilled. Garnish with the lemon slices and/or parsley. Serves 4.

GREEN BEANS AND SHALLOTS, GARNI

½ cup Mayonnaise*
12 cherry tomatoes, halved
1 teaspoon prepared mustard
1½ pounds trimmed fresh or 3 (10-ounce) packages frozen cut green beans
12 ounces mushrooms, sliced thin
¼ cup minced parsley
¼ cup chopped shallots
1 small green pepper, shredded
2 tablespoons minced fresh or 2 teaspoons crumbled dried basil
Lemon wedges

Mix the Mayonnaise with the prepared mustard. Toss the tomatoes with just enough dressing to coat. Cook the beans in salted water until crisp-tender; cook frozen beans a little less than instructions specify. Drain and toss with the mushrooms, parsley, shallots, green pepper, basil, and remaining dressing. Chill several hours. At serving time, place on a cool, shallow salad bowl or platter and place the tomatoes and lemon wedges on the sides. Serves 8.

WHITE BEAN AND TUNA SALAD IN TOMATO SHELLS

4 medium ripe tomatoes
¼ cup Mayonnaise*
2 cloves garlic, minced
½ teaspoon oregano
¼ teaspoon sugar
¼ teaspoon pepper
1 (20-ounce) can white kidney beans, rinsed and drained
1 (6½-ounce) can tuna, drained and broken into small pieces
1 small red onion, chopped
Lettuce leaves (optional)

Cut a thin slice off the top of each tomato; scoop out and reserve pulp, leaving sturdy shells. Drain upside down on paper towels. Chop pulp coarse; reserve. In a large bowl, mix the remaining ingredients except the lettuce with the tomato pulp. Stuff the tomatoes and place on lettuce leaves if desired. Serve chilled. Serves 4.

BEET SALAD WITH EGG

3 cups diced cooked beets
4 hard-cooked eggs, coarsely chopped
2 tablespoons minced chives or scallions
3–4 tablespoons Mayonnaise*
3 tablespoons sour cream
2 tablespoons vinegar
½ teaspoon sugar

Mix the beets with the eggs and chives. Combine the remaining ingredients, starting with 3 tablespoons of the Mayonnaise and adding more if you wish. Fold into the beet-egg mixture. Reseason. You may want to add a little salt. Chill. Serves 6 to 8.

BROCCOLI AND BERMUDA ONION SALAD

2 cups small fresh broccoli flowerets
1 small Bermuda onion, cut in quarters and sliced thin
1 dill pickle, sliced thin
½ cup Vinaigrette with Pimiento*
5 cups torn romaine lettuce

Put the broccoli, onion, pickle, and vinaigrette in a large salad bowl and marinate in the refrigerator at least 1 hour. Add the lettuce and toss. Serve promptly. Serves 6.

WHITE BEAN AND SALMON SALAD

1 (20-ounce) can cannellini (white kidney beans), rinsed and drained
2 tablespoons lemon juice
2 tablespoons minced parsley
¼ teaspoon pepper
6 large lettuce leaves
1 (7¾-ounce) can salmon, drained (reserve 2 tablespoons liquid)
1 medium onion, sliced thin
2 tablespoons oil
8 ripe olives (for garnish)

Mix well the cannellini, lemon juice, parsley, and pepper. Line a large shallow bowl with the lettuce. Layer the bean mixture, salmon, and onion on the lettuce. Beat together the reserved salmon liquid and oil. Pour over the salad and garnish with the olives. Chill. Serves 4.

BLUEBERRY-RADISH SALAD

1 teaspoon grated orange peel
Juice of 1 orange
⅓ cup oil (not olive)
2 tablespoons minced parsley
½ teaspoon salt
¼ teaspoon pepper
4 cups escarole or other greens, torn
1½ cups coarsely shredded radishes
1 cup fresh blueberries

Combine and mix well the orange peel, juice, oil, parsley, salt, and pepper. Line a platter with the escarole. Top with the radishes, then sprinkle with the blueberries. Just before serving, add the dressing and toss. Serve at room temperature. Serves 4 to 6.

BROCCOLI AND RED CABBAGE SALAD

2 cups small fresh broccoli flowerets
4 cups shredded red cabbage
⅓ cup Creamy Dressing*
2 tablespoons dill or sweet pickle juice
2 scallions, with tops, minced
⅛ teaspoon pepper

Combine the broccoli and red cabbage. Mix together the remaining ingredients and pour over. Toss to mix. Chill. Serves 4 to 6.

BRUSSELS SPROUTS SALAD

⅓ cup sour cream
1 tablespoon white wine vinegar
2 tablespoons capers, drained
½ teaspoon basil
¼ teaspoon salt
¼ teaspoon pepper
1 (10-ounce) package frozen Brussels sprouts, cooked until crisp-tender,
    drained, and halved if large
1 medium red onion, chopped
1 large rib celery, sliced diagonally

In a medium bowl, mix well the sour cream, vinegar, capers, basil, salt, and pepper. Add the cooled Brussels sprouts, onion, and celery; toss until well coated. Chill 1 hour. Serves 4 as a side dish.

CELERY VICTOR

(Originated by a chef in San Francisco)

4 heads celery, leaves trimmed and reserved for garnish
Chicken or beef broth
Bouquet garni (2 sprigs parsley, 1 bay leaf, 1 sprig fresh or 1 teaspoon dried
    thyme, tied in cheesecloth)
1 medium onion, sliced
1 cup French Dressing*
8 anchovy fillets (for garnish)
8 strips pimiento (for garnish)

Trim the celery roots carefully, being careful not to cut too deeply (you do not want ribs to fall off). Scrape outside ribs. Halve each head lengthwise. Place in a large skillet in a single layer. Pour the broth over barely to cover; add the bouquet garni and onion. Bring to a boil, cover, and simmer until crisp-tender, about 10 to 12 minutes. Remove, drain completely, and cool. Place on a serving plate or on 8 individual salad plates. Pour the dressing over and chill several hours. Garnish with the anchovy fillets, pimientos, and some celery leaves, if you wish. Serves 8.

CARROT SALAD WITH ORANGE

2 pounds carrots, cut into thin diagonal slices
4 scallions, with tops, chopped fine
¼ cup finely chopped parsley
2 tablespoons grated orange peel
2 tablespoons orange juice
⅓–½ cup French Dressing*

Cook the carrots in salted water or steam them until crisp-tender, about 12 to 15 minutes. Drain and cool. Put in a serving bowl with the scallions and parsley. Add the orange peel and juice to ⅓ cup French Dressing, pour over, and toss. If you want the carrots more moist, add the remaining dressing and toss again, but do not make the salad too wet. Serve at room temperature. Serves 8.

CAULIFLOWER-ROMAINE SALAD

½ cup oil
2 tablespoons chili sauce
2 tablespoons lemon juice or wine vinegar
1 teaspoon prepared horseradish
½ teaspoon salt
⅛ teaspoon pepper
1½ cups thinly sliced cauliflowerets
3 cups packed romaine lettuce, cut crosswise in ¼-inch shreds

Mix the oil, chili sauce, lemon juice or vinegar, 1 tablespoon water, horseradish, salt, and pepper. Place the cauliflowerets and romaine in a bowl, pour the dressing over, toss lightly, and chill. Serves 6.

CITRUS-AVOCADO SALAD

1 cup well-drained grapefruit sections
1 (11-ounce) can mandarin oranges, drained
1 large ripe avocado, peeled and sliced
A few celery tops or watercress sprigs
⅓ cup Honey Dressing*

Arrange the grapefruit, oranges, avocado, and celery tops on 4 individual salad plates. Spoon the dressing over and chill. Serves 4.

SPICY CHICK-PEA SALAD

1 (20-ounce) can chick-peas
½ medium green pepper, slivered
1 small red onion, sliced thin and separated into rings
1 canned green chili, drained and chopped
¼ cup olive oil
2 tablespoons red wine vinegar
2 tablespoons capers, drained
½ teaspoon salt

Rinse the chick-peas and drain well. In a large bowl, toss to mix all the ingredients. Chill several hours or overnight. Serves 4 as a side dish.

COLESLAW WITH MAYONNAISE

1 large or 2 medium heads cabbage, shredded fine
1½ cups Mayonnaise*
1 cup sour cream
1 teaspoon salt
¼ teaspoon pepper
2 teaspoons lemon juice
1 teaspoon sugar

Mix the cabbage with the remaining ingredients. Allow to mellow in the refrigerator 1½ to 2 hours. Serves 8.

COLESLAW WITH PARSLEY

½ cup oil, part olive
3 tablespoons white wine vinegar
1 teaspoon salt
½ teaspoon pepper
1½ teaspoons sugar
Dash hot pepper sauce
1 head cabbage (about 1½ pounds)
½ cup minced parsley

Beat together all of the ingredients except the cabbage and parsley. Shred the cabbage, reserving a few outer leaves to line the bowl. Toss the cabbage thoroughly with the parsley and dressing. Chill at least 2 hours, stirring several times at intervals. Place in a salad bowl lined with cabbage leaves. Serves 6.

CORN SALAD

2 (10-ounce) packages frozen whole-kernel corn, thawed, or 2 (12-ounce)
    cans whole-kernel corn
1 medium green pepper, diced
1 medium red onion, sliced
2 medium tomatoes, peeled and diced
3 scallions, with tops, chopped
2 tablespoons vinegar or lemon juice
¼ teaspoon pepper
½ teaspoon salt
½ cup Mayonnaise*
Minced parsley (for garnish)

Drain the corn, reserving the liquid, and put the corn into a serving bowl
with the green pepper, onion, tomatoes, and scallions. Add the vinegar
or lemon juice, pepper, and salt to the Mayonnaise. Thin, if you wish,
with a little liquid from the corn. Pour over the vegetables and toss gently
but thoroughly. Chill. Serve garnished with a little minced parsley. Serves
6 to 8.

CUCUMBER IN MUSTARD-YOGURT SAUCE

½ cup plain yogurt
1½ teaspoons prepared mustard
¼ teaspoon salt
3 dashes hot pepper sauce
1 large cucumber, peeled and sliced thin

In a medium bowl, mix well the yogurt, mustard, salt, and pepper sauce.
Fold in the cucumber. Cover and chill. Serves 4.

CUCUMBERS STUFFED WITH PEAS AND BEANS

4 large cucumbers
2 (10-ounce) packages tiny frozen peas
2 (10-ounce) packages frozen French-cut or small whole green beans
2 tablespoons minced chives or scallions
1 cup Mayonnaise with tarragon*

Cut the cucumbers in halves lengthwise. Parboil for 2 minutes. Cool,
and scoop out most of the seeds. Cook the peas and beans according to
package directions. Chill. Mix with the chives and stir in 3 tablespoons
Mayonnaise. Fill the cucumbers with the mixture and chill. Top with
the remaining chilled Mayonnaise before serving. Serves 8.

DATE-ORANGE SALAD

1 cup dates, pitted and cut in lengthwise strips
2 tablespoons lime or lemon juice
1 scallion, with top, minced
½ cup Honey Dressing*
3 oranges, peeled
6 cups torn lettuce

Put dates, lime or lemon juice, scallion, and dressing in a salad bowl and marinate in the refrigerator at least 30 minutes. Remove all white membrane from the oranges and slice thin crosswise. Just before serving, add the orange slices to the date mixture, add the lettuce, and toss. Serves 6.

EGG SALAD

8 hard-cooked eggs
1 medium onion, cut up
¼ pound ham, cut up
½ cup strong chicken broth
1 tablespoon olive oil
1 teaspoon lemon juice
1 teaspoon salt
¼ teaspoon pepper
¼ teaspoon dry mustard
Lettuce

Peel the eggs and cut them up. Put the remaining ingredients in a processor or blender. Process until blended but not too fine. Mix with the eggs and chill. Serve on lettuce leaves or shredded lettuce. Serves 6 to 8.

This salad has many uses. It may be used as a sandwich filling, to fill avocado halves, to fill cherry tomatoes, etc.

EGG SALAD VARIATIONS

Stir in any of the following:

⅓ cup chopped toasted almonds or sunflower seeds
2 tablespoons minced green pepper
1 tablespoon curry powder and 2 tablespoons currants
3 tablespoons bean sprouts and 1 tablespoon minced parsley
1 tablespoon tomato paste

EGGPLANT AND SWISS CHEESE SALAD

⅓ cup olive oil
1 medium eggplant (about 1 pound), peeled and cut in 1-inch cubes
1 large onion, chopped
1 cup chopped celery
1 clove garlic, minced
1 (16-ounce) can tomatoes, drained and cut up
½ teaspoon salt
1 teaspoon basil
2 tablespoons vinegar
1 tablespoon sugar
8 ounces Swiss cheese, cut in ¼-inch cubes

In a large skillet, heat the oil and sauté the eggplant 5 minutes, or until tender. Remove with a slotted spoon; set aside. To the skillet add the onion, celery, and garlic; sauté until the onion is tender. Add the tomatoes, salt, basil, vinegar, and sugar. Simmer, uncovered, 15 minutes. Add eggplant. Chill overnight. Gently mix in the cheese cubes. Can be refrigerated up to 2 weeks. Serves 6.

EGGPLANT-YOGURT SALAD

5 tablespoons lemon juice (juice of about 2 lemons)
1½ teaspoons salt
2 medium eggplants (about 2 pounds), peeled and cut in 1-inch chunks
⅓ cup scallions, with tops, minced
2 tablespoons olive oil
¼ teaspoon pepper
1 medium clove garlic, crushed
1 cup plain yogurt
1 large tomato, peeled and cut in wedges (optional, for garnish)

Bring 6 cups water, 2 tablespoons lemon juice, and 1 teaspoon salt to a boil. Add the eggplants; cover and simmer until tender, about 7 minutes. Drain and cool. In a bowl, combine the eggplants, remaining 3 tablespoons lemon juice, scallions, oil, remaining ½ teaspoon salt, pepper, and garlic; mix well. Stir in the yogurt just until blended. Chill. Garnish with tomato wedges, if you wish. Serves 4 to 6.

ENDIVE-KUMQUAT SALAD

2 large heads Belgian endive, sliced thin crosswise
2 cups thin-sliced fresh kumquats or 1 (10-ounce) jar kumquats, drained
    and sliced

Dressing

⅓ cup olive oil
2 tablespoons red wine vinegar
½ teaspoon salt
¼ teaspoon pepper
½ teaspoon sugar
½ teaspoon dry mustard

Toss the endive and kumquats with just enough dressing to coat—start
with ⅓ cup. To make the dressing, combine the dressing ingredients and
mix thoroughly. This salad is particularly attractive served in a glass bowl.
Serve at room temperature. Serves 4.

ASSORTED FRUITS WITH COTTAGE CHEESE

Choose from among:
2 medium bananas, sliced
2 large oranges, peeled and sectioned
1 large grapefruit, peeled and sectioned
2 medium apples, cored, peeled, and cut into bite-size pieces
3 medium pears, cored, peeled, and cut into bite-size pieces (canned pears
    may be substituted)
3 medium peaches, peeled and sliced, or 1 (16-ounce) can sliced peaches,
    drained
Shredded lettuce

1 pound cottage cheese
½ cup Mayonnaise*
2 teaspoons lemon juice
½ cup sugar or syrup (or more)

Choose several of the fruits and place them in piles on the lettuce on a
platter. Cover and chill. Meanwhile, combine the cottage cheese, Mayonnaise, lemon juice, and ½ cup sugar or syrup. Taste for sweetness; you
may want to add more sugar or syrup. Chill until ready to serve. Spoon
a little dressing over the fruit and pass the rest. The number of servings
depends on the amount of fruit used. Serve immediately. Serves 6 to 8.

FRUIT PLATE WITH COTTAGE CHEESE

1 (20-ounce) can unsweetened pineapple chunks
1 (11-ounce) can mandarin oranges, drained
2 large bananas, sliced
½ cup chopped dates
2 tablespoons cider vinegar
¼ cup salad oil
1 teaspoon curry powder
¼ teaspoon salt
Crisp salad greens
2 pounds cottage cheese
½ cup slivered or coarsely chopped toasted almonds (for garnish)

Drain the pineapple, reserving ½ cup syrup. Combine the pineapple, oranges, bananas, and dates. Combine the reserved pineapple syrup with the vinegar, oil, curry powder, and salt; mix well. Pour over the fruit and marinate at room temperature 30 minutes. Arrange the salad greens on 6 serving plates or a platter. Spoon the cheese onto the greens and top with the fruit mixture. Sprinkle with the almonds. Serve immediately at room temperature. Serves 6 to 8.

SUMMER FRUIT SALAD WITH HONEY DRESSING

½ cup lime juice
½ cup sugar
1 large banana, sliced diagonally
1 pint blueberries
2 large nectarines, sliced
1 pint strawberries, hulled and halved
1 cup watermelon balls
1 cup seedless green grapes
1 kiwi fruit, peeled and sliced
Dark sweet cherries with stems (optional, for garnish)
½ cup Honey Dressing*

Mix the lime juice and sugar and pour over the sliced banana. In a large serving bowl, preferably glass, layer the banana (drained; reserve the lime juice mixture), blueberries (reserve ½ cup for garnish), nectarines, strawberries, watermelon, and grapes. Garnish with the reserved blueberries, kiwi, and cherries. Drizzle with the reserved lime juice mixture. To serve, top with the dressing. Serve at room temperature. Serves 6.

FRUIT PLATE WITH BRANDIED DATE SAUCE

1 cup finely chopped dates
½ cup orange juice
2 tablespoons brandy
1 (20-ounce) can pineapple chunks, chilled and drained
1 cup strawberries, hulled and halved
1½ cups grapes, seeded and halved
1 (16-ounce) can peach slices, chilled and drained

In a small saucepan, bring to a boil the dates, ¾ cup water, and orange juice, then simmer 10 minutes, or until dates are very soft. Remove from heat, stir in the brandy, and chill. Yield: 1½ cups sauce.

To serve, mix the fruit together and serve with the sauce on the side. Serves 6.

FRUIT SALAD

1 (8-ounce) can sliced pineapple
½ cup Curried Cheese Dressing*
2 cups packed shredded iceberg lettuce
1 (17-ounce) can apricot halves, drained
2 unpeeled medium red apples, cut in thin wedges
¼ cup toasted shredded coconut

Drain the pineapple and reserve ¼ cup syrup. Mix the syrup into the dressing. Arrange the lettuce and fruits on 4 to 6 individual salad plates. Spoon the dressing over. Sprinkle with the coconut. Chill. Serves 4 to 6.

GRAPE-CARROT-WALNUT SALAD

1½ cups grapes, halved and seeded or seedless
1 large carrot, coarsely shredded
½ cup Lemon French Dressing*
5 cups torn Boston or bibb lettuce
⅓ cup coarsely chopped walnuts

Combine the grapes, carrot, and dressing in a salad bowl. Toss well and chill. Just before serving, add the lettuce, toss, and sprinkle with the walnuts. Serves 6.

GRAPEFRUIT-BANANA-CELERY SALAD

1 cup thinly sliced celery
½ cup packed torn celery leaves
1 cup well-drained grapefruit sections
2 medium bananas, sliced
Celery Seed and Honey Dressing*
¼ cup chopped walnuts

Combine the celery and leaves, grapefruit, and bananas in a salad bowl.
Add ⅓ cup dressing, or to taste; toss lightly. Sprinkle with the walnuts.
Chill. Serves 4.

GREEK SALAD

8 cups torn romaine lettuce
½ Bermuda onion, sliced
1 medium cucumber, sliced
1 medium green pepper, cut in rings
1 pound feta cheese, cubed
20 ripe olives
½ cup oil, preferably olive
¼ cup vinegar, preferably white
2 tablespoons chopped fresh or 2 teaspoons dried dillweed

Toss all the ingredients except the last three. Stir the oil, vinegar, and
dillweed together and pour over. Toss to coat ingredients with dressing.
Chill. Serves 6.

This can also be served as a main dish.

MIXED GREENS SALAD BOWL WITH BEETS

6 cups torn mixed greens (iceberg, romaine, escarole, watercress, and
    spinach)
⅓ cup French Dressing*
1 (16-ounce) can diced or sliced beets, drained
1 hard-cooked egg, grated or chopped

In a serving bowl, toss the greens with the dressing until well coated.
Top with the beets and egg. Serve immediately. Serves 6.

HERRING-BEET SALAD

1 (6-ounce) jar pickled herring, cut up
6 medium beets, cooked and cut into eighths
3 medium potatoes, cooked, peeled, and diced
2 dill pickles, diced
⅓ cup sour cream
⅓ cup Mayonnaise*
2 tablespoons red wine
2 teaspoons sugar

Drain the herring. Mix the herring with the beets, potatoes, and pickles. Combine the sour cream, Mayonnaise, wine, and sugar. Mix thoroughly, pour over the herring, and toss. Chill. Serves 6.

LENTIL SALAD

1 pound dried lentils
1 teaspoon salt
1 teaspoon ground cumin
5 scallions, with tops, chopped
½ cup minced parsley
½ cup Lemon French Dressing*

Simmer the lentils in 6 cups water with the salt and cumin about 30 minutes, until tender. Cool and drain. Stir in the scallions, parsley, and dressing. Toss and adjust seasoning. Serve at room temperature or chilled. Serves 8.

OKRA WITH LEMON

1 pound young okra
2 tablespoons lemon juice (about)
2 tablespoons olive oil
½ teaspoon salt
Pinch sugar
Lemon wedges (optional)

Boil or steam the okra until just crisp-tender, about 4 to 5 minutes. Drain and cool. Mix 1½ tablespoons lemon juice and the oil, salt, and sugar. Add more lemon juice to taste. Place the okra on a serving dish. Pour the dressing over the okra and chill. Garnish with the lemon wedges. Serves 4.

KASHA SALAD WITH NUTS

1 large onion, minced
1 tablespoon butter
1½ cups kasha (buckwheat)
2½ cups water or part chicken broth
½ cup minced celery
1 teaspoon salt
1 teaspoon thyme
½ cup slivered almonds or chopped pecans
2 tablespoons minced parsley
⅓ cup sour cream
½ cup French Dressing*

Sauté the onion in butter over medium heat 2 minutes. Stir in the kasha, add the water, and cook 12 minutes, stirring several times. Add the celery, salt, and thyme and cook 5 minutes. Remove from heat and drain if necessary. Fluff with a fork. Add the nuts and parsley. Cool. Just before serving, stir in a mixture of the sour cream and French Dressing. Chill and serve. Serves 8.

CURRIED LENTILS WITH VEGETABLES

2 medium onions, sliced thin
3 medium carrots, sliced thin (about 1 cup)
3 tablespoons oil
1 (16-ounce) can tomatoes, cut up, with their liquid
1 cup dried lentils, rinsed
1 tablespoon grated fresh ginger
1 teaspoon curry powder
1 teaspoon ground cumin
1 teaspoon turmeric
2 cloves garlic, crushed
2 tablespoons lemon juice
½ teaspoon salt

Sauté the onions and carrots in the oil until tender, about 5 minutes (do not brown). Add the tomatoes with their liquid, lentils, ½ cup water, ginger, curry powder, cumin, turmeric, and garlic; cover and simmer until the lentils are tender, about 25 to 30 minutes. Cool; add the lemon juice and salt; chill at least 4 hours, or overnight. Serves 4 to 6.

MUSHROOM-ENDIVE SALAD

1 pound medium mushrooms
½ cup French Dressing*
1-2 tablespoons Mayonnaise*
1 tablespoon chopped fresh or 1 teaspoon dried oregano
1 pound Belgian endive

Wipe the mushrooms with a damp paper towel. Cut the stems off close to the caps. Cut into slices about ⅓ inch thick. Mix the French Dressing with the Mayonnaise and oregano. Place the mushrooms in a bowl, pour ½ cup dressing over, and let stand 2 or 3 hours at room temperature, turning to coat them on all sides. Cut the endive in rounds about the thickness of the mushrooms. About ½ hour before serving, combine with the mushrooms and toss with remaining dressing. Serve promptly. The salad should not be too wet, especially if it is to be served on the dinner plate. (This recipe can be doubled or tripled successfully.) Serves 6.

ORANGE-GRAPEFRUIT-AVOCADO SALAD

3 tablespoons oil
2 tablespoons lime juice
1 teaspoon sugar
½ teaspoon salt
⅛ teaspoon pepper
1 large avocado
2 large grapefruit, peeled and sectioned (reserve juice)
Lettuce
2 large oranges, peeled and sliced crosswise

Mix well the oil, lime juice, sugar, salt, and pepper; set aside. Halve the avocado lengthwise, peel, and cut crosswise in ½-inch-thick slices. Turn slices in the reserved grapefruit juice to prevent discoloration. Line a platter with lettuce. Alternate avocado slices and grapefruit sections. Place the orange slices in front of the grapefruit and avocado. Drizzle dressing over all. Serve chilled. Serves 4 to 6.

ORANGE-ONION SALAD

3 cups packed torn iceberg or romaine lettuce
3 medium oranges, peeled, pith removed, sliced thin
1 medium red onion, sliced thin
¼ cup Blue Cheese Dressing with Parsley*

Combine the lettuce, oranges, and onion in a salad bowl. Add the dressing; toss lightly. Serve chilled. Serves 4.

HEART OF PALM SALAD

2 (16-ounce) cans hearts of palm, drained
½ cup French Dressing*
Salad greens (optional)

Divide the hearts of palm among 8 salad plates. If some of the stalks are large, split them lengthwise. Pour the dressing over them. The hearts of palm may be served on a bed of greens. Serve at room temperature. Serves 8.

DILLED CUCUMBER-PASTA SALAD

2 medium cucumbers
1 medium onion, chopped
1 teaspoon salt
½ cup plain yogurt
1 scallion, including top, sliced thin
2 tablespoons fresh dillweed
⅛ teaspoon dry mustard
¼ teaspoon pepper
1 tablespoon vinegar (preferably white)
1 tablespoon oil
½ pound pasta (small shells or twists), cooked, drained, and cooled

Peel the cucumbers, halve lengthwise, and slice thin. Combine with the onion and salt in a colander or sieve. Cover with a saucer and weight down to press out excess water. Allow to stand 2 hours.

Combine the yogurt, scallion, dillweed, mustard, pepper, vinegar, and oil and mix well. Chill at least 1 hour. Add the cucumbers to the pasta and pour the dressing over sparingly. Chill. Serves 6.

AVOCADO-MUSHROOM PASTA

1 cup Lemon French Dressing*
1 clove garlic, minced
¼ cup minced parsley
½ pound pasta, cooked, drained, and cooled
½ pound mushrooms, sliced
1 medium avocado, peeled and cubed

Combine the dressing with the garlic and parsley and mix with the pasta and mushrooms. Add the avocado; chill 1 to 2 hours. Toss and serve. Serves 4 to 6.

BROCCOLI-PASTA SALAD

2 cloves garlic, minced
½ cup olive oil
1 pound pasta (elbow macaroni), cooked and drained
1 (10-ounce) package frozen chopped broccoli, cooked and drained
1 cup cherry tomatoes, halved
½ teaspoon salt
¼ teaspoon pepper

In a small saucepan over low heat, cook the garlic in the oil about 10 minutes, or until garlic is lightly browned. Remove garlic. In a large bowl, combine the pasta, broccoli, and tomatoes. Pour the garlic oil over all. Season with salt and pepper. Toss carefully. Cover and chill. Serves 6.

CHINESE PASTA-VEGETABLE SALAD

¾ pound pasta (fusilli), cooked, drained, and cooled
2 cups fresh or 1 (16-ounce) can bean sprouts, drained
1 cup frozen peas, thawed
1 medium green pepper, chopped
1 medium onion, minced
1 (8-ounce) can water chestnuts, drained and sliced
¼ pound mushrooms, sliced
¾ cup Mayonnaise*
2 tablespoons soy sauce
1 teaspoon prepared mustard
Dash hot pepper sauce
1 teaspoon grated fresh ginger
¼ teaspoon pepper

Combine the pasta with the bean sprouts, peas, green pepper, onion, water chestnuts, and mushrooms. Stir the Mayonnaise together with the soy sauce, mustard, hot pepper sauce, ginger, and pepper. Pour over the pasta and vegetables. Chill. Serves 6 to 8.

GREEK FETA-PASTA SALAD

1 pound pasta (vermicelli), cooked, drained, and cooled
2 medium peeled tomatoes, cut in wedges
1 medium cucumber, peeled and sliced thin
1 large green pepper, cut in strips
12 ripe olives, pitted
1½ cups feta cheese, crumbled
8 radishes, sliced thin
4 scallions, including tops, sliced thin
2 tablespoons finely chopped parsley
¼ teaspoon oregano
1 cup Vinaigrette with Pimiento*

Combine the pasta with the vegetables, cheese, and parsley. Add the oregano to the vinaigrette and pour over. Toss lightly. Serve immediately. Serves 6 to 8.

This can also be a main dish serving 4.

SALMON-PASTA SALAD

1 pound pasta (small shells or twists), cooked, drained, and cooled
1 (7¾-ounce) can salmon, drained (reserve liquid)
1 medium cucumber, peeled, seeded, and diced
1 cup green peas, cooked and drained
¾ cup Mayonnaise*
1 tablespoon lemon juice
1 tablespoon prepared white horseradish
1 teaspoon prepared mustard
¼ teaspoon salt
Spinach leaves (optional)

Combine the pasta, salmon, cucumber, and peas. Mix the Mayonnaise together with 1 tablespoon liquid from salmon and the remaining ingredients, except the spinach. Pour over pasta mixture and toss gently to blend. Chill. Serve on a bed of spinach, if desired. Serves 6.

This could also serve 4 as a main course.

PASTA-OLIVE SALAD

¾ pound pasta (small shells), cooked and drained
1 (7-ounce) can tuna, drained and broken up
1 red onion, sliced
12 ripe olives, pitted and sliced
12 stuffed green olives, halved
½ cup ricotta cheese
¼ cup wine vinegar
½ cup olive oil
½ teaspoon salt
¼ teaspoon pepper
1 tablespoon chopped fresh or ¼ teaspoon dried basil
1 tablespoon minced parsley

Combine the pasta, tuna, onion, and olives. Beat together the cheese, vinegar, oil, salt, pepper, basil, and parsley until creamy. Pour over the pasta and vegetables; toss gently to combine. Chill. Serves 4 to 6.

This can be an appetizer serving more people or a light main dish serving 4.

CHINESE NOODLES

½ cup soy sauce
½ cup oil (not olive)
¼ cup vinegar
2 tablespoons chili sauce
2 tablespoons sugar
½ teaspoon salt
1 pound thin Chinese noodles
2 tablespoons sesame oil
2 tablespoons toasted sesame seeds
2 cucumbers, peeled, sliced thin, and cut in halves
1 cup radishes or carrots, cut in thin rounds

Combine the soy sauce, oil, vinegar, chili sauce, sugar, and salt. Mix thoroughly and refrigerate. Cook the noodles in boiling salted water 2 to 3 minutes, no longer. Drain and toss with the sesame oil and seeds. Chill. When ready to serve, pour part of the sauce over the noodles. Don't make them too wet. Surround with the cucumbers and radishes and pass the remaining sauce. Serves 8.

NOODLES WITH SPICY PEANUT SAUCE

1 (8-ounce) package fine egg noodles, cooked and drained
3 tablespoons oil
2 tablespoons peanut butter
2 tablespoons soy sauce
1 teaspoon sugar
¼ cup chopped scallions, with tops
½ teaspoon ground ginger
Dash hot pepper sauce
1 small cucumber, peeled, seeded, and cut into slivers

Toss the noodles with 1 tablespoon oil, coating well; chill. In a large bowl, combine the peanut butter, soy sauce, remaining 2 tablespoons oil, 1 tablespoon water, sugar, scallions, ginger, and hot pepper sauce; stir until well blended and creamy. Add the noodles; toss to coat well. Top with the cucumber; chill. Serves 4.

MACARONI SALAD WITH VEGETABLES

1 pound elbow macaroni (regular or whole wheat)
2 teaspoons salt
6 scallions, with tops, chopped
½ cup chopped celery
1 red or green pepper or 3 green chilies, chopped
1 tablespoon prepared mustard
1 teaspoon oregano
½ cup French Dressing*

Boil the macaroni in deep water with the salt until tender, not mushy, about 8 minutes. Drain. Toss with the vegetables. Add the mustard and oregano to the dressing. Pour over the salad. Chill. Serves 6 to 8.

POLISH BLACK-EYED PEA SALAD

2 (10-ounce) packages frozen black-eyed peas
1 pound Polish sausage, cooked
½ cup French Dressing*

Cook the peas according to the package directions. Drain and cool. Cut the sausage in small chunks. Combine the peas and sausage. Toss with the dressing and chill. Serves 6 to 8.

MINTED GREEN PEA SALAD

1 (10-ounce) package frozen green peas or 1½ pounds fresh green peas (1½ cups shelled)
3 tablespoons Mayonnaise*
1 teaspoon lemon juice
½ teaspoon sugar
¼ teaspoon dried or 1 tablespoon chopped fresh mint
⅛ teaspoon salt
½ cup chopped celery
8 leaves Boston lettuce
Lemon slices (optional, for garnish)
Mint leaves (optional, for garnish)

Thaw the frozen peas in a colander under very hot running water; set aside to drain. (If using fresh peas, shell and cook until barely tender and drain.) In a large bowl, blend the Mayonnaise, lemon juice, sugar, mint, and salt. Stir in the celery and peas. Spoon onto a lettuce-lined platter. Garnish with lemon slices and mint if you wish. Chill before serving. Serves 4.

GREEN AND RED PEPPER SALAD

4 medium green peppers
4 medium red peppers
2 cloves garlic, crushed
⅓ cup Lemon French Dressing*

Hold the peppers on a fork over an open flame until the skins are charred on all sides. If a gas or other flame is not available, place the peppers on a baking sheet and broil about 12 to 15 minutes, turning to char evenly. Cool, rub skins off, and wash in cold water. Remove stems and seeds and cut the peppers in strips ⅓ to ½ inch wide. Place in a bowl with the garlic and dressing. Chill overnight or longer, stirring once or twice to ensure that all the peppers are coated with the dressing. Serves about 12.

This would also make an interesting appetizer.

PEACH-CELERY-LETTUCE SALAD

3 cups packed torn iceberg lettuce
1 (16-ounce) can sliced peaches, drained (reserve 2 tablespoons syrup)
1 cup diagonally sliced celery
¼ cup Ginger Dressing*
¼ cup chopped walnuts (optional)

In a salad bowl, combine the lettuce, peaches, and celery. Chill. Mix
the dressing with 2 tablespoons of the reserved syrup from the peaches,
add to the salad, and toss lightly. Sprinkle with walnuts if you wish. Serve
at once. Serves 4 to 6.

PEAR-CARROT-CHEESE SALAD

2 medium ripe pears, peeled and cut in eighths, or 1 (8½-ounce) can sliced
    pears, drained
3 large carrots, coarsely shredded
2 scallions, with some tops, sliced thin
⅓ cup coarsely shredded sharp Cheddar cheese
1 pimiento or roasted red pepper, drained and cut up
¼ cup Lemon French Dressing*

In a salad bowl, combine the pears, carrots, onions, cheese, and pimiento.
Chill. Add the dressing; toss gently. Serve at once. Serves 4.

PEAR-CARROT SALAD WITH BLUE CHEESE DRESSING

2 medium carrots, coarsely shredded
2 large ripe pears, peeled, quartered, and cored, or 4 canned pear halves,
    drained and halved
¼ cup Blue Cheese Dressing* (made without parsley)
¼ cup pecan or walnut halves

Arrange the carrots and pears on 4 individual salad plates. Spoon the
dressing over. Sprinkle with the nuts. Serve promptly. Serves 4.

POTATO AND GREEN BEAN SALAD

1 pound warm cooked cut green beans
4 warm cooked large potatoes, peeled and cubed (about 4 cups)
2 scallions, with tops, sliced thin
¼ cup oil
2 tablespoons white wine vinegar
1 medium clove garlic, crushed
1 small red onion, sliced thin
½ teaspoon oregano
1 teaspoon salt
⅛ teaspoon pepper
Lettuce (optional)

Place the beans, potatoes, and scallions in a bowl. In a jar, mix well the oil, vinegar, garlic, onion, oregano, salt, and pepper. Pour over vegetables and toss gently. Cover and chill several hours or overnight. Serve in lettuce-lined bowl if desired. Serves 6.

CUCUMBER-POTATO SALAD

1 tablespoon plus about ¾ teaspoon salt
1 medium cucumber, peeled if waxed, and sliced very thin (about 1½ cups sliced)
1 (2-pound) package frozen southern-style hash brown potatoes, partially broken up
7 scallions, with some tops, sliced thin, plus more (optional, for garnish)
1 cup chicken broth or water
1 cup plain yogurt
½ teaspoon minced garlic
½ teaspoon sugar
¼ teaspoon dried mint
Radishes (for garnish)

Sprinkle 1 tablespoon salt over the cucumber in a bowl. Toss and chill at least 2 hours. Rinse the cucumbers well with cold water to remove the salt; squeeze dry. Meanwhile, in a skillet, combine the potatoes, scallions, and broth; bring to a boil. Cover, then simmer until potatoes are tender and broth is absorbed, 5 to 10 minutes. Chill. Add the cucumber. Mix the yogurt, about ¾ teaspoon salt (or to taste), garlic, sugar, and mint. Add to the potatoes and cucumber; toss gently just to coat. Cover; chill well. Garnish with radishes and, if desired, scallions. Serves 4.

CURRIED POTATO SALAD

⅓ cup chicken broth
2–3 tablespoons curry powder
5 warm cooked large potatoes, peeled and cubed
6 scallions, with some tops, minced
1 teaspoon salt
½ cup Mayonnaise*
2 tablespoons lemon juice
6 inner ribs celery, sliced thin
1 large tart apple, cored and diced

In a small saucepan, heat the broth; blend in the curry powder. Cook 1 to 2 minutes; cool slightly. In a bowl, toss the potatoes gently with the scallions, curry-broth mixture, and salt; let stand until most of broth is absorbed. Mix the Mayonnaise, lemon juice, celery, and apple and add to potato mixture. Toss gently to coat. Cover and chill at least 2 hours. Serves 6.

POTATO SALAD WITH HAM

6 large potatoes
2 cups diced or slivered celery
2 tablespoons minced onion
1 pound ham, slivered
1 teaspoon salt
¼ teaspoon pepper
¼ cup cider vinegar
½ cup sour cream
¼ cup Mayonnaise*
Lettuce leaves (optional)

Boil the potatoes in their jackets about 20 minutes, until tender but not mushy. Cool, peel, and dice or sliver them. Add the celery, onion, and ham. Combine the salt, pepper, vinegar, sour cream, and Mayonnaise and pour over the potatoes. Toss gently. Serve on lettuce leaves, if you wish. Serves 8.

HERBED NEW POTATO SALAD

¾ cup Mayonnaise*
½ cup buttermilk or plain yogurt
2 tablespoons snipped fresh or 2 teaspoons dried dillweed
3 tablespoons minced chives or scallions
½ teaspoon salt
⅛ teaspoon pepper
2½ pounds cooked small new potatoes, unpeeled and quartered
Watercress sprigs (for garnish)

In a bowl, mix the Mayonnaise, buttermilk, dillweed, chives, salt, and pepper. Fold in the potatoes. Cover and chill at least 1 hour. Just before serving, spoon into a serving dish. Garnish with the watercress. Serves 6.

PRUNE-CHEESE SALAD

3 cups packed torn salad greens
¾ cup pitted prunes, cut up
¾ cup diced mozzarella or cream cheese
¼ cup Creamy Dressing*
2 tablespoons toasted slivered almonds or other chopped nuts

Combine the greens, prunes, and cheese in a salad bowl. Chill. Add the dressing; toss lightly. Sprinkle with the almonds. Serve at once. Serves 4.

RICE SALAD

2 tablespoons Mayonnaise*
2 tablespoons pineapple juice
½ teaspoon salt
¼ teaspoon pepper
2½ cups cold cooked rice
2 scallions, with tops, sliced
1 medium rib celery, sliced thin

In a medium bowl, mix well the Mayonnaise, pineapple juice, salt, and pepper. Add the remaining ingredients; toss until well coated. Chill. Serves 4.

Salmon-Shrimp Mold (page 78)

Allen Vogel

Turkey Tonnato (page 84)

Gazpacho from Madrid (page 31)

Will Rousseau

Spinach Soup (page 37),
Tomato Aspic Ring
with Chicken Salad
(page 61), Devil's Food
Cake (page 186)

Will Rousseau

Nectarine Mousse Parfaits
(page 173), Scandinavian
Cherry Soup (page 28),
Lemon Mold with Plums
(page 171), Pineapple Buttermilk Sherbet (page 181),
Melon with Berries (page
164)

Woman's Day Studio

Will Ro[u]

Pasta Salad with Vegetables (page 67)

RADISH-POTATO SALAD

1 teaspoon prepared mustard
2 tablespoons cider vinegar
1 cup sour cream
1 teaspoon salt
1/8 teaspoon pepper
Dash hot pepper sauce (optional)
4 cooked large potatoes, peeled and sliced or diced
1 cup sliced or chopped radishes
4 scallions, with tops, minced
Paprika (for garnish)

In a large bowl, mix well the mustard, vinegar, sour cream, salt, pepper, and the hot pepper sauce (if desired). Add the potatoes, radishes, and about 1/4 cup scallions; toss gently. Sprinkle with the remaining scallions and with paprika, if desired. Chill. Serves 4.

BROWN RICE WITH NUTS AND MUSHROOMS

1 cup brown rice
1/3 cup slivered toasted almonds
1/2 pound mushrooms, sliced
1 tablespoon minced chives or scallions
1/4 cup French Dressing*

Cook the rice according to package directions, drain, and cool. Stir in the remaining ingredients and adjust seasoning. Toss and chill. Serves 4.

BROWN RICE WITH VEGETABLES

3 cups cooked brown rice, drained and cooled
1 cup cooked cut green beans, drained and cooled
12 cherry tomatoes, halved
1 medium red onion, cut in half and sliced thin
18 pitted ripe olives
1 clove garlic, crushed
1/2 cup Lemon French Dressing*

Combine the cooked rice with the vegetables. Stir the garlic into the dressing, pour over the rice mixture, and toss. Chill. Serves 6.

RICE PILAF WITH VEGETABLES

2 cups rice
¼ cup butter
2 tablespoons olive oil
1 teaspoon salt
¼ teaspoon pepper
3½ cups chicken broth
¾ cup cooked cut green beans
12 pitted ripe olives
8 cherry tomatoes, halved
1 small red onion, sliced thin
¾ cup Lemon French Dressing*

Sauté the rice in the butter and oil in a heavy saucepan. Stir until straw-colored. Add the salt, pepper, and broth. Cover and simmer 15 minutes, without stirring. The rice should be tender and the liquid absorbed. When rice is cooked, remove from heat. Cool. Add the vegetables. Pour the dressing over. Mix thoroughly and chill. Serves 6 to 8.

BROWN RICE SALAD WITH WATERCRESS

5 cups chicken broth
1½ teaspoons salt
2½ cups raw brown rice
1 cup minced watercress
1 cup diced radishes
⅓ cup minced scallions, with tops
¼ cup oil
2 tablespoons red wine vinegar
1 teaspoon prepared mustard
½ teaspoon pepper
Lettuce leaves
Radish roses (for garnish)

In a large saucepan or Dutch oven, bring the chicken broth and 1 teaspoon salt to a boil. Stir in the rice and return to a boil. Reduce heat to low, cover tightly, and simmer until rice is tender and liquid absorbed, about 45 minutes. Cool completely. Fluff rice with a fork. Toss in the watercress, radishes, and scallions. Mix well the oil, vinegar, mustard, remaining ½ teaspoon salt, and pepper. Pour over the rice mixture and toss just until blended. Chill. Serve in a lettuce-lined bowl. Garnish with radish roses. Serves 8 to 10.

PEACH-RICE SALAD

½ cup plain yogurt
2 tablespoons lemon juice
2 tablespoons honey
½ teaspoon salt
2 cups cold cooked rice
2 medium peaches, sliced (about 1 cup sliced)
1 rib celery, sliced diagonally
4 tablespoons coarsely chopped walnuts or pecans

In a serving bowl, mix well the yogurt, lemon juice, honey, and salt.
Add the rice, peaches, celery, and 3 tablespoons nuts; toss to coat well.
Garnish with remaining nuts. Chill. Serves 4.

RUSSIAN SALAD

2 cups diced cooked beef
½ cup diced dill pickles
½ cup diced cooked beets
½ cup diced cooked potatoes
1 medium cucumber, peeled and diced
¼ cup chopped olives, green or ripe
1 cup kidney beans, drained
½ cup sauerkraut, drained
2 tablespoons vodka (optional)
½–¾ cup French Dressing* (or part Mayonnaise*)

Have all of the ingredients cold. You *must* use the first four ingredients
and the dressing. Use as many of the others as you wish and have readily
available. Mix all together and toss with the vodka (if using) and dressing. Chill. Serves 6 to 8.

SHRIMP-PASTA-CAULIFLOWER SALAD

1 pound pasta (small shells), cooked, drained, and cooled
¾ pound small shrimp, cooked, shelled, drained, and cooled
1 medium head cauliflower, broken into flowerets, cooked, drained, and
    cooled (about 2 cups)
3 scallions, including tops, minced
2 tablespoons chopped parsley
¾–1 cup Avocado Dressing*

Combine the pasta, shrimp, cauliflowerets, scallions, and parsley. Pour
the dressing over and toss gently to blend. Chill. Serves 6.

This could also be a main course, serving 4.

SPINACH-CITRUS SALAD

3 cups packed torn spinach leaves, stems removed
1 large orange, peeled and sectioned
1 medium grapefruit, peeled and sectioned .
1 medium red onion, sliced and separated into rings
½ cup Honey–Poppy Seed Dressing*

Combine the spinach, orange, grapefruit, and onion; pour the dressing
over all. Toss and serve at room temperature or chilled. Serves 4.

SPINACH SALAD WITH SESAME SEEDS

2 tablespoons oil
2 tablespoons soy sauce
2 tablespoons wine vinegar
1 small clove garlic, crushed (optional)
¼ teaspoon salt
¼ teaspoon pepper
¼ teaspoon sugar
⅛ teaspoon ground ginger
½ pound spinach, torn
2 tablespoons toasted sesame seeds
1 hard-cooked egg, chopped (for garnish)

Mix the oil, soy sauce, vinegar, garlic (if using), and seasonings. Pour
over the spinach. Toss lightly and chill. Sprinkle with the sesame seeds
and egg. Serves 4 to 6.

SPAGHETTI SQUASH SALAD

1 spaghetti squash (about 2 pounds)
¼ cup French Dressing*
½ teaspoon sugar
¼ teaspoon nutmeg
1 tablespoon chopped chives
1 (8-ounce) can tomatoes, drained and coarsely chopped, or 1 large ripe
    tomato, peeled and chopped
Greens (optional)

In a large pot, cook the squash in boiling water to cover about 40 minutes, or until easily pierced with a fork. (The edible portion of the squash should be crisp-tender.) Remove and let cool until easy to handle. Meanwhile, in a large bowl, mix the dressing, sugar, nutmeg, and chives. Halve the squash lengthwise; scoop out and discard the seeds. Remove the pulp and separate with a fork into strands. Add to the dressing, with the tomatoes. Toss to coat well. Return to the squash shells and chill. Serve garnished with greens if you wish. Serves 4.

SUMMER SQUASH WITH SOUR CREAM

3 medium summer squash, sliced ¼ inch thick
2 tablespoons oil
2 tablespoons cider vinegar
½ teaspoon salt
⅓ cup sour cream
1 tablespoon minced chives

In a large saucepan, cook the squash in boiling salted water to cover 1 minute. Drain and cool. In a medium bowl, blend the oil, vinegar, and salt; stir in the sour cream and chives. Fold in the squash and chill at least 30 minutes. Serves 4.

MARINATED TOMATOES WITH BLUE CHEESE

3 large tomatoes, peeled and cut in chunks or sliced
¼ cup Blue Cheese Dressing with Parsley*

Combine the tomatoes with the dressing and chill at least 30 minutes. Serves 4.

TOMATO ASPIC WITH HERBS

2 envelopes unflavored gelatin
2 (12-ounce) cans tomato or cocktail vegetable juice
½ teaspoon salt
1 teaspoon sugar
¼ teaspoon pepper
2 tablespoons lemon juice
2 tablespoons minced chives or scallions
2 tablespoons minced parsley
1 tablespoon chopped fresh or 1 teaspoon dried basil
1 tablespoon chopped fresh or 1 teaspoon dried tarragon
1 tablespoon Worcestershire sauce
Lettuce
2 hard-cooked eggs, sliced (for garnish)
1 cup Mayonnaise*

Soften the gelatin in ½ cup tomato juice. Add the remaining tomato juice, salt, sugar, pepper, lemon juice, and chives. Heat and stir until the gelatin is dissolved. Remove from heat and add the herbs and Worcestershire. Adjust the seasoning and pour into 8 individual cups or a ring or other mold. Chill at least 2 hours, until set. Unmold and serve on lettuce and garnish with the hard-cooked eggs. Pass the Mayonnaise. Serves 8.

TOMATOES STUFFED WITH AVOCADO

8 medium ripe tomatoes
2 medium avocados
2 teaspoons lemon juice
2 tablespoons minced chives or scallions, with tops
1 clove garlic, crushed
½ cup Mayonnaise*

Prepare the tomatoes by cutting off the top and scooping out the seeds and flesh. Turn the tomatoes upside down to drain. Peel and dice the avocados and sprinkle with the lemon juice. Add the chives and garlic to the Mayonnaise, stir in some of the chopped tomato flesh, and mix well. Toss gently with the avocados. Fill the tomato shells with the mixture and chill. Serves 8.

TOMATOES WITH BASIL

6 medium ripe tomatoes
½ teaspoon salt
¼ teaspoon pepper
½ teaspoon sugar
Chopped fresh basil
2 tablespoons olive oil

Plunge the tomatoes into boiling water for a few seconds. Peel and slice. Then place on a serving plate with the slices overlapping slightly. Sprinkle with the salt, pepper, sugar, and basil. Dribble the oil over. Chill. Serves 6.

TOMATOES IN CURRY MARINADE

3 large tomatoes, peeled and cut in wedges
1 teaspoon curry powder
2 tablespoons strong chicken broth
½ cup Mayonnaise*
1 tablespoon lemon juice
⅛ teaspoon pepper
⅓ cup minced watercress

Arrange the tomatoes in a serving dish. Combine the curry powder and chicken broth in a small pan and simmer, stirring, 2 minutes. Cool. Beat into the Mayonnaise, add the lemon juice, and season with pepper. Pour over the tomatoes and sprinkle with the watercress. Chill. Serves 4.

CHERRY TOMATOES, GUACAMOLE STYLE

2 cups cherry tomatoes, halved
½ medium avocado, peeled and cut up
1 teaspoon lemon juice
½ teaspoon chili powder
1 small clove garlic
2 tablespoons Mayonnaise*
⅓ cup half-and-half

Place the cherry tomatoes in serving bowl. Place all the other ingredients in a blender or processor and purée until smooth. Pour over the tomatoes and chill. Serves 4.

TOMATO HALVES STUFFED WITH MARINATED CHERRY TOMATOES

3 large tomatoes, cut in half crosswise
1½ cups cherry tomatoes, cut in wedges
1 tablespoon vinegar
3 tablespoons oil
¼ teaspoon salt
⅛ teaspoon pepper
2 tablespoons minced parsley
1 tablespoon capers, drained and minced

Scoop pulp out of the large tomatoes and reserve for another use. Combine all the other ingredients and spoon into the tomato halves. Chill at least 30 minutes. Serves 6.

MARINATED TOMATOES, ITALIAN STYLE

3 large tomatoes, peeled and sliced
⅓ cup minced parsley
1 small clove garlic, minced
2 tablespoons capers, drained and chopped
3 anchovy fillets, cut up
½ cup olive oil
¼ teaspoon pepper

On a serving platter, layer the tomatoes, sprinkled with the parsley. Combine all the other ingredients, mix well, and pour over. Let stand in the refrigerator at least 1 hour before serving. Serves 4.

TOMATOES WITH SOUR CREAM MARINADE

3 large tomatoes, peeled and cut in chunks
½ cup sour cream
½ cup finely chopped ripe olives
1 tablespoon minced fresh dillweed
½ teaspoon salt
¼ teaspoon pepper
½ teaspoon sugar

Place the tomatoes in a serving dish. Combine all the other ingredients, mix well, and pour over. Chill several hours. Serves 4.

TOMATO-MOZZARELLA SALAD

2 large tomatoes, peeled, seeded, and cubed (about 1½ cups)
8 ounces mozzarella cheese, cubed (about 1¼ cups)
¼ cup chopped mild onion
3 tablespoons oil
2 tablespoons lemon juice
2 tablespoons chopped fresh or 1½ teaspoons dried basil
½ teaspoon salt
¼ teaspoon pepper

In a medium bowl, mix well all the ingredients. Serve at room temperature. Serves 4.

MARINATED VEGETABLE PLATTER

½ pound cooked green beans, drained
3 large potatoes, cooked, peeled, and diced
2 medium yellow squash, sliced, cooked, and drained
3 medium tomatoes, peeled and sliced
1 medium red onion, sliced thin and separated into rings
½ cup French Dressing*

Arrange the vegetables attractively on a serving platter; sprinkle with the dressing. Cover and chill. Serves 4 to 6.

MARINATED VEGETABLE SALAD

1 (10-ounce) package frozen Fordhook lima beans, cooked and drained
1 (9-ounce) package frozen cut green beans, cooked and drained
1 (10-ounce) package frozen whole-kernel corn, cooked and drained
1 medium red onion, minced
1 clove garlic
½ cup olive oil
3 tablespoons red wine vinegar
½ teaspoon salt
¼ teaspoon pepper

Combine the vegetables in a large bowl. While still warm, add the rest of the ingredients. Toss lightly to mix. Cover and chill several hours or overnight. Remove garlic before serving. Serves 6.

ROMANIAN VEGETABLE POTPOURRI
(*Ghivetch*)

¼ cup olive oil
2 medium onions, sliced thin
2 large cloves garlic, crushed
1 medium eggplant (about 1 pound), peeled and cut in ½-inch dice
2 medium tomatoes, peeled and diced
1 medium green pepper, cut in strips
1 small yellow summer squash, cut in 1½-inch strips
1 medium potato, diced (unpeeled)
1 cup green peas
1 cup chicken broth
1 teaspoon salt
½ teaspoon pepper
1 tomato, chopped coarsely (for garnish)

In a large pan, heat the oil and sauté the onions and garlic until tender, 5 to 7 minutes. Stir in the eggplant, diced tomatoes, green pepper, squash, potato, peas, broth, salt, and pepper. Bring to a boil. Cover and simmer, stirring occasionally, 20 minutes, or until vegetables are tender and liquid has been absorbed. Serve at room temperature or chilled. Garnish with the chopped tomato. Serves 4 to 6.

CRACKED WHEAT SALAD I
(Iranian *Tabbouleh*)

1½ cups cracked wheat (bulgur)
¼ cup chopped fresh or 1 tablespoon dried mint
1 large cucumber, peeled and diced
3 medium tomatoes, peeled, seeded, and diced
1 large green pepper, diced
1 large onion, diced
⅓ cup chopped parsley (flat-leaf) or coriander
½–¾ cup Lemon French Dressing*

Soak the cracked wheat in water 40 minutes. Drain and dry. Combine with the remaining ingredients except the dressing. Pour ½ cup dressing over and mix thoroughly. If you want a little more dressing, add it, but this salad should not be too wet. Chill in the refrigerator at least 1 hour before serving. Serves 8.

CRACKED WHEAT SALAD II
(Bulgur)

1½ cups cracked wheat (bulgur)
½ cup minced onion
2 tablespoons oil
1 cup broth (any kind)
1 teaspoon salt
½ teaspoon thyme
½ teaspoon ground allspice
¼ teaspoon pepper
2 tablespoons minced chives or scallions
2 tablespoons minced parsley or coriander

Soak the cracked wheat in 2 cups water 30 minutes. Sauté the onion in the oil until limp but not brown. Drain the cracked wheat and stir into the onion. Cook, stirring, 2 minutes. Add the broth, salt, thyme, allspice, and pepper. Cover and simmer about 10 minutes. Drain and stir in the chives and parsley. Chill at least 1 hour before serving. Serves 6.

WINTER BUFFET SALAD

3 cups shredded red cabbage
2 cups shredded carrots
2 cups thinly sliced celery
2 cups peeled and thinly sliced white turnips (about 4 small)
2 cups thinly sliced cauliflowerets
2 cups thinly sliced peeled broccoli stalks
1 cup thinly sliced radishes
3 or 4 broccoli flowerets for decoration
1¼ cups dressing—especially good with Green French Dressing*; Russian
    Dressing*; Vinaigrette with Herbs*; Lemon French Dressing*

Arrange all the vegetables except the broccoli flowerets in separate mounds on a serving platter. To keep crisp, put an ice cube in each mound. Decorate the platter with the broccoli flowerets. Place one or two dressings in small bowls and serve with the salad. Serves 10 to 12.

ZUCCHINI SALAD

½ cup olive oil
3 tablespoons wine vinegar
1 small clove garlic, crushed or minced
½ teaspoon salt
⅛ teaspoon pepper
1½ pounds small zucchini, cut up
½ cup thinly sliced scallions, with tops
Lettuce cups

Mix the oil, vinegar, garlic, salt, and pepper thoroughly. Pour over the zucchini and scallions, and toss. Cover and chill for 1 hour or longer. Serve in lettuce cups, spooning on any dressing remaining in the bowl. Serves 6.

MARINATED ZUCCHINI

4 medium-small zucchini (about 1½ pounds)
¼ cup dry white wine
⅓ cup oil, preferably olive
1 teaspoon salt
½ teaspoon pepper
⅛ teaspoon tarragon
Parsley sprigs (for garnish)

Cut the zucchini in ¾-inch strips. Cut the strips diagonally in ½-inch pieces; set aside. In a large skillet, bring to a boil the wine, oil, salt, pepper, and tarragon. Add the zucchini; return to the boil. Cover, then simmer about 5 minutes, stirring occasionally. Remove to a serving dish. Cover and chill at least 3 hours. Garnish with the parsley. Serves 4.

TOMATO-ZUCCHINI SALAD WITH BLUE CHEESE

1 pint cherry tomatoes, halved
2 small zucchini, sliced thin
1 small onion, sliced thin and separated into rings
⅓ cup blue cheese, crumbled
⅓ cup oil, preferably olive
2 tablespoons red wine vinegar
⅛ teaspoon pepper

Combine the tomatoes, zucchini, onion, and cheese. Combine the oil, vinegar, and pepper, and pour over. Chill several hours or overnight. Serves 4.

Dressings

ANCHOVY DRESSING

1 (2-ounce) can anchovies
⅓ cup olive oil
¼ cup red wine vinegar
1 tablespoon Dijon-style mustard
⅛ teaspoon pepper

In a bowl, mash the anchovies and mix with the oil to make a smooth paste. Add the remaining ingredients and mix well. Yield: about ¾ cup.

AVOCADO DRESSING

1 medium avocado, peeled, pitted, and cubed
1 cup plain yogurt
1 tablespoon lemon juice
½ teaspoon salt
¼ teaspoon basil or tarragon
¼ teaspoon pepper

Whirl all the ingredients in blender or processor until smooth. Yield: about 1½ cups.

BLUE CHEESE DRESSING WITH PARSLEY

½ cup crumbled blue cheese
⅓ cup oil
2 tablespoons cider vinegar
2 tablespoons water
½ cup parsley sprigs
⅛ teaspoon salt

Combine the ingredients in a blender or processor and purée. Yield: about 1 cup.

CELERY SEED AND HONEY DRESSING

⅓ cup sugar
1 teaspoon dry mustard
1 teaspoon celery seed
½ teaspoon salt
½ teaspoon paprika
3 tablespoons honey
3 tablespoons cider vinegar
1 tablespoon lemon juice
½ cup oil, at least part olive

In a bowl, combine the sugar, mustard, celery seed, salt, and paprika.
Beat in the honey, vinegar, lemon juice, and oil. Yield: about 1¼ cups.

CREAMY DRESSING

⅓ cup Mayonnaise*
⅓ cup buttermilk
1 tablespoon cider vinegar
Dash salt or garlic salt
⅛ teaspoon pepper

Combine all of the ingredients and mix thoroughly. Yield: about ⅔ cup.

CHIVE SAUCE

½ cup Mayonnaise*
1 tablespoon prepared mustard, preferably Dijon-style
3 tablespoons minced chives
½ teaspoon salt
⅛ teaspoon pepper
¼ cup heavy cream, whipped stiff

In a bowl, with a rubber spatula, gently but thoroughly fold together
all the ingredients. Chill. Yield: 1½ cups.

Very good with vegetables, raw or cooked.

RAW CRANBERRY-ORANGE RELISH

2 cups cranberries
2 large oranges, unpeeled, seeded, and cut up
¾–1 cup sugar
3 tablespoons orange liqueur: Cointreau, curaçao, or Triple Sec

Put the cranberries and oranges with ¾ cup sugar in a blender or processor. Process briefly to cut up; do not make a smooth purée. Stir in the liqueur and more sugar to taste. Yield: about 2½ cups.

This is particularly good served as an accompaniment to ham, turkey, or chicken.

CREAMY COCKTAIL SAUCE

1 cup Mayonnaise*
½ cup sour cream
½ cup ketchup
3 teaspoons lemon juice
2 teaspoons prepared horseradish
½ teaspoon sugar
Few drops hot pepper sauce

Mix all the ingredients together and chill. Yield: about 2 cups.

This is good with seafood. For delicate seafood such as crab meat, omit the hot pepper sauce.

CUCUMBER SAUCE

½ cup Mayonnaise*
1 cup cucumber, peeled, halved, seeded, and chopped
1 tablespoon lemon juice
1 tablespoon minced fresh dillweed
½ teaspoon salt

Stir all the ingredients together and chill. Yield: 1½ cups.

CURRIED CHEESE DRESSING

¼ cup Mayonnaise*
¾ cup cottage cheese
¼ cup fruit syrup
2 teaspoons curry powder
¼ teaspoon salt
1 cup raisins (optional)

In a bowl, combine the ingredients except the raisins. Beat well and fold in the raisins, if you wish. Yield: about 1½ cups (more with raisins).

FRENCH DRESSING

¼ cup wine vinegar
1 teaspoon salt
¼ teaspoon pepper
Pinch of sugar (optional)
½ teaspoon dry mustard
¾ cup olive oil

Mix the vinegar with the combined seasonings. Pour in the oil very slowly, stirring all the time. Mix thoroughly. A good way is to shake it in a tightly closed jar. Chill before serving. Yield: about 1 cup.

GREEN FRENCH DRESSING

¾ cup oil, at least part olive
¼ cup wine vinegar
1 teaspoon prepared mustard
½ teaspoon salt
¼ teaspoon pepper
½ teaspoon sugar (optional)
½ cup parsley sprigs or 3 tablespoons minced parsley

Combine all of the ingredients in a blender or covered jar. If using a blender, use parsley sprigs; if a jar, use minced. Whirl or shake until thoroughly blended. Yield: about 1 cup.

Rousseau

Ratatouille (page 71)

William Helms

Glazed Oranges (page 165), Cheese Twists (page 7),
Rice Pilaf with Vegetables (page 122)

André Gillardin

French Beef Salad (page 48)

Tuna Pâté (page 20), Italian Tuna Pie
(page 81), Salade Niçoise (page 66)

Irwin Horowitz

Summer Fruits with Lime Cream Dressing (page 163)

Cookies: Oatmeal-Raisin (page 205), Double-Peanut (page 205), Banana-Pecan Squares (page 199), Thumbkins (page 206), Date-Nut Bars (page 202), Kasha Crackles (page 203), Nut Crisps (page 204), Chocolate Refrigerator (page 202), Oatmeal and Apple Butter Bars (page 204)

Chocolate Fantasy (page 175), Ladyfinger Ice Cream Cake (page 176),
Peach Ice Cream Bombe with Raspberry Purée (page 178)

LEMON FRENCH DRESSING

½ cup salad oil, at least part olive oil
3 tablespoons lemon juice
½ teaspoon dry mustard (optional)
½ teaspoon paprika
Pinch of sugar (optional)
½ teaspoon salt

Put all the ingredients in a jar, cover tightly, and shake. Chill. Shake again before serving. Yield: about ¾ cup.

GINGER DRESSING

⅓ cup Mayonnaise*
2 tablespoons peach or other fruit syrup
1 tablespoon cider vinegar or lemon juice
¼–½ teaspoon grated fresh ginger
Pinch salt

Combine the ingredients, using ¼ teaspoon ginger. Mix thoroughly and add more ginger to taste. Yield: about ½ cup.

GREEN SAUCE

¾ cup oil, preferably olive
2 cups loosely packed sprigs parsley, preferably flat-leaf
3 tablespoons lemon juice
2 tablespoons capers, drained (optional)
2 cloves garlic, crushed
3 anchovy fillets
½ teaspoon salt
¼ teaspoon pepper

Whirl all the ingredients in a blender or processor until almost smooth, or chop all the ingredients fine and beat together. Chill. Yield: about 2 cups.

Especially good with raw vegetables, as a dip or sauce.

GREEN GODDESS DRESSING

¾ cup Mayonnaise*
½ cup sour cream
2 tablespoons minced scallions, with tops
½ teaspoon salt
¼ teaspoon pepper
1 teaspoon tarragon

Combine the ingredients. Stir, and chill several hours. Yield: about 1½ cups.

HONEY DRESSING

⅓ cup sugar
¼ teaspoon dry mustard
1 teaspoon celery seed
½ teaspoon salt
½ teaspoon paprika
3 tablespoons honey, slightly warmed
3 tablespoons cider vinegar
1 tablespoon lemon juice
½ cup oil (at least part olive)

Combine the sugar, mustard, celery seed, salt, and paprika. Beat in the honey, vinegar, lemon juice, and oil. Mix thoroughly. Yield: about 1¼ cups.

HONEY–POPPY SEED DRESSING

2 tablespoons lime or lemon juice
⅓ cup oil (not olive)
2 tablespoons honey
1 tablespoon poppy seeds
½ teaspoon prepared mustard
¼ teaspoon salt
⅛ teaspoon pepper

Combine all the ingredients and mix very thoroughly. Chill. Yield: about ½ cup.

LIME CREAM DRESSING

1 cup sour cream
1 (3-ounce) package cream cheese
¼ cup lime juice
2 tablespoons honey

Smooth the sour cream and cream cheese together. Stir in the lime juice and honey. This may be done in a blender or processor. Blend until smooth. Yield: about 1½ cups.

LORENZO DRESSING

¾ cup chopped watercress leaves (packed down)
⅔ cup French Dressing* or Lemon French Dressing*
½ cup chili sauce or ketchup
2 teaspoons sugar
¼ teaspoon pepper

Combine all of the ingredients and mix thoroughly. Taste for seasoning. Yield: about 1¾ cups.

MAYONNAISE

1 egg
½ teaspoon salt
½ teaspoon dry mustard
¾ cup oil (part but not all olive)
1 tablespoon lemon juice or vinegar

Put the egg in a blender with the salt and mustard. Set the blender at its lowest speed; add the oil very slowly. After using 2 or 3 tablespoons, add the rest of the oil in a very slow stream. Thin with lemon juice or vinegar. (Lemon juice is particularly good with fish.) Yield: about 1¼ cups.

VARIATIONS:

Add to about 1 cup of Mayonnaise*:
½ teaspoon curry powder and a little crushed garlic
½–¾ cup chili sauce
2 tablespoons capers, drained and chopped
2–3 tablespoons chopped fresh or 1 teaspoon dried herbs, such as tarragon, parsley, dill, chives, or a mixture.

MUSTARD DRESSING

1 tablespoon prepared mustard
2 tablespoons vinegar
2 tablespoons water
1 teaspoon sugar
¼ teaspoon salt
5 tablespoons oil

Combine all the ingredients and mix thoroughly. Yield: about ⅔ cup.

PESTO

(Basil Sauce)

2 cups chopped fresh basil
2 tablespoons chopped parsley
3 tablespoons olive oil
2 cloves garlic, cut up
3 tablespoons pine nuts (pignoli) or walnuts
2 tablespoons grated Parmesan or Romano cheese

Place all the ingredients in a blender and whirl until smooth. Do not purée too long. Yield: 1⅓ cups.

NOTE: If fresh basil is not available, substitute 1¾ cups chopped parsley and 1 tablespoon dried basil for the fresh basil and omit the 2 tablespoons parsley.

ROQUEFORT DRESSING WITH SOUR CREAM

2 ounces Roquefort or blue cheese, crumbled
1 egg
½ teaspoon salt
½ teaspoon dry mustard
½ cup olive oil
½ cup sour cream

Blend the cheese, egg, salt, and mustard in a blender. Pour in the oil slowly with the machine at slowest speed. Add the sour cream and blend ½ minute. Yield: about 1½ cups.

RUSSIAN DRESSING I

1 cup Mayonnaise*
½ cup chili sauce
½ cup ketchup
1 tablespoon minced scallions, chives, or onion
1 tablespoon India relish
2 hard-cooked eggs, chopped

Mix the Mayonnaise with the other ingredients and chill. Yield: about 2¼ cups.

NOTE: Real Russian Dressing has 2 tablespoons caviar added just before serving!

RUSSIAN DRESSING II

¾ cup Mayonnaise*
¼ cup chili sauce
2 tablespoons lemon juice
2 tablespoons pickle relish (optional)
2 tablespoons minced scallions

Combine all the ingredients and stir until thoroughly blended. Yield: about 1½ cups.

SOUR CREAM SAUCE

1¼ cups sour cream
2 egg yolks, slightly beaten
2 tablespoons prepared horseradish
2 tablespoons lemon juice
½ teaspoon salt
¼ teaspoon pepper

Combine all the ingredients and blend well. Chill. Especially good for vegetables. Yield: about 1¾ cups.

SOY DRESSING

2 tablespoons soy sauce
2 tablespoons lemon juice
4 tablespoons oil
1 tablespoon cider or rice wine vinegar
½ clove garlic, crushed
½ teaspoon salt
½ teaspoon sugar
¼ teaspoon ground ginger or ½ teaspoon grated fresh ginger

Combine all the ingredients and mix thoroughly. Yield: about ½ cup.

THOUSAND ISLAND DRESSING

1 cup Mayonnaise*
½ cup chili sauce
2 hard-cooked eggs, chopped
3 tablespoons minced onion

Combine all the ingredients and mix well. Chill a few hours. Yield: about
2 cups.

TOMATO MAYONNAISE

1 cup Mayonnaise*
1 (8-ounce) can tomato purée (you may add puréed roasted peppers if
    desired)
1 clove garlic, crushed

Combine and chill at least 30 minutes before serving. Yield: 2 cups.

WHITE WINE–LEMON MAYONNAISE

½ cup dry white wine
1 teaspoon lemon juice
1 cup Mayonnaise*

Stir the ingredients together thoroughly. Yield: about 1½ cups.

VINAIGRETTE WITH HERBS

¾ cup olive oil
¼ cup wine vinegar
½ teaspoon salt
¼ teaspoon pepper
1 tablespoon minced parsley
2 teaspoons minced chives
1 teaspoon finely chopped capers

In a bowl, combine all the ingredients and beat until blended. Yield: about 1 cup.

VINAIGRETTE WITH PIMIENTO

¾ cup olive oil
¼ cup red wine vinegar
½ teaspoon salt
¼ teaspoon pepper
1 pimiento, drained and chopped
1 hard-cooked egg, chopped fine

Combine the oil, vinegar, salt, and pepper in a jar or bowl. Shake or beat until thoroughly blended. Stir in the pimiento and egg. Yield: about 1¼ cups.

YOGURT MAYONNAISE

1 egg or egg yolk
½ teaspoon salt
½ cup peanut or vegetable oil
1 tablespoon vinegar or lemon juice (or more)
½ cup plain yogurt

If using a blender or processor, use the whole egg; if mixing by hand, use the yolk only. Put the egg and salt in a bowl and mix slowly with a fork or whisk. Add the oil a few drops at a time. When the mixture starts to thicken, add the oil in a very thin stream, stirring steadily. When really thick, thin with 1 tablespoon vinegar or lemon juice. If using a machine, keep at slow speed. Add more lemon juice or vinegar for taste. Stir in the yogurt. Yield: about 1½ cups.

Especially good with fruit or seafood.

YOGURT-SESAME DRESSING

⅔ cup plain yogurt
3 tablespoons toasted sesame seeds
2 tablespoons cider vinegar
2 tablespoons honey

Mix all the ingredients well. Yield: about 1 cup.

Sandwiches and Sandwich Fillings

RELUCTANT to leave the gaming table long enough to dine, the Fourth Earl of Sandwich ordered meat and other good things served between slices of bread so that he could eat as he played. Now, two centuries later, he would be surprised if he could see the number of concoctions that bear his name.

There are dainty tea sandwiches—the thinnest bits of bread hiding a sliver of cucumber and a sprig of cress, or a long thin slice of bread spread with soft cheese, rolled, and sliced into pinwheels. Dozens of these tiny morsels make an enticing display on a tea table or tea tray.

Luncheon sandwiches are heartier; the bread may be thicker, it may be French bread or pita (pocket bread), and the sandwich may even be open-faced, as some Europeans prefer. Of course, the closed sandwich is essential for those who eat en route.

One cannot think of a picnic without thinking of sandwiches, either as the mainstay or an accompaniment to fried chicken or other picnic treats. Here is where that monumental concoction of countless ingredients and many names—"hero" and "grinder" are the most common—comes into its own.

If only the Earl of Sandwich, First Lord of the Admiralty, could see—and taste—his namesake now!

CHEESE-NUT SANDWICHES

½ pound Cheddar cheese, shredded
⅓ cup chopped walnuts
½ cup Mayonnaise*
8 slices rye bread
4 lettuce leaves

Mix well the cheese, walnuts, and ¼ cup Mayonnaise. Spread 4 slices bread with the cheese mixture. Top each with a lettuce leaf. Spread the remaining 4 slices bread with the remaining ¼ cup Mayonnaise. Place the bread, Mayonnaise side down, on the lettuce. Halve each sandwich. Serves 4 to 6.

CREAM CHEESE AND CHIPPED BEEF SANDWICHES

12 ounces cream cheese, at room temperature
½ cup chipped beef
2–2½ teaspoons Worcestershire sauce
¼ cup soft butter
16 slices rye or pumpernickel bread

Combine the cheese, beef, and 2 teaspoons Worcestershire sauce. Add
more Worcestershire to taste. Let stand a few hours in the refrigerator
to blend flavors. Butter the bread or mix the butter into the spread. Dark
bread is especially good for these sandwiches. Spread the slices of bread.
Cover with remaining bread and press top down. Remove crusts if you
wish. Cut in halves. Serves 8.

OLIVE AND CREAM CHEESE SANDWICHES

Proceed as for Cream Cheese and Chipped Beef Sandwiches*. Reduce
the cheese to 8 ounces and substitute ¾ cup chopped ripe olives for the
beef. Use 8 slices of rye bread. Serves 4.

CHICKEN CLUB SANDWICHES

12 very thin slices whole wheat bread
2 tablespoons whipped butter
2 tablespoons Mayonnaise*
8 ounces sliced cooked chicken
1 medium tomato, peeled and sliced
1 medium red or other sweet onion, sliced
1 medium zucchini (about 4 ounces), sliced
4 large lettuce leaves
16 pimiento-stuffed olives (optional)

Spread 8 slices of bread with butter and another 4 slices with Mayonnaise. On 4 buttered slices layer the chicken and tomato. Cover with
the Mayonnaise-spread bread and layer the onion, zucchini, and lettuce.
Top with the remaining buttered bread. If you wish, for each sandwich,
push a toothpick into an olive and then into the sandwich about halfway
along one side. Repeat on the other sides. Cut diagonally into quarters.
Serves 4.

ELEGANT CHICKEN SANDWICHES

12 slices very thin-sliced white bread
¼ cup soft butter
1 (2¾-ounce) can pâté de foie gras (at room temperature)
¾–1 pound thin-sliced cooked chicken breasts
Parsley sprigs (for garnish)

Remove the crusts from the bread and spread slices with the butter.
Spread with the foie gras and place slices of chicken on top. Cut in halves
or diagonally into quarters. You may cover with second slices of buttered bread if you wish, but they are more elegant open-faced. Serves 6.

CHICKEN AND EGG SALAD SANDWICHES

4 hard-cooked eggs, chopped
1 cup chopped cooked chicken
1 teaspoon lemon juice
½ teaspoon salt
¼ teaspoon paprika
¼–⅓ cup Mayonnaise*
12 slices white or whole wheat bread

Combine the eggs and chicken. Add the lemon juice, salt, and paprika
to the Mayonnaise and stir ¼ cup into the egg-chicken mixture. Add more
Mayonnaise to taste. Spread the salad on 6 slices of bread, cover with
the remaining slices, pat down. Cut the sandwiches in halves. Serves 6.

CHICKEN SALAD SANDWICHES

1 cup chopped cooked chicken
⅓ cup fine-chopped celery
1 teaspoon lemon juice
¼ cup Mayonnaise*
12 slices thin white bread
Soft butter

Combine the chicken, celery, lemon juice, and Mayonnaise. Spread 6
slices of bread with butter, cover with the chicken salad, and top with
the remaining bread. Press firmly to hold sandwiches together. Cut off
crusts and cut sandwiches in halves. Serves 6.

CURRIED CHICKEN SALAD SANDWICHES

2½ cups diced cooked chicken
½ cup diced celery
½ cup diced apple
½ teaspoon lemon juice
1 teaspoon minced onion
½ teaspoon salt
¼ teaspoon pepper
2 teaspoons curry powder
⅓ cup Mayonnaise*
12 slices thin-sliced bread

Mix the chicken with the celery. Sprinkle the apple with the lemon juice and add to the chicken. Combine the onion, salt, pepper, and curry powder with the Mayonnaise. Stir into the chicken mixture and spread on 6 slices of bread. Top with the remaining bread and push down so the sandwich will stay well closed. Serves 6.

CHICKEN SALAD SANDWICHES WITH WATER CHESTNUTS

Add ½ cup diced water chestnuts and 1 teaspoon soy sauce to Chicken Salad Sandwiches*. Serves 6.

CHICKEN LOAF

2 broiler-fryers (about 4½ pounds total)
1 cup soft bread crumbs
¼ cup heavy cream
1 teaspoon salt
⅛ teaspoon pepper
½ teaspoon rosemary, crushed
1 teaspoon curry powder
1 egg, slightly beaten
2 tablespoons butter, melted
½ cup sliced pimiento-stuffed olives

Remove the skin from the chickens and cut and scrape the meat from bones, discarding sinews. Chop fine, or put meat through a food chopper, using medium blade. Add remaining ingredients except olives, and mix well. Gently stir in the olives. Pack into an oiled 1-pound coffee can. Bake at 350° F. 1 hour. Cool slightly, then remove from can; chill. Serve sliced thin. Serves 6.

CHICKEN-PINEAPPLE ROLLS

2 cups diced cooked chicken
1 (8-ounce) can crushed pineapple packed in its own juice, drained
½ cup chopped celery
¼ cup Mayonnaise*
1 scallion, with top, minced
¼ teaspoon salt
¼ teaspoon ground ginger
2 tablespoons butter, softened
4 round hard rolls or 6 small rolls, split
8 small lettuce leaves (optional)

In a medium bowl, mix well the chicken, pineapple, celery, Mayonnaise, scallion, salt, and ginger; cover and chill overnight. Spread the butter on the rolls, fill with the chicken mixture, place a lettuce leaf inside each if you wish, and cut in half. Serves 4.

EGG-SARDINE SPREAD

3 hard-cooked eggs
1 (4⅜-ounce) can skinless, boneless sardines, drained
2 tablespoons butter, softened
¼ cup finely chopped scallions (about 4, with tops)
1 tablespoon prepared mustard
1 tablespoon lemon juice
½ teaspoon salt
Dash hot pepper sauce

In a large bowl, with a fork, mash the eggs and sardines to a paste. Add the remaining ingredients and mix well. Yield: about 1¾ cups.

EGG SANDWICHES FOR A PARTY

2 dozen hard-cooked eggs, chopped
½ cup minced parsley
1 cup minced celery
2 tablespoons minced onion or chives
1 teaspoon salt
½ teaspoon paprika
¼ cup melted butter
½-¾ cup Mayonnaise*
1 tablespoon fines herbes or 2 teaspoons curry powder
1-2 loaves very thin-sliced bread

Combine all of the ingredients except the bread, and mix thoroughly. Putting melted butter into the spread is much easier than buttering the slices of bread. Spread the egg mixture on half the bread. You cannot be sure how many slices you will need. Cover each sandwich and push the top slice of bread firmly into place. Trim off the crusts and cut each sandwich in halves or in thirds, making them finger shapes. These are inexpensive and good. If made ahead, pile onto serving plates, cover with a damp dish towel, and keep cool. Serves about 12.

EGG SANDWICHES WITH HAM

5 hard-cooked eggs, chopped
½ pound ham, chopped
1 teaspoon prepared mustard
¼ teaspoon pepper
⅓ cup Mayonnaise*
3 tablespoons soft butter (about)
16 slices bread (whole wheat, white, or rye)

Combine the eggs and ham. Add the mustard and pepper to the Mayonnaise, and add to the egg-ham mixture. Butter the bread lightly. Spread the mixture on 8 slices of bread, cover with the remaining bread, and press in place firmly. You may cut off crusts if you wish. If you want to save time, put the soft butter into the spread. Serves 8.

FOUR-MEAT LOAF

2 pounds meat loaf mixture (ground beef, pork, lamb, and veal)
1 medium onion, chopped fine
1 tablespoon butter
1 cup soft stale-bread crumbs
2 scallions, with tops, minced
1 egg, slightly beaten
⅓ cup milk
1 teaspoon thyme
1½ teaspoons salt
½ teaspoon pepper
1 tablespoon Worcestershire sauce
½ cup coarsely chopped water chestnuts
6 chicken livers, parboiled and cut into large pieces
Prepared mustard (for garnish)
3 tablespoons chopped pimiento (for garnish)

Put the meat loaf mixture in large bowl. Sauté the onion in the butter, stirring, until tender. Add the onion to meat; add the bread crumbs, scallions, egg, milk, thyme, salt, pepper, Worcestershire, and water chestnuts. Mix well. Gently stir in the chicken livers. Pack in a 9 × 5 × 3-inch loaf pan. Bake at 350° F. 1 hour 20 minutes. Let stand a few minutes, then remove to a platter and cool. Spread top with mustard and sprinkle pimiento over. Chill. Slice thin to serve. Serves 6 to 8.

HAM LOAF

1½ pounds cooked ham, ground or chopped fine
1 small onion, minced
½ cup packed minced parsley
¾ cup soft bread crumbs
¾ cup milk
¼ cup Dijon-style mustard
2 tablespoons light brown sugar
1 egg, slightly beaten

Combine all the ingredients; blend well. Pack firmly into a round 1-quart casserole. Bake at 325° F. 1 hour 15 minutes, or until hot and lightly browned. Cool and chill. Unmold and slice. Serves 6.

HAMWICHES

8 slices whole wheat bread (toasted if desired)
2 tablespoons butter, softened
2 tablespoons Mayonnaise*
½ teaspoon prepared mustard
¼ teaspoon pepper
1 cup diced cooked ham
1 hard-cooked egg, mashed
¼ cup chopped celery

Spread 4 slices bread with butter. In a small bowl, mix well the remaining ingredients. Spread on buttered bread. Top with remaining slices of bread. Press down, cut in half and chill. Serves 4.

HEROS

1 long loaf French bread
Soft butter
6 slices Swiss or Port Salut cheese
6 slices smoked tongue or ham
6 slices chicken
2 sliced peeled tomatoes
Lettuce
Mayonnaise*

Slice the bread lengthwise and butter the lower half. Pile the ingredients on the bread. Spread a little Mayonnaise on the top side of the bread and close the sandwich. Cut in about 6-inch lengths. Serves about 6.

ANTIPASTO HEROS

3 tablespoons olive oil
1 small clove garlic, crushed
4 crusty hero rolls (6–7 inches long)
1 (12-ounce) jar roasted red peppers, drained and split
1 (4⅜-ounce) can skinless, boneless sardines, drained and cut up
1 medium red onion, sliced thin and separated into rings
¼ cup shredded provolone cheese

Mix the olive oil with the garlic and let stand at least 1 hour. Split the rolls lengthwise and brush with some olive oil. Add the peppers and drizzle with the remaining oil. Layer with the sardines, then the onion rings. Sprinkle with the cheese. Cut in half crosswise. Serves 4.

ITALIAN HEROS

Proceed as for Heros*, substituting Italian bread for French, mozzarella for Swiss cheese, salami for tongue, and sliced red onion for chicken. You may sprinkle these with oregano and/or crushed red pepper and drizzle over the mixture 2 tablespoons olive oil and 1 tablespoon red wine vinegar. Serves about 6.

HERO VARIATIONS

Substitute long or round hard rolls for the bread. Choose several meats from: bologna, salami, ham, smoked tongue, corned beef, luncheon meats, chicken, and turkey. Use Swiss, Cheddar, provolone, mozzarella, Port Salut, or any firm cheese; always tomatoes and lettuce; sometimes sliced onions, cucumbers, sweet peppers, or coleslaw. Build to suit yourself. Be generous—it's a hero!

MEAT OR MINCED MEAT SANDWICH

Use about ½ pound of any cooked meat, sliced thin, for 4 sandwiches. Flavor with butter and prepared mustard, horseradish, or ketchup. Minced cured meats make excellent sandwiches. For 4, use about 1 cup meat mixed with ⅓ cup mayonnaise or any or several of the following: prepared mustard, chili sauce, minced celery, minced onion, minced chives, sliced dill pickles, kosher pickles, or relish. Make on the bread of your choice. Serves 4.

PEANUT BUTTER AND CHEESE SANDWICHES

½ cup peanut butter
½ cup shredded Cheddar cheese
½ cup shredded carrots
¼ cup orange marmalade
8 thin slices whole wheat bread

Mix well the peanut butter, cheese, carrots, and marmalade. Spread on 4 slices bread; top with remaining slices. Cut in half and serve. Serves 4.

SALAMI IN A BUN

1 tablespoon Mayonnaise*
½ teaspoon prepared mustard
2 teaspoons prepared horseradish
4 frankfurter buns
4 (1-ounce) slices salami
1 large dill pickle, quartered lengthwise

Mix the Mayonnaise, mustard, and horseradish. Spread on the buns.
Wrap 1 slice salami around each pickle spear. Place in the buns. Serves 4.

HEARTY STEAK SANDWICHES

1 large onion, sliced
1 large green or red pepper, cut in strips
2 tablespoons butter
4 thin chopped-beef sandwich steaks (2 ounces each)
4 club or Italian rolls (about 5 inches long), split
1 tablespoon bottled steak sauce

In a medium skillet, sauté the onion and pepper in the butter until tender.
Meanwhile, cook the steaks to your taste. In each roll place a steak, folded
in half; spread with steak sauce and top with the onion-pepper mixture.
Cool. Serves 4.

TUNA AND WATERCRESS SANDWICHES

8 slices bread
2 tablespoons whipped butter
4 tablespoons Mayonnaise*
1 (6½-ounce) can water-packed tuna, drained and flaked
2 cups packed watercress leaves

Spread 4 slices of bread with the butter and the other 4 slices with 2 tablespoons Mayonnaise. Mix the tuna and remaining 2 tablespoons Mayonnaise. On the buttered slices place the watercress and then the tuna mixture. Top with remaining bread. Serves 4.

TURKEY CLUB SANDWICH

2 ounces blue cheese, crumbled, or Swiss cheese, grated
¼ cup Mayonnaise*
2 tablespoons soft butter
12 slices white or whole wheat bread
8 ounces thinly sliced cooked turkey
1 large tomato, peeled and sliced thin
1 medium sweet onion, sliced thin
Lettuce leaves

Blend the cheese into the Mayonnaise. Butter 8 slices of bread and spread the other 4 with the Mayonnaise-cheese mixture. On 4 slices of buttered bread layer the turkey and tomato. Cover with the cheese-spread slices, then the onion and lettuce. Top with the remaining bread. Secure by pushing in a toothpick at the sides and cut in half, or at the 4 corners and cut diagonally in quarters. (If you want less bread, omit the center slice. Butter only 4 slices of bread.) Serves 4.

TURKEY SPREAD

¾ pound cooked turkey with skin, ground fine
2 hard-cooked eggs
½ cup walnuts
1 small onion
½ cup Mayonnaise*
1–2 tablespoons brandy
Dash hot pepper sauce
Pepper to taste

Grind the eggs, walnuts, and onion in a blender or processor; add to the turkey with the Mayonnaise, brandy to taste, hot pepper sauce, and pepper. Mix well. Pack into a container, cover, and chill at least 4 hours or overnight. Yield: 2¼ cups.

VEGETARIAN PITA

3 tablespoons peanut butter
8 ounces plain yogurt
2 cups shredded lettuce
1 medium tomato, chopped coarse
1 medium cucumber, peeled and chopped coarse
1 small onion, chopped coarse
4 pita (pocket breads)
1 cup alfalfa sprouts

Beat the peanut butter and yogurt in a small bowl until well combined; set aside. In a large bowl, mix well the lettuce, tomato, cucumber, and onion. Cut about 1 inch off each pita and fill with the vegetable mixture, yogurt dressing, and sprouts. Serves 4.

WATERCRESS SANDWICHES

1 (8-ounce) package cream cheese, at room temperature
2 tablespoons cream
3 tablespoons soft butter
1 teaspoon Worcestershire sauce
2 cups tightly packed watercress
20 slices thin white bread

Mix thoroughly the cheese, cream, butter, and Worcestershire. Stir in the watercress. Spread on half the bread; cover with the remaining bread and press firmly in place. Cut off crusts; cut in halves. If serving with cocktails or tea, cut in thirds. Yield: 10 regular or 30 finger-size sandwiches.

Desserts

DESSERTS served cold are certainly no novelty, but today there are many varieties to end the meal elegantly—of course including a number that meet the requirements of today's health-oriented eaters. Desserts vary from fresh fruits to a rich Vienna Café Cake, with many other delicious recipes in between. You will find appealing desserts that will appropriately conclude a light or hearty luncheon or dinner on a note of triumph. Moreover, the long, varied list of dessert sauces changes not only the flavor but also the consistency of many a sweet, multiplying the choices.

Small portions can eliminate any feeling of guilt. After all, a meal is often judged by its finale—the last thing you eat is likely to be the one thing you remember and talk about when you leave the table.

Fruit Desserts

AMBROSIA

5 large oranges, peeled
4 medium bananas, sliced
¼ cup orange juice
½ cup sugar
¾ cup flaked coconut

Be sure to remove all the white pith when peeling the oranges. Section the oranges or cut them into pieces. Mix with the bananas. Add the orange juice at once. Combine the sugar and coconut; add to the fruit and toss gently. Serve at once. Serves 6.

APPLESAUCE

2 pounds apples (Golden Delicious, McIntosh, or any cooking apples)
2–4 tablespoons sugar (optional)
Dash nutmeg or cinnamon

Cut the apples in halves, remove seeds and stems, and cut up. Put in a saucepan and add water just to cover. Add the sugar. The amount depends on how you are serving the sauce. If it is to accompany pork or other main dishes, you will need no sugar. For a dessert, start with 2 tablespoons in the water and add more to taste. Simmer, uncovered, until soft. Process in a blender or processor. Adjust seasoning. Cool. Serves 4 to 6.

BAKED APPLES WITH MAPLE SYRUP

6 medium apples (McIntosh or Rome)
½ cup raisins, plumped and chopped
1½ teaspoons nutmeg
⅓ cup light brown sugar
6 teaspoons butter
½ cup maple syrup

Core and peel the apples and place in a flat pan. Mix the raisins with 1 teaspoon nutmeg and sugar, and put in the center of the apples. Sprinkle the remaining ½ teaspoon nutmeg over the apples; then top each with a teaspoon of butter and a spoonful of maple syrup. Bake at 350° F. about 30 minutes, until tender. Cool to room temperature or chill. Pass the remaining syrup. Serves 6.

POACHED APPLES

1 cup sugar
½ teaspoon vanilla extract
Grating of nutmeg
4 medium apples (not Delicious), peeled, cored, and halved
Heavy cream, plain or whipped (optional)

Add the sugar, vanilla, and nutmeg to 2 to 3 cups water. Bring to a boil. Add the halved apples and poach 6 to 8 minutes. Chill. Serve with a little chilled liquid spooned over and cream, if you wish. Serves 4 to 6.

FRUIT KEBABS

Choose several fruits such as:
1 banana, sliced thick
Pineapple chunks
Seedless or seeded grapes
Pitted sweet cherries
Melon pieces or balls
Orange sections
Strawberries
Grapefruit sections
Papaya pieces
Kiwi fruit slices
Peach chunks
Pear pieces

String the fruits on skewers—long bamboo ones are appropriate. You may sprinkle with sugar, honey, grated coconut, or white wine. If using bananas, peaches, or pears, sprinkle with a little lemon or orange juice. Choose the quantity of fruit depending on the number of people to be served. The kebabs may be chilled for a short time.

SUMMER FRUITS WITH LIME CREAM DRESSING

½ cup lime juice
½ cup sugar
1 large banana, sliced diagonally
1 pint box blueberries
2 large nectarines, sliced
1 pint box strawberries, hulled and halved
1 cup watermelon balls
1 cup seedless white grapes
1 kiwi fruit, peeled and sliced (for garnish)
Dark sweet cherries with stems (for garnish)
Lime Cream Dressing*

In a bowl, stir the lime juice, ½ cup water, and sugar until the sugar dissolves. Add the banana and set aside. In a large serving bowl, preferably glass, layer the blueberries (reserving ½ cup for garnish), nectarines, strawberries, banana, watermelon, and grapes. Garnish with the reserved blueberries and the kiwi and cherries. Pour the lime syrup over the fruits, cover loosely, and chill. To serve, spoon an assortment of fruits and berries with some of the syrup into dessert bowls. Pass the dressing. Serves 6 to 8.

MACÉDOINE OF FRUITS WITH MADEIRA

2 cups melon balls (honeydew or watermelon)
2 cups cantaloupe or other yellow-fleshed melon balls
2 cups canned or fresh pitted cherries
2 cups cut-up bottled crab apples or any red berries
½–1 cup orange juice
1 cup Madeira
Chopped fresh mint (optional, for garnish)

Drain the fruits and combine in a serving bowl. Pour all the juice from
the fruits and the orange juice in a saucepan and simmer 5 minutes. Add
the Madeira and pour over the fruit. Chill several hours. Garnish with
some chopped fresh mint, if you wish. Serves 8.

EASY GRAPE DESSERT

2½–3 pounds seedless white grapes
1½ cups sour cream
¾ cup light or dark brown sugar

Pull the grapes from their stems and wash and dry them. Mix the sour
cream and sugar. Put the grapes into the cream mixture and stir well.
Chill several hours. Serves 6 to 8.

MELON WITH BERRIES

½ cup hulled, halved strawberries
½ cup red raspberries
½ cup blueberries
¼ cup orange juice
2 tablespoons sugar
½ large or 1 small honeydew melon, chilled

Combine the berries, juice, and sugar in a medium bowl. Chill. Cut the
melon in 4 wedges; remove the seeds and peel. Arrange on a serving platter or individual plates. Spoon the berries and juice over the melon. (This
recipe is easy to double.) Serves 4.

ORANGE SLICES WITH CRANBERRY SAUCE

6 large oranges, peeled and sliced
1½ cups cranberry juice cocktail
¼ cup sugar
1 (3-inch) cinnamon stick

Place the orange slices in a serving bowl and set aside. In a saucepan, cook and stir the remaining ingredients until the sugar dissolves. Boil until reduced by half. Remove the cinnamon stick and pour the sauce over the orange slices. Serve chilled or at room temperature. Serves 6.

GLAZED ORANGES

8 large oranges, peeled and sectioned
¼ cup grated orange peel
¼ cup Grand Marnier or curaçao
1 cup light brown sugar

Put the oranges into a serving bowl, preferably glass. Sprinkle the peel over. Heat the liqueur, sugar, and ⅓ cup water until glaze thickens enough to coat a spoon. Pour over the oranges. Toss and chill. Serves 8.

PEACHES IN RASPBERRY SAUCE

1 cup sugar
6 large peaches
2 (10-ounce) packages frozen raspberries
2 tablespoons orange-flavored liqueur (Cointreau, curaçao, or Triple Sec)

Mix 2 cups water and the sugar in a saucepan and boil for 5 minutes. Plunge the peaches for 1 minute into boiling water to facilitate peeling. Peel, cut in halves, and remove pits. Simmer the peaches in the syrup 5 or 6 minutes, or until soft but not mushy. Drain, cool, and chill. Meanwhile, thaw the raspberries and purée in a blender or processor—if in a blender, add the liqueur before blending. Strain, and add a tablespoon or two of the syrup and the liqueur, if not already used. Pour over the peaches and chill. Serves 6.

GLAZED PEACHES WITH STRAWBERRY CREAM

6 large peaches
1 cup sugar
1 pint fresh or 1 (10-ounce) package frozen strawberries
2 tablespoons rum or brandy
½ cup heavy cream, whipped

Plunge the peaches in boiling water for a minute and peel them. In a saucepan, combine all but 2 tablespoons sugar with ¾ cup water and poach the peaches in this syrup 5 minutes. Remove with a slotted spoon and cool. Simmer the syrup 5 minutes, uncovered. Cool slightly and pour over the peaches. Turn to coat all sides. Chill. Purée the strawberries with the remaining 2 tablespoons sugar and the rum or brandy. Fold in the whipped cream and chill 2 hours. When almost ready to serve, spoon the strawberry cream over the peaches. Serves 6.

PEACH-BLUEBERRY SHORTCAKE

6–8 large peaches, peeled and sliced
1 cup blueberries, thawed if frozen
Sugar
1¾ cups flour
1 tablespoon baking powder
1 teaspoon salt
⅓ cup shortening
¾ cup milk
2 tablespoons butter, softened
1 cup heavy cream, whipped and sweetened

Sweeten the fruit to taste and let stand at room temperature ½ hour, stirring occasionally. In a bowl, mix the flour, 2 tablespoons sugar, and the baking powder and salt. Cut in the shortening with a pastry blender or 2 knives until the mixture resembles coarse crumbs. Add the milk and mix quickly with a fork just until the dough leaves the sides of the bowl (the dough will be sticky). Spoon into a greased 8-inch round layer pan. Bake at 450° F. 10 to 15 minutes, until golden brown. Invert onto a rack, then turn top side up. Carefully slice the cake in half horizontally with a serrated knife and spread the bottom layer with the butter. Assemble just before serving. Spread the bottom layer of the cake with half the whipped cream. Using a slotted spoon, add half the fruit. Top with the top half of the cake. Spread with the remaining cream and arrange the remaining fruit attractively. Serves 6.

STRAWBERRY SHORTCAKE

Substitute 2 pint boxes strawberries for the peaches and blueberries. Halve the strawberries and proceed as for Peach-Blueberry Shortcake*, but omit the softened butter. Serves 6.

POACHED PEARS IN RED WINE

1¼ cups sugar
1 cup dry red wine
8 pears (preferably Anjou or Comice), peeled

Combine the sugar and ½ cup water and boil for 2 to 3 minutes to dissolve the sugar. Add the wine, bring to a boil, and add the pears. Simmer until tender, about 10 minutes. (The time will depend upon the size of the pears.) Remove the pears. Reduce the liquid, cool, and pour over the pears. Chill. You may cut the pears in halves and core them, cooking several minutes less. Serves 8.

POACHED PEARS WITH CURRANT JELLY

2 cups sugar
¼ cup lemon juice
12 firm medium pears
½ cup currant jelly
Mint leaves (for garnish)

Combine 4 cups water, the sugar, and 3 tablespoons lemon juice in a large saucepan or Dutch oven. Bring to a boil, stirring until the sugar dissolves. Reduce heat, cover, and simmer 5 minutes. Meanwhile, peel the pears, leaving the stems on, and rub with the remaining tablespoon lemon juice. Add the pears to the syrup, in two batches if necessary. Cover. Simmer the pears, turning occasionally, 20 minutes, or until tender when pierced at the bottom. With a slotted spoon, carefully lift the pears to a serving dish. Stir the jelly in a small saucepan over low heat until melted. Spoon over the pears. Chill thoroughly. Garnish with mint. Serves 12.

POACHED PEARS

4 large pears
1 cup sugar
1½ teaspoons vanilla extract

Peel the pears and poach in the sugar, 3 cups water, and vanilla for about 10 minutes, until they feel tender when you pierce them with a fork. Do not overcook. Remove from syrup, cool, and chill. Reduce the syrup to about half and chill. Spoon some of the syrup over the pears. Serves 4.

LADYFINGERS WITH PINEAPPLE-LEMON CREAM

¼ cup sugar
2 tablespoons cornstarch
⅛ teaspoon salt
2 egg yolks
1 (8-ounce) can crushed pineapple, well drained (reserve ½ cup syrup)
1 tablespoon butter, softened
1 teaspoon grated lemon peel
1 tablespoon lemon juice
8 to 10 ladyfingers, split
Confectioners' sugar

In a small saucepan, mix the sugar, cornstarch, and salt. Beat the egg yolks and reserved pineapple syrup until blended; gradually stir into the sugar mixture. Stir over medium heat until mixture thickens and is smooth, then cook 1 minute longer. Remove from heat and stir in the pineapple, butter, and lemon peel and juice. Chill. Fill the ladyfingers and sprinkle lightly with confectioners' sugar. Yield: 1¼ cups, enough for 8 to 10 ladyfingers. Serves 4.

STRAWBERRIES WITH RASPBERRY SAUCE

3 pint boxes strawberries, washed and hulled
¼ cup sugar
2–3 (10-ounce) packages frozen raspberries
3 tablespoons brandy or framboise

Put the strawberries in a bowl, preferably glass. Sprinkle with 3 tablespoons sugar. Purée the thawed raspberries in a processor or blender with the remaining tablespoon sugar. Strain and add the brandy or framboise. Pour over the berries and chill 1 hour or more. Serves 8.

RHUBARB WHIP

2 pounds rhubarb, cut up
⅔ cup sugar
1 envelope unflavored gelatin
⅛ teaspoon salt
¼ teaspoon vanilla extract
2 egg whites, at room temperature
1 cup strawberries (optional, for garnish)

In a large saucepan, bring the rhubarb and 1 cup water to a boil; cover, then simmer until soft, about 10 minutes. Purée in a blender or processor, or press the rhubarb through a colander over a bowl. This should make about 2 cups liquid and purée. In a small saucepan, mix the puréed rhubarb, sugar, gelatin, and salt. Stir over low heat until the gelatin is dissolved; stir in the vanilla. Chill until slightly thickened. In a large bowl, beat the rhubarb mixture and egg whites at high speed until very light and doubled in volume, about 10 minutes. Turn into a large serving dish. Chill until set. Garnish with strawberries if desired. Serves 6.

Gelatin Molds, Parfaits, and Light Puddings and Sauces

COFFEE JELLY

3 envelopes unflavored gelatin
¾ cup sugar
2½ cups hot *strong* coffee
2 tablespoons lemon juice
1 tablespoon brandy
Whipped cream (optional)

Soften the gelatin in ¾ cup cold water. Add the sugar and coffee, heat, and stir until the gelatin is dissolved. Stir in the lemon juice and brandy. Chill until set. Serve topped with whipped cream if you wish. Serves 4 to 6.

BAKED CUSTARD

6 eggs
½ cup sugar
Pinch salt
1 quart milk, scalded
1 teaspoon vanilla extract

Beat the eggs with a fork just enough to break up the whites and yolks. Add the sugar and salt. Gradually stir in the scalded milk and flavor with the vanilla. Strain into 8 buttered custard cups. Set in a large pan of hot water, with the water up to about ½ inch from the tops of the cups. Bake at 350° F. about 30 minutes. You can put the custard in a large mold or serving dish instead of individual cups; in this case, bake 10 minutes longer. The custard is done when a knife inserted in the center comes out clean. Chill immediately. Serves 6.

MOCHA MOUSSE WITH COFFEE SAUCE

6 egg yolks, beaten
½ cup sugar
1½ cups strong espresso coffee
¼ pound semisweet chocolate, grated
2 envelopes unflavored gelatin
1½ cups heavy cream, whipped

Sauce

2 cups cold espresso
1 cup sugar
2 tablespoons arrowroot or cornstarch
½ cup Kahlúa or other coffee liqueur

Simmer the egg yolks, sugar, coffee, and chocolate until thickened. Soften the gelatin in 6 tablespoons cold water. Add to the mixture and stir and heat until the gelatin is dissolved. Cool. Fold in the whipped cream. Pour into a mold or bowl and chill several hours. Unmold onto a cold plate. Serves 8.

SAUCE: Heat the coffee and sugar. Stir the arrowroot into ½ cup cold water. When smooth, pour into the coffee and cook and stir until smooth and thickened. Remove from the heat, stir in the liqueur, and chill. Pour over the mousse.

LEMON MOLD WITH PLUMS

1 (6-ounce) package lemon-flavored gelatin dessert
2 tablespoons sherry
¾ cup seedless white grapes
3 medium plums, sliced thin (about 1½ cups)
Whipped cream (optional)
Grape clusters (optional, for garnish)
Mint leaves (optional, for garnish)

Dissolve the gelatin in 2 cups boiling water in a large bowl. Stir in 1½ cups cold water and the sherry; mix well. Pour about ¾ cup gelatin into a rinsed but not dried 5-cup ring mold. Chill about 1 hour, or until slightly thickened. Arrange the grapes on the gelatin. Chill until set. Add the remaining gelatin mixture; chill until just slightly thickened. Gently push the plums through the gelatin around the side of the mold. Chill 3 hours, or until firm. Unmold onto a moistened serving platter. Fill the center with whipped cream and garnish with grape clusters and mint sprigs if you wish. Serves 8.

CHILLED LEMON SOUFFLÉ

1 envelope unflavored gelatin
½ cup sugar
⅛ teaspoon salt
⅔ cup milk
2 eggs, separated, at room temperature
2 teaspoons grated lemon peel
⅓ cup lemon juice
½ cup heavy cream, whipped
Strawberries or mint leaves (optional, for garnish)

Stir the gelatin, ¼ cup sugar, salt, and milk in a heavy saucepan over medium heat about 3 minutes, until the sugar and gelatin dissolve. Beat the egg yolks slightly and stir a small amount of hot mixture into them, then add to the gelatin mixture. Stir over low heat about 2 minutes, until the custard thickens slightly and coats a metal spoon. Remove from the heat, stir in the lemon peel and juice, and chill until thickened. Beat the egg whites in a small bowl until soft peaks form. Gradually beat in the remaining ¼ cup sugar until the meringue is stiff and glossy. Fold into the gelatin mixture with the whipped cream. Pour into a 1-quart soufflé dish or casserole. Chill several hours or overnight, until set. Garnish with strawberries or mint leaves if you wish. Serves 6.

NESSELRODE PIE

¼ cup dark rum
⅓ cup mixed candied fruit, chopped
⅓ cup golden raisins, chopped
½ cup sugar
1 envelope unflavored gelatin
¼ teaspoon salt
1½ cups milk
3 eggs, separated, at room temperature
½ cup heavy cream
1 Unbaked Crumb Crust*
½ square (½ ounce) semisweet chocolate, shaved or shredded
Whipped cream
Candied fruit (optional, for garnish)

Sprinkle the rum over the fruit and raisins; set aside. Combine ¼ cup sugar, the gelatin, and salt in a saucepan. Gradually stir in the milk. Stir over medium heat until the gelatin and sugar dissolve. Beat some warm milk mixture into the egg yolks. Add the yolks to the saucepan and stir over low heat until the mixture thickens and coats a metal spoon. Chill until the mixture mounds slightly when dropped from a spoon. In a small bowl, beat the egg whites until foamy. Gradually beat in the remaining ¼ cup sugar. Beat until stiff. Fold into the gelatin mixture with the fruit and rum. Turn into the crust. Sprinkle with the shaved chocolate. Chill until set, several hours or overnight. Garnish with whipped cream, and with candied fruit if you wish. Serves 8 to 10.

CRÈME FRAÎCHE

1 cup heavy cream
2 tablespoons buttermilk
Sugar (optional)

Combine the cream and buttermilk in a jar or a bowl and mix well. Cover and leave in a warm place overnight. (An oven with just the pilot light on is ideal.) In the morning, stir, cover, and refrigerate until ready to use. You may add sugar to taste if you wish. Yield: about 1 cup.

This is particularly good over strawberries (as shown in the photograph on the back of the jacket) or over raspberries.

NECTARINE MOUSSE PARFAITS

4 medium nectarines
1 tablespoon lemon juice
20 large marshmallows, cut into pieces, or 2 cups miniature marshmallows
½ cup heavy cream, whipped stiff
Whipped cream (optional)

Peel 2 nectarines, cut into pieces, and purée with the lemon juice in a blender, food processor, or food mill, or by forcing through a sieve with a wooden spoon. You should have 1 cup. Set aside. Partially melt the marshmallows in a double boiler or heatproof bowl set over simmering water, stirring occasionally. Add the purée, stir until well blended, and remove from the heat. Cool. Fold in the whipped cream. Turn into an 8-inch-square metal pan. Cover and freeze until firm. Let soften 30 minutes in the refrigerator, then layer into 4 parfait glasses with the remaining 2 nectarines, peeled and cut in thin wedges. Serve with whipped cream as a topping if you wish. Serves 4.

SPANISH CREAM

3 cups milk
1 envelope unflavored gelatin
⅛ teaspoon salt
½ cup sugar
3 eggs, separated, at room temperature
1 teaspoon vanilla extract
1 tablespoon sherry
Whipped or plain cream or fruits (optional)

Pour the milk into a double boiler and soften the gelatin in it for 5 minutes. Place over hot water, add the salt and sugar, and stir until dissolved. Gradually stir into the slightly beaten egg yolks, return the mixture to the double boiler, and cook until slightly thickened, stirring constantly. Remove from heat, pour into a bowl, and add the vanilla and sherry. Beat the egg whites until stiff and fold into the gelatin mixture. Turn into a wet bowl or mold and chill. Turn out onto a platter to serve, with or without cream, whipped cream, or puréed fruits. Serves 6 to 8.

STRAWBERRY CROWN

1 envelope unflavored gelatin
1 (3-ounce) package strawberry-flavored gelatin dessert
1 pint box strawberries, hulled and halved lengthwise (about 2 cups),
    reserving some whole for garnish
1 cup plain yogurt

Soften the unflavored gelatin in 2 tablespoons cold water. In a large bowl, dissolve the strawberry gelatin in 2½ cups boiling water. Stir in the unflavored gelatin. Pour ½ cup of the mixture into a 6-cup mold. Chill until thickened. Lightly press some strawberry halves, cut side up, into the gelatin and spoon on ¼ cup liquid gelatin mixture. Chill until set. Chill the remaining gelatin mixture until it has the consistency of unbeaten egg whites. Fold in the yogurt and the remaining strawberry halves. Turn into the mold and chill until set. Unmold to serve. Garnish with the reserved whole strawberries. Serves 6.

ZABAGLIONE

4 egg yolks
½ cup sugar
1½ cups Marsala

Beat the egg yolks thoroughly with the sugar, heating in a double boiler. Pour in the Marsala slowly while continuing to beat. Cook until thickened, about 5 minutes. Cool. Serves 6.

JELLIED ZABAGLIONE

6 egg yolks
⅓ cup sugar
1 teaspoon grated lemon peel
¾ cup Marsala
½ envelope unflavored gelatin
2 tablespoons brandy
1½ cups heavy cream, whipped

Beat the egg yolks thoroughly with the sugar. Add the lemon peel and Marsala. Heat in a double boiler, beating, for 5 minutes. Meanwhile soften the gelatin in ¼ cup cold water. Add the brandy and pour into the Zabaglione mixture. Heat and stir until the gelatin is dissolved, about 2 minutes. Cool. Fold in the whipped cream. Pour into 6 or 8 glasses or a serving bowl. Chill several hours. You may unmold from the serving bowl, if you wish. Serves 6 to 8.

Ice Creams and Sherbets

CHOCOLATE FANTASY

1 quart firmly packed chocolate ice cream
½ cup heavy cream, whipped, or 1 cup whipped topping
1 cup Chocolate Sauce*
2 tablespoons toasted sliced almonds

Cut the ice cream container open from top to bottom with scissors. Remove the ice cream in one piece and place top side down on a chilled serving platter. Freeze while preparing the sauce or until serving time. Pipe or spoon whipped cream in rosettes or dollops around the base and on top of the ice cream. Drizzle with some of the sauce. Sprinkle with the almonds. Serve at once. Pass the remaining whipped cream and sauce. Serves 6.

TRIPLE STRAWBERRY TREAT

1 quart firmly packed strawberry ice cream
1 (10-ounce) package frozen sliced sweetened strawberries, partially thawed
1 tablespoon lemon juice
1 pint box fresh strawberries, rinsed, hulled, and sliced
Whipped cream or topping

Cut the ice cream container open from top to bottom with scissors. Remove the ice cream in one piece and place top side down on a chilled serving platter. Freeze until serving time. Purée the frozen strawberries with the lemon juice in a blender or processor. Spoon the fresh strawberries around the base of the ice cream. Drizzle some purée over the ice cream and top with a large sliced strawberry. Serve immediately. Pass the remaining purée and the whipped cream. Serves 6 to 8.

FROZEN FIG MOUSSE

½ cup sour cream
1 (7-ounce) can Kadota figs, drained (reserve ½ cup syrup) and chopped
   fine
½ cup heavy cream, whipped
2 tablespoons brandy

Fold the sour cream and figs into the whipped cream. Fold in the reserved
½ cup syrup and brandy just until combined (mixture will be thin). Pour
into a 4-cup mold or individual dessert dishes. Freeze until firm. If using a mold, unmold onto a chilled serving plate; refreeze. Remove from
the freezer about 15 minutes before serving. Serves 6.

LADYFINGER ICE CREAM CAKE

10 ladyfingers
½–¾ cup apricot preserves
1 tablespoon lemon juice
½ gallon carton vanilla ice cream
½ cup heavy cream, whipped, or 1 cup whipped topping

Split the ladyfingers, keeping them attached in 2 strips of 6 and 2 strips
of 4. Mix the preserves with the lemon juice and spread a thin layer on
the flat side of the ladyfingers. Remove the ice cream from the carton
and place on a chilled serving platter. Cover the sides with the ladyfingers, rounded sides out. Pipe or spoon the cream on top. Decorate
with the remaining apricot preserves. Serve immediately or freeze until
serving time. Serves 12.

MOCHA PARFAITS

1 cup heavy cream
2 tablespoons sugar
2 teaspoons instant coffee
¼ teaspoon vanilla extract
2 pints chocolate ice cream, preferably dark chocolate

In a small bowl, whip the cream, sugar, coffee, and vanilla until soft
peaks form. Alternate with layers of ice cream in parfait, sherbet, wine,
or tall drink glasses. Cover and freeze until firm. Remove from freezer
10 to 15 minutes before serving. Makes 8 to 10 parfaits, depending on
size of glasses.

FROZEN GRAND MARNIER ORANGE PARFAITS

½ cup Grand Marnier
¼ cup orange juice
¾ cup sugar
4 egg whites, at room temperature
Pinch salt
2 cups heavy cream, whipped
2 tablespoons grated orange peel
½ cup graham cracker or cookie crumbs

Combine the Grand Marnier, orange juice, and ½ cup sugar. Stir to dissolve the sugar and set aside. Whip the egg whites with the pinch of salt until soft peaks form. Beat in the remaining ¼ cup sugar, a tablespoon at a time. Add the Grand Marnier mixture and fold into the whipped cream. Chill 30 minutes and spoon half the mixture into 8 cold parfait glasses. Mix the orange peel and crumbs and sprinkle half into the parfaits. Pile in the remaining mousse and top with the remaining crumbs. Freeze 4 hours or overnight. Serves 8.

RASPBERRY-NUT ROLL

2 (10-ounce) packages frozen raspberries, thawed
¾ cup sugar
2 teaspoons unflavored gelatin
¼ teaspoon almond extract
¾ cup heavy cream, whipped
¼ cup finely chopped nuts (almonds, pecans, pistachios, or walnuts)
Fresh mint sprigs (optional, for garnish)

Purée the berries by forcing through a sieve, or purée in a blender or processor, then strain. Add ½ cup sugar and enough cold water to make 3 cups mixture. Soften the gelatin in ¼ cup cold water, then dissolve over hot water. Stir into the berry mixture. Pour into 2 ice cube trays and freeze 1½ hours, or until mushy. Turn into a mixing bowl and beat well. Pour mixture into a lightly oiled 46-ounce juice can (mixture will not fill can). Put in freezer and push solidified mixture toward sides of can every ½ hour, leaving center hollow. This will take 1½ to 2 hours. Meanwhile, add the remaining ¼ cup sugar and the almond extract to the cream and beat until stiff. Fold in the nuts. Pour into center of can, cover with waxed paper, and freeze. To unmold, remove bottom, run a spatula or knife around inside of can, then wrap can in a hot cloth until dessert slides out. Cut in ¾-inch-thick slices and decorate with mint sprigs if desired. Serves 6 to 8.

PEACH ICE CREAM BOMBE WITH RASPBERRY PURÉE

1 quart peach ice cream
2 cups sliced peaches
2 tablespoons sugar
1 tablespoon lemon juice
1 (10-ounce) package frozen raspberries, partially thawed
Mint sprig (optional, for garnish)

Line a deep 1-quart mold with plastic wrap, letting enough extend to wrap over the top. Pack the ice cream firmly into the mold. Fold the plastic wrap over the ice cream and freeze until firm. Just before serving, toss the peaches with the sugar and lemon juice; set aside. Purée the raspberries in a blender or processor and force through a sieve. To serve, unmold the ice cream onto a chilled platter. Peel off the plastic wrap. Surround with the peaches. Spoon some raspberry purée over the ice cream. Garnish with a mint sprig if you wish. Serve immediately with the remaining purée on the side. Serves 8.

VANILLA-STRAWBERRY BOMBE

2 pint boxes fresh strawberries or 2 (16-ounce) bags frozen unsweetened
    whole strawberries, thawed
Sugar
2–3 pints vanilla ice cream, slightly softened

Chill well a 1½-quart melon- or dome-shaped mold or mixing bowl. If using a mixing bowl, place 2 (18 × 2-inch) strips of foil or waxed paper crosswise in the bowl, extending ends over the rim, to help with unmolding. In a blender or processor, purée 1 pint strawberries. Pour into a 9-inch-square pan. Stir in ⅓ to ½ cup sugar, depending on the sweetness of the berries; mix well. Freeze until mushy. Meanwhile, working quickly, pack the ice cream on bottom and sides of a mold or bowl to form a 1-inch shell. Freeze about 15 minutes to harden. Stir the partially frozen strawberry mixture and fill center of lined mold. Cover tight and freeze overnight or longer. To unmold, dip mold in cool water or wrap in a hot dish towel. Invert onto a chilled plate and tap mold gently. If using a bowl, pull ends of foil to help remove ice cream. Place in freezer until serving time. Meanwhile, slice the remaining 1 pint berries and sweeten to taste. (If desired, reserve a few whole berries for garnish.) Let sliced berries stand at room temperature 30 minutes, stirring occasionally. To serve, slice bombe or cut in wedges and serve with sweetened berries. Serves 8.

VANILLA-BLUEBERRY BOMBE

Substitute 2 pint boxes fresh or 2 (16-ounce) bags frozen blueberries for the strawberries. Add 1 teaspoon lemon juice to the purée and proceed as for Vanilla-Strawberry Bombe*. Serves 8 to 10.

BUTTERSCOTCH SAUCE

1 cup light brown sugar
3 tablespoons butter
2 teaspoons cornstarch
1 teaspoon vanilla extract

Boil the sugar, butter, and cornstarch mixed with 1½ cups water until mixture forms a soft ball when dropped into cold water. Add vanilla, cool, and chill. Terrific on ice cream. Yield: about 1 cup.

CHOCOLATE SAUCE

2 ounces unsweetened chocolate, shaved or cut up
1 cup sugar
1 tablespoon instant coffee
¼ cup butter
½ teaspoon vanilla extract

Melt the chocolate with the sugar, coffee, and 3 tablespoons water. Bring to a boil and simmer about 5 minutes. Remove from heat and stir in the butter and vanilla. Cool, or chill if to be served on ice cream. Yield: about 1½ cups.

CRANBERRY SHERBET

3 cups cranberries
¼ cup orange juice or 2 tablespoons lemon juice
1 envelope unflavored gelatin
2 cups granulated sugar or 2½ cups light brown sugar (about)

Cook the cranberries in 3 cups boiling water until they pop open. Drain. Purée in a blender or processor with the orange or lemon juice. Soften the gelatin in ¼ cup cold water. Add part of the sugar to the gelatin mixture and heat and stir until dissolved. Stir in the cranberry purée. Add more sugar to taste. Pour into a bowl or ice cube trays and freeze until firm, about 4 hours. Serves 6 to 8.

LEMON SHERBET

2 cups sugar
1 cup lemon juice
2 egg whites, stiffly beaten

Boil the sugar and 3½ cups water together for 5 minutes. Add the lemon juice and cool. Pour into a bowl and freeze until almost frozen. Remove and beat with an eggbeater. Fold in the egg whites and refreeze. Serves 6.

FROZEN LIME SHERBET CAKE

1 (12–13-ounce) angel food cake
2 pints lime or other sherbet, very slightly softened
Whipped cream or whipped topping (optional, for garnish)
Mint sprigs (optional, for garnish)

Insert toothpicks midpoint at several places around the outside of the cake. Using the toothpicks as guides, split the cake with a serrated knife or a long thread. With a narrow spatula, quickly spread 1 pint sherbet on the bottom layer. Then quickly spread the remaining sherbet on the top layer, swirling it attractively. Carefully place top on bottom layer; freeze until surface is hardened. Cover and freeze until firm. Remove from freezer 10 to 15 minutes before serving. Garnish with rosettes or dollops of whipped cream and mint sprigs. Serves about 10.

ORANGE YOGURT SHERBET

1 envelope unflavored gelatin
2 cups orange juice
1 cup sugar
¼ teaspoon salt
2 teaspoons grated orange peel
2 cups plain yogurt

In a medium saucepan, sprinkle the gelatin over ½ cup orange juice. Let stand 1 minute. Stir over low heat until the gelatin dissolves; stir in the sugar and salt. Remove from heat; stir in the remaining orange juice, the orange peel, and yogurt. Turn into a 9-inch-square metal pan; freeze about 2 hours, or until almost firm. Beat until fluffy. Return to the pan; freeze until firm. Serves 6.

PINEAPPLE BUTTERMILK SHERBET

½ cup sugar
½ cup orange juice
1 large ripe pineapple (about 4 pounds)
1 cup buttermilk
Mint sprigs (optional, for garnish)
Strips of orange peel (optional, for garnish)

Stir the sugar and orange juice in a small heavy saucepan over medium heat until the sugar dissolves. Cool. Halve the pineapple lengthwise, including the crown. With a small sharp knife (a curved grapefruit knife works well), cut around the pulp, leaving a shell about ½ inch thick. Scrape out any remaining loose pieces and juice with a spoon. Cover and refrigerate or freeze the pineapple shells. Cut out and discard the hard core from the pulp. Cut the pulp into cubes and drain well, reserving the juice. Measure 2 cups fruit and ½ cup juice. Chop very fine in a processor and mix with the juice, or purée in a blender with the juice. Add the orange syrup and buttermilk; whirl or stir just until blended. Pour into an 8-inch-square metal pan, cover, and freeze about 3 hours, or until semifrozen. Stir until smooth. Refreeze several hours, or until firm enough to spoon or scoop into the pineapple shells. Cover and freeze until firm. Let stand at room temperature 10 to 15 minutes before serving. Garnish with mint sprigs and orange peel if you wish. Serves 8.

PLUM YOGURT SHERBET

2 (16-ounce) cans purple plums
1 cup sugar
1 teaspoon grated lemon peel
2 cups plain yogurt
¼ teaspoon salt

Drain plums, reserving 1 cup syrup. Remove the pits and whirl plums in blender or processor. Simmer the purée, reserved syrup, and sugar in a saucepan until the sugar dissolves. Cool. Add the lemon peel, yogurt, and salt; mix well and turn into 2 ice cube trays or an 8-inch-square metal pan. Freeze until almost firm. Turn into a chilled large bowl and beat until smooth. Turn into a 6-cup ring mold or bowl; freeze until firm. To unmold, dip mold in warm water 5 to 10 seconds. Loosen around edges with a sharp knife. Invert onto a chilled serving plate. Return to freezer until firm. Serves 6.

RASPBERRY SHERBET

3 (10-ounce) packages frozen raspberries
¾ cup sugar
2 tablespoons brandy or rum (optional)
2 egg whites, beaten stiff

Thaw the raspberries and whirl in a blender or mash. Strain. Add the sugar to 1 cup water and boil 3 to 4 minutes. Cool and combine with the raspberry purée and the liqueur, if using. Freeze until mushy. Fold in the egg whites and refreeze until firm. Serves 6.

RED, RED RASPBERRY SHERBET

3 (10-ounce) packages frozen raspberries
¾ cup sugar
2 tablespoons brandy, rum, or framboise

Thaw the raspberries and add the sugar and liqueur. Whirl in a blender. Strain the purée and freeze at once. Serves 4 to 6.

Cakes and Pies

ALMOND CAKE WITH PEACHES AND CREAM

4 cups thin-sliced peaches (about 2 pounds or 8 medium)
1 cup plus 2 tablespoons sugar
6 eggs, separated, at room temperature
⅛ teaspoon salt
1 teaspoon grated lemon peel
1 tablespoon lemon juice
½ teaspoon cinnamon
½ teaspoon almond extract
1 cup unblanched whole almonds, ground
½ cup fine dry bread crumbs
1 cup heavy cream, whipped

In a medium bowl, toss the peaches with 2 tablespoons sugar; set aside. In a large bowl, beat the egg whites with the salt until soft peaks form. Gradually, 1 tablespoon at a time, beat in the remaining 1 cup sugar until stiff glossy peaks form. Without washing beaters, in a medium bowl beat the yolks, lemon peel and juice, cinnamon, and almond extract until well blended. Fold a fourth of the egg white mixture into the yolk mixture; pour yolk mixture over whites. Sprinkle the almonds and crumbs over mixture; fold gently but thoroughly to blend well. Turn into a 13 × 9-inch pan greased *on bottom only*, lined with waxed paper, then greased again. Bake at 350° F. 30 to 40 minutes, or until top springs back when pressed lightly with a finger. Cool in pan on rack; cake will fall in center. Run spatula around sides of pan; turn out cake; peel off paper. Invert onto serving plate. Spoon peaches with juices into middle of cake. Chill until serving time. Cut in squares; top with whipped cream. Serves 10.

COFFEE CHEESECAKE

Vanilla Wafer Crust (recipe follows)
3 (8-ounce) packages cream cheese, softened
¾ cup sugar
3 eggs, at room temperature
1 tablespoon plus 1 teaspoon instant coffee
½ cup sour cream

Prepare the crust and chill. Beat the cheese until light and fluffy. Gradually beat in the sugar. Add the eggs one at a time, beating well after each; dissolve the coffee in 2 tablespoons hot water and beat into the mixture with the sour cream. Pour into the crust and bake at 350° F. 1 hour, or until firm in center. Cool on a cake rack; chill. Run a spatula around the edge of the cake to loosen; then remove sides of pan. Serves 10.

VANILLA WAFER CRUST

1 cup vanilla wafer crumbs
2 tablespoons sugar
½ teaspoon cinnamon
½ teaspoon instant coffee
¼ cup butter, melted

Combine all the ingredients and press on the bottom of a 9-inch springform or other loose-bottomed pan. Chill.

CINNAMON CHEESECAKE

Cookie Dough Crust (recipe follows)
2 (8-ounce) packages cream cheese, softened
1 cup sugar
2 tablespoons grated orange peel
2 tablespoons grated lemon peel
1 tablespoon lemon juice
1 teaspoon vanilla extract
4 eggs, at room temperature
1 teaspoon cinnamon

Prepare the crust, bake, and cool. Beat together the cheese, ¾ cup sugar, grated orange and lemon peels, lemon juice, and vanilla until smooth. Add the eggs one at a time, beating well after each. Pour into the crust and sprinkle with a mixture of the cinnamon and remaining ¼ cup sugar. Bake at 350° F. 45 minutes, or until set. Cool on a cake rack, then chill. Run a spatula around the edge of the cake to loosen; then remove sides of pan. Serves 8 to 10.

COOKIE DOUGH CRUST

1 cup flour
¼ cup sugar
½ teaspoon salt
½ cup butter
1 egg yolk
2 teaspoons grated lemon peel

Mix together the flour, sugar, and salt. Cut in the butter until particles are fine. Add the egg yolk and lemon peel. Mix well with a fork until blended. Gather into a ball and press onto a piece of waxed paper to form a pancake shape. Chill 10 minutes. Put in a 9-inch springform or other loose-bottomed pan and press with your fingers, stretching to cover the bottom and halfway up the sides. Bake at 400° F. 12 to 14 minutes, or until lightly browned.

COCONUT CAKE

2 cups cake flour
2 teaspoons baking powder
½ teaspoon salt
¾ cup butter, softened
1½ cups sugar
3 eggs
⅔ cup milk
1 teaspoon vanilla extract
1 cup shredded coconut
Orange Filling (recipe follows)
1 cup heavy cream
1 tablespoon confectioners' sugar
3 tablespoons orange-flavored liqueur (optional)

Sift together the flour, baking powder, and salt; set aside. In a large bowl, cream the butter. Gradually beat in the sugar, beating until light and fluffy. Add the eggs one at a time, beating well after each. Add the flour mixture alternately with the milk, beating after each addition until smooth. Add the vanilla; stir in the coconut. Pour into 2 greased and floured 9-inch cake pans. Bake at 350° F. 40 minutes, or until tops spring back when pressed lightly. Cool in pans on racks 10 minutes; remove from pans; cool thoroughly on racks. Place one layer on a serving plate; spread with the filling. Top with the remaining layer. Whip the cream with the confectioners' sugar and liqueur. Frost the top of the cake with the whipped cream mixture or serve it on the side. Serves 12.

ORANGE FILLING

½ cup sugar
2 tablespoons cornstarch
Dash salt
1 tablespoon grated orange peel
1 cup orange juice
1 tablespoon lemon juice
1 tablespoon butter

In a small saucepan, mix well the sugar, cornstarch, and salt. Stir in the orange peel and juices. Stir over low heat 5 minutes, or until thickened. Remove from the heat and stir in the butter; cool. Yield: about 1¼ cups.

DEVIL'S FOOD CAKE WITH WHITE SEVEN-MINUTE FROSTING AND CHOCOLATE CURLS

1½ cups sugar
1½ cups milk
2 eggs and 1 egg yolk
3½ ounces unsweetened chocolate
½ cup butter
2 cups cake flour
½ teaspoon salt
1½ teaspoons baking soda
1 teaspoon vanilla extract
Seven-Minute Frosting (recipe follows)
Chocolate Curls (recipe follows)
¾ cup pecans or walnuts (optional)

Combine ½ cup sugar, ½ cup milk, 1 egg yolk, and the chocolate in a double boiler. Cook and stir until the mixture is smooth and slightly thickened. Remove from heat and cool. Cream the butter with the remaining 1 cup sugar until light and fluffy. Beat the 2 eggs well and mix with the creamed butter and sugar. Sift the flour with the salt and add alternately with the remaining 1 cup milk. Dissolve the baking soda in 1 tablespoon hot water, add to the batter, and flavor with the vanilla. Blend in the cooled chocolate mixture and pour into 2 (9-inch) layer cake pans lined with waxed paper. Bake at 350° F. 30 minutes. Cool on racks 5 minutes before removing from the pans. Turn out and remove the waxed paper. Cool. Frost with the Seven-Minute Frosting and decorate with the Chocolate Curls, and with the nuts, if you wish. Serves 8 to 10.

SEVEN-MINUTE FROSTING

2 egg whites
1½ cups sugar
¼ teaspoon cream of tartar
Pinch salt
1 teaspoon vanilla extract

Place the egg whites, sugar, cream of tartar, ⅓ cup water, and salt in the top part of a double boiler. Cook over moderate heat, beating constantly until the mixture forms peaks. (It should take about 7 minutes.) Remove from the heat and add the vanilla. Beat until the frosting is of spreading consistency. Yield: about 2½ cups.

CHOCOLATE CURLS

1 ounce unsweetened chocolate, at room temperature

Use a vegetable peeler to scrape curls. Chill before decorating the cake.

ORANGE-RAISIN-NUT CAKE

¾ cup butter, softened
2 cups sugar
3 eggs
Grated peel of 1 orange
Grated peel of 1 lemon
3 cups flour
1½ teaspoons baking powder
1½ teaspoons baking soda
¾ teaspoon salt
1 cup chopped raisins
1 cup chopped walnuts or pecans
1½ cups buttermilk
Juice of 1 orange
Juice of 1 lemon

Cream the butter with 1½ cups sugar until fluffy. Beat in the eggs one
at a time until mixture is light and well blended. Stir in the orange and
lemon peels. Stir together in another bowl the flour, baking powder, soda,
salt, raisins, and nuts. Stir the flour mixture into the butter-sugar mixture alternately with the buttermilk until well blended. Pour into a
greased 3-quart fluted tube pan. Bake at 350° F. 1 hour, or until a
toothpick inserted into the center comes out clean. Meanwhile, mix the
remaining ½ cup sugar with the orange and lemon juices until the sugar
is dissolved. Place the cake in the pan on a rack. Prick with a skewer
at ½-inch intervals. Slowly pour the orange-lemon mixture over the hot
cake. Let cool in pan before removing. Wrap airtight and let stand at
room temperature 2 days before serving. Serves about 18.

ORANGE-COCONUT CHEESECAKE

Coconut Crust (recipe follows)
1 cup orange juice
2 envelopes unflavored gelatin
¾ cup sugar
2 eggs, separated, at room temperature
½ teaspoon salt
2 cups (1 pound) fine-curd creamed cottage cheese, at room temperature
Grated peel of 1 orange
2 tablespoons lemon juice
1 cup heavy cream, whipped
1 cup flaked coconut, toasted
1 teaspoon grated orange peel

Prepare the crust and chill. Pour the orange juice into a saucepan and sprinkle with the gelatin. Let stand 5 minutes, then stir in the sugar, egg yolks, and salt. Stir over low heat until the sugar and gelatin are dissolved and the mixture coats a metal spoon. Set aside to cool. In a large bowl, beat the cheese until fairly smooth. Beat in the grated peel of the orange, lemon juice, and cooled thickened gelatin mixture. Beat the egg whites until stiff peaks form, and fold into cheese mixture. Fold in the whipped cream. Pour into the crust and chill overnight, or until firm. Combine the coconut and 1 teaspoon orange peel and sprinkle over the top. Serves 8 to 10.

COCONUT CRUST

1 cup finely crushed vanilla wafers
⅓ cup flaked coconut
1 teaspoon grated orange peel
2 tablespoons melted butter

Combine all the ingredients. Press on the bottom of a 10-inch springform or other loose-bottomed pan and chill.

SPONGE CAKE WITH STRAWBERRIES

Cake

1 cup flour
1 teaspoon baking powder
5 eggs, at room temperature
¾ cup sugar
3 tablespoons butter
¼ cup heavy cream
2 teaspoons grated lemon peel
1 teaspoon lemon extract
1 teaspoon vanilla extract

Filling and Topping

1 quart strawberries, hulled and halved (reserve a few whole and unhulled
    for garnish)
½ cup sugar
1½ cups heavy cream, whipped

CAKE: Sift together the flour and baking powder; set aside. In a large bowl, beat the eggs and sugar at high speed about 10 minutes, or until lemon-colored, fluffy, and thickened. Meanwhile, in a small saucepan over low heat, melt the butter in the cream; set aside to cool slightly. Fold the flour mixture into the egg mixture, then fold in the cream mixture, peel, and extracts. Divide the batter evenly into 2 well-greased and floured 9-inch cake pans. Bake at 350° F. 22 to 25 minutes, or until top springs back when touched lightly. Cool in pans on racks 5 minutes. Remove from pans; cool thoroughly on racks.

FILLING AND TOPPING: Gently toss the berries with the sugar. Let stand at room temperature until they draw juice, about 1 hour. Place 1 cake layer on a serving plate. Spoon half the berries and juice over; top with all but 1 cup whipped cream. Place the second cake layer on the cream; press down lightly. Spoon the remaining berries and juice on the cake; mound the remaining whipped cream in the center. Garnish with the whole berries. Serves 10.

VIENNA CAFÉ CAKE

2 cups flour
⅔ cup unsweetened cocoa
1¼ teaspoons baking soda
¼ teaspoon baking powder
½ teaspoon salt
⅔ cup butter, softened
1⅔ cups sugar
3 eggs, at room temperature
1 teaspoon vanilla extract
1½ cups milk
Coffee Cream Frosting (recipe follows)
Sliced almonds (for garnish)

Grease and flour 3 (9-inch) cake pans; set aside. Mix well the flour, cocoa, baking soda, baking powder, and salt; set aside. In a large bowl, scraping down the sides occasionally, beat the butter, sugar, eggs, and vanilla until fluffy. Gradually stir in the flour mixture alternately with the milk just until blended. Pour batter into prepared pans. Adjust racks to divide oven into thirds; stagger pans on racks. Bake at 350° F., rotating pans once to ensure even layers, 20 to 25 minutes, or until a toothpick inserted in the center comes out clean. Cool in pans on racks 10 minutes; invert cakes on racks; remove pans; turn cakes right side up; cool completely. Fill and frost top with the Coffee Cream Frosting. Garnish with the almonds. Serves about 10.

COFFEE CREAM FROSTING

1 cup heavy cream
2 tablespoons sugar
1½ teaspoons instant coffee

Beat the cream until it starts to thicken; beat in the sugar and coffee until stiff. Yield: 2 cups.

SWEDISH-STYLE CHEESE PIE

1 tablespoon butter, softened
3 eggs, at room temperature
¼ cup sugar
¼ cup flour
¼ cup finely chopped blanched almonds
1 teaspoon vanilla extract
1 teaspoon grated lemon peel
1½ cups pot cheese (dry, uncreamed cottage cheese) or sieved small-curd
    cottage cheese
¾ cup milk
Whipped cream

Spread the butter in a 9-inch pie pan and set aside. Combine the eggs and sugar and beat until light and fluffy. Add the flour, almonds, vanilla, lemon peel, cheese, and milk and mix well. Pour into the pie pan and bake at 300° F. 1 hour, or until set. Serve at room temperature with whipped cream. Serves 6 to 8.

PUMPKIN PIE

2 cups cooked or canned pumpkin
1 (13-ounce) can evaporated milk
2 eggs, slightly beaten
¾ cup packed light brown sugar
2 teaspoons cinnamon
½ teaspoon ground ginger
⅛ teaspoon salt
1 (9-inch) unbaked pie shell
Whipped cream (optional)
Grated nutmeg (optional)

Beat the pumpkin, milk, eggs, sugar, cinnamon, ginger, and salt until smooth and well blended. Pour into the pie shell. Bake at 350° F. 50 minutes, or until set. Cool on a rack. Top with whipped cream and nutmeg if you wish. Serves 6 to 8.

CHEESE PIE WITH RHUBARB GLAZE

Sweet-Crisp Pie Shell (recipe follows)
3 eggs, at room temperature
⅓ cup sugar
½ teaspoon salt
8 ounces pot cheese (dry, uncreamed cottage cheese)
2 tablespoons flour
1 cup sour cream
1 teaspoon vanilla extract
2 teaspoons grated orange peel
Rhubarb Glaze (recipe follows)
Whipped cream
Finely shredded orange peel (optional)
Fresh mint leaves (optional)

Prepare the shell, bake, and cool. Beat the eggs until light; gradually add the sugar, beating until light and fluffy. Add the salt and pot cheese; beat until well blended. Add the flour, sour cream, vanilla, and orange peel and mix well. Pour into the pie shell and bake at 350° F. on the center rack 30 to 40 minutes, or until set. Cool. Pour the Rhubarb Glaze on top and chill 30 minutes, or until glaze is firm. Garnish with whipped cream, and with orange peel and mint if desired. Serves 6 to 8.

SWEET-CRISP PIE SHELL

1 cup flour
1 tablespoon sugar
6 tablespoons butter
1 egg yolk
1 tablespoon ice water

Combine the flour and sugar; cut in the butter until particles are very fine. Beat the egg yolk with the ice water and pour over the dry mixture, stirring with a fork to dampen. Work with your hands until dough is smooth and holds together. Roll dough on a lightly floured board into a 9-inch circle. Transfer to a 9-inch pie pan and press firmly to bottom and sides, stretching to build up edges. Flute edges and prick bottom. Chill 30 minutes. Bake at 350° F. on rack in low position 10 minutes. Chill.

RHUBARB GLAZE

2 cups diced rhubarb
1 envelope unflavored gelatin
¼ cup sugar

In a saucepan, combine the rhubarb and ½ cup water. Slowly bring to a boil, cover, and simmer 6 to 8 minutes. Strain through a fine sieve or cheesecloth. Measure ¾ cup liquid. In a mixing bowl soften the gelatin in ¼ cup cold water. Combine the rhubarb liquid and sugar in a saucepan. Bring to a boil and pour over the gelatin, stirring until dissolved. Cool until slightly thickened.

STRAWBERRY TART

1½ (8-ounce) packages cream cheese, softened
1 (9-inch) graham-cracker crust
2 pints ripe strawberries, hulled
1 tablespoon sugar
½ cup red currant jelly

Spread the cheese in the crust. Arrange the berries, pointed side up, on the cheese. Sprinkle with the sugar and chill. Heat the jelly until smooth. Cool and spoon over the berries to glaze. Chill until ready to serve. Serves 6 to 8.

UNBAKED CRUMB CRUST

1½ cups graham cracker or zwieback crumbs
¼ cup sugar
½ cup melted butter

Mix the crumbs and sugar thoroughly with the melted butter. Press this mixture evenly onto the bottom and sides of a buttered 9-inch pie plate. Chill about 1 hour, until firm. Yield: 1 crust.

PECAN TART

½ cup butter
1 cup flour
¾ cup dark brown sugar
1 cup heavy cream
1½ cups pecan halves

Cut the butter into the flour until mixture has the consistency of small peas. Press into a 10-inch pie pan. Bake at 400° F. 10 to 12 minutes. Cool. Stir the sugar into the cream and, when dissolved, stir in the pecans. Pour into the pie shell. Bake at 400° F. 30 minutes. Cool. Serves 8.

GREEK CHEESE PIE WITH PRUNES

Walnut Crumb Crust (recipe follows)
1 (8-ounce) package cream cheese, softened
3 tablespoons honey
Grated peel and juice of 1 lemon
¼ teaspoon cinnamon
1 cup plain yogurt
1 cup finely chopped prunes

Prepare the crust, bake, and cool thoroughly. Cream the cheese until light and fluffy; add the honey, lemon peel and juice, and cinnamon; cream until well blended. Carefully fold in the yogurt a little at a time until smooth (overfolding may break down yogurt curds). Fold in the prunes. Pour into the crust and chill at least 24 hours before serving. Serves 6 to 8.

WALNUT CRUMB CRUST

1¼ cups fine vanilla wafer crumbs
¼ cup finely chopped walnuts
2 tablespoons sugar
5 tablespoons butter, softened

Combine the vanilla wafer crumbs, walnuts, and sugar. Work in the butter and press firmly onto the bottom and sides of a 9-inch pie pan. Bake at 375° F. 8 minutes.

BERRY PIE

Pastry for a 2-crust 9-inch pie
1 quart strawberries, blueberries, or blackberries
1–1½ cups sugar
3 tablespoons quick-cooking tapioca
Milk (optional)

Fit half the crust into a 9-inch pie pan. Cut slits in the other half and place a moist tea towel over. Mix the berries with 1 cup sugar (use more sugar depending on the sweetness of the berries) and the tapioca and pour into the pie shell. Place the top crust over, wet the edges, and crimp. Be sure the crust is slashed in several places so steam can escape. Put a piece of foil under the pie while baking in case it leaks. You may brush the top crust with a little milk before baking if you wish. Bake at 450° F. 20 minutes, reduce heat to 400° F., and bake 10 minutes more. Cool. Serves 6.

CRANBERRY-PEAR CRISP

1 (12-ounce) package cranberries (about 3 cups)
2 large unpeeled pears, cored and sliced thin
1 cup sugar
1 teaspoon cinnamon
¼ cup flour
¼ cup packed light brown sugar
¼ cup butter
¾ cup old-fashioned oats
¾ cup chopped walnuts
Half-and-half or heavy cream (optional)

In a lightly greased shallow 1½-quart baking dish, thoroughly mix the cranberries, pears, sugar, cinnamon, and 1 tablespoon flour; set aside. In a bowl, mix the remaining flour with the brown sugar. With a pastry blender, cut in the butter until the mixture resembles coarse crumbs. Stir in the oats and walnuts and sprinkle evenly over the fruit mixture. Bake at 375° F. 40 minutes, or until lightly browned. Let stand until cool. Serve with half-and-half or cream, if you wish. Serves 8.

JELLIED ORANGE-CHEESE PIE WITH STRAWBERRIES

Graham Cracker Crust (recipe follows)
2 (8-ounce) packages cream cheese, softened
½ cup sugar
1 cup orange juice
2 tablespoons lemon juice
1 envelope unflavored gelatin
1½ cups sliced fresh strawberries
⅓ cup currant jelly

Prepare and chill the crust. Cream the cheese until soft, add the sugar, and cream until light and fluffy. Blend in the orange and lemon juices until smooth. Soften the gelatin in ¼ cup cold water, then dissolve over low heat. Cool and beat into the cheese mixture. Pour into the crust and chill until firm. An hour before serving, arrange the strawberries over the top. Melt the jelly over low heat, stirring constantly. Remove from the heat and stir until cool. Spoon over the strawberries and chill not more than 1 hour. (If chilled too long, topping will become runny.) Serves 6 to 8.

GRAHAM CRACKER CRUST

1¼ cups fine graham cracker crumbs
2 tablespoons sugar
1 teaspoon grated lemon peel
6 tablespoons melted butter

Combine all the ingredients and press firmly onto the bottom and sides of a 9-inch pie pan. Chill.

APPLE FLAN

1 cup flour
3 tablespoons sugar
¼ teaspoon salt
½ cup plus 2 tablespoons butter
2 tablespoons ice water
3 medium (1 pound) tart, firm apples, peeled, cored, quartered, and sliced
    thin
2 tablespoons lemon juice
1 egg, beaten
½ cup apricot preserves

Combine the flour, 1 tablespoon sugar, and salt. Cut in ½ cup butter until particles resemble small peas. Sprinkle with the ice water; mix thoroughly with a fork. Form into a ball; flatten into a 6-inch circle. Wrap and chill at least 1½ hours, or until firm enough to roll. Toss the apples with the lemon juice and remaining 2 tablespoons sugar; set aside. On a cookie sheet, using a lightly floured stockinette-covered rolling pin, roll out the pastry ⅛ inch thick. Place a 9-inch layer cake pan on the pastry; cut around edge with a knife or pastry wheel. Remove excess pastry and reserve. Prick dough with a fork and bake at 400° F. for 15 minutes, or until golden. Cool on the cookie sheet on a rack. Reserving the juice, arrange the apples in closely overlapping circles on the crust, leaving ½ inch of outer edge uncovered. On a lightly floured surface, hand-roll the reserved pastry into a 27-inch-long roll. Press around outer edge of crust. Brush with the egg. Melt the remaining 2 tablespoons butter and drizzle over the apples with the reserved sugar-lemon juice. Bake at 400° F. 20 minutes, or until the apples are almost tender. Remove from oven and spoon the preserves over the apples. Bake 5 minutes longer, or until preserves have melted and edge of crust is golden brown. Cool on the cookie sheet on the rack 10 minutes, then loosen with a wide spatula and slide onto rack to cool. Serve at room temperature, cut in wedges. Serves 6.

SHERRIED CREAM PUFFS

½ cup butter
1 teaspoon sugar
⅛ teaspoon salt
1 cup flour
4 large eggs, at room temperature
Sherry Custard Filling (recipe follows)
Sherry Sugar Glaze (recipe follows)

In a heavy 2-quart saucepan, heat 1 cup water, the butter, sugar, and salt until the butter melts. Bring to a boil, remove from the heat, and add the flour all at once. Beat with a wooden spoon until thoroughly blended. Stir over medium heat about 2 minutes until the mixture forms a ball, leaves the sides of the pan, and begins to form a film on the bottom of the pan. Put the mixture in a large bowl and beat at low speed 1 minute to cool slightly. Add the eggs all at once and beat at medium speed, scraping the sides of the bowl while beating, about 2 minutes, until the batter is thick and begins to cling to the beaters. Beat about 2 minutes longer, lifting up the beaters slightly to allow the dough to run off a bit. Mixture will be very thick. Using 2 tablespoonfuls each, drop 16 mounds about 1½ inches apart on an ungreased cookie sheet. Bake at 425° F. 20 minutes, reduce heat to 375° F., and bake 15 minutes longer, until golden and firm. Turn off the oven. Remove the puffs and make a small slit in the side of each with a small knife. Return to oven for 10 minutes, leaving the door slightly ajar. Remove to racks to cool. Not more than 2 hours before serving, split each puff with a sharp knife and fill with about 3 tablespoons filling. Drizzle with the glaze and refrigerate until ready to serve. Yield: 16 puffs.

SHERRY CUSTARD FILLING

½ cup sugar
3 tablespoons cornstarch
2¾ cups milk
4 egg yolks, slightly beaten
¼ cup sweet sherry

In a heavy 2-quart saucepan, mix the sugar and cornstarch well. Stir in the milk. Stir over medium heat until the mixture thickens and comes to a boil. Simmer 1 minute. Beat a small amount of the hot mixture into the egg yolks. Pour back into the saucepan and stir over medium heat until the mixture thickens and boils. Remove from the heat and stir in the sherry. Place waxed paper directly on the surface of the filling and chill until ready to use. Yield: about 3 cups.

SHERRY SUGAR GLAZE

1 cup confectioners' sugar
2 tablespoons sweet sherry

Beat the sugar with the sherry, adding a little more sherry if necessary, to make a glaze consistency.

Cookies

BANANA-PECAN SQUARES

1½ cups flour
½ teaspoon baking soda
½ teaspoon salt
½ cup butter
¾ cup sugar
1 egg
1 teaspoon vanilla extract
1 cup mashed banana
½ cup chopped pecans
9 pecan halves (optional, for garnish)

Sift together the flour, baking soda, and salt and set aside. In a medium bowl, cream the butter and sugar until light and fluffy. Beat in the egg, vanilla, and banana (the mixture will look curdled). Stir in the flour mixture until well blended, then the chopped nuts. Spread in a greased 9-inch-square pan. Space the pecan halves on the dough if you wish. Bake at 350° F. 25 minutes, or until browned and a toothpick inserted in the center comes out clean. Cool in the pan. Cut into 3-inch squares. Yield: 9 squares.

BROWNIES

1 cup flour
¾ teaspoon baking powder
¼ teaspoon salt
3 ounces unsweetened chocolate
½ cup butter
1½ cups sugar
3 eggs, beaten
¾ cup coarsely chopped pecans
1 teaspoon vanilla extract

Sift together the flour, baking powder, and salt. Melt the chocolate and butter in a double boiler. Gradually stir the sugar into the beaten eggs and add to the melted chocolate mixture. Blend in the flour and then the pecans and vanilla. Bake in a greased 9-inch-square pan at 350° F. 35 to 40 minutes. Cut into rectangular pieces and cool on a rack. Yield: about 3 dozen brownies.

CHOCOLATE WHOLE WHEAT BROWNIES

½ cup whole wheat flour
½ teaspoon baking powder
¼ teaspoon salt
½ cup butter, softened
⅔ cup sugar
2 (1-ounce) squares unsweetened chocolate, melted and cooled
2 eggs
1 teaspoon vanilla extract
¾ cup chopped walnuts

Sift together the flour, baking powder, and salt and set aside. Cream the butter and sugar until fluffy. Beat in the chocolate, eggs, and vanilla. Stir in the flour mixture and ½ cup nuts. Spread in a greased 8-inch-square pan. Sprinkle with the remaining nuts. Bake at 350° F. 20 minutes, or until the brownies pull away from the sides of the pan and a toothpick inserted in the center comes out clean. Cool in the pan on a rack. Cut into 2-inch squares. Yield: 16 brownies.

BUTTERSCOTCH BROWNIES

½ cup flour
⅛ teaspoon salt
1 teaspoon baking powder
¼ cup butter
1 cup light brown sugar
1 egg
1 teaspoon vanilla extract
½ cup finely chopped walnuts

Sift together the flour, salt, and baking powder. In a saucepan, melt the butter and stir in the sugar. Continue stirring until dissolved. Cool slightly before beating in the egg and vanilla. Blend in the flour mixture. Add the nuts and pour into a greased 8-inch-square pan. Bake at 350° F. for 30 minutes. Cut into 1 × 2-inch bars. Yield: 32 brownies.

MERINGUE KISSES

1 egg white, at room temperature
Pinch salt
½ cup superfine sugar
¼ teaspoon vanilla extract

Beat the egg white with the salt until very frothy. Beat in the sugar a tablespoon at a time. Continue beating until the meringue stands in a stiff peak and the sugar is dissolved. Fold in the vanilla. Drop by teaspoonfuls onto well-greased baking sheets. Bake at 250° F. for about 45 minutes, until dry but not browned. Leave in the oven for 10 minutes after turning it off. Yield: about 2 dozen.

COFFEE MERINGUE KISSES

Fold 2 teaspoons instant coffee into the Meringue Kisses* with the vanilla.

CHOCOLATE MERINGUE KISSES

Add 1 teaspoon unsweetened cocoa to the Meringue Kisses* with the vanilla.

CHOCOLATE REFRIGERATOR COOKIES

2 cups flour
½ teaspoon baking powder
1 teaspoon cinnamon
¼ teaspoon salt
½ cup butter, softened
⅔ cup sugar
1 egg
¼ cup chocolate syrup
¾ cup chopped walnuts, pecans, or almonds

Sift together the flour, baking powder, cinnamon, and salt and set aside. In a large bowl, cream the butter and sugar until light and fluffy. Beat in the egg and chocolate syrup. Stir in the dry ingredients. Shape into a roll 2 inches in diameter. Roll in the nuts. Wrap in waxed paper and chill several hours or overnight. Cut in slices ⅜ inch thick. Place 1 inch apart on greased cookie sheets. Bake at 350° F. for 15 minutes, or until the edges are lightly browned. Remove to a rack to cool. Yield: 36 cookies.

DATE-NUT BARS

1 cup flour
½ cup sugar
½ teaspoon nutmeg
½ teaspoon baking powder
¼ teaspoon salt
2 eggs
¼ cup oil
1 tablespoon lemon juice
1 (8-ounce) package chopped dates
1 cup chopped walnuts
Topping: 1 tablespoon sugar mixed with ½ teaspoon nutmeg

Mix the dry ingredients well in a 9-inch-square pan. Add the eggs, oil, and lemon juice. Mix and stir with a rubber spatula until well blended. (The bater will be thick.) Stir in the dates and walnuts. Bake at 350° F. about 30 minutes, until lightly browned and a toothpick inserted in the center comes out clean. Sprinkle with the topping. Cool in the pan on a rack. Cut in 4 × 1-inch bars or 2-inch squares. Yield: 16 bars.

KASHA CRACKLES

1½ cups flour
1½ teaspoons baking powder
1 teaspoon nutmeg
½ teaspoon salt
½ cup kasha (roasted buckwheat)
½ cup raisins
¾ cup shortening
1 cup packed light brown sugar
1 egg

Mix well the flour, baking powder, nutmeg, salt, kasha, and raisins; set aside. In a medium bowl, cream the shortening and sugar until fluffy. Beat in the egg. Stir in the flour mixture until blended. Roll into 1-inch balls and place 1½ inches apart on greased cookie sheets; flatten slightly. Bake at 350° F. 10 to 12 minutes, until lightly browned. Remove to a rack to cool. Yield: 48 cookies.

LACE COOKIES

½ cup sugar
½ cup flour
Pinch salt
¼ teaspoon baking powder
½ cup old-fashioned oats
2 tablespoons heavy cream
2 tablespoons light corn syrup
⅓ cup melted butter
1 tablespoon vanilla extract

Sift the sugar, flour, salt, and baking powder into a bowl. Add the remaining ingredients and mix together until well blended. Using a ¼-teaspoon measuring spoon, drop about 4 inches apart onto ungreased baking sheets. Bake at 375° F. 6 to 8 minutes, until lightly browned. Let cool a few seconds before removing from the baking sheets. Yield: about 6 dozen (2-inch) cookies.

NUT CRISPS

1 cup flour
½ teaspoon baking powder
½ teaspoon salt
¾ cup butter, softened
⅓ cup white sugar
⅓ cup packed light brown sugar
1 egg
½ teaspoon vanilla extract
1 cup oven-toasted rice cereal
½ cup coarsely chopped walnuts
Walnut pieces (for garnish)

Sift together the flour, baking powder, and salt; set aside. Cream the butter and sugars until light and fluffy. Beat in the egg and vanilla. Stir in the flour mixture until well blended. Stir in the cereal and chopped walnuts. Drop by rounded tablespoonfuls 2 inches apart onto a greased cookie sheet. Press a walnut piece on each. Bake at 375° F. about 10 minutes, until browned around the edges. Remove to a rack to cool. Yield: 24 cookies.

OATMEAL AND APPLE BUTTER BARS

1¼ cups flour
1 cup packed dark brown sugar
¾ cup butter, cut into pieces
1¼ cups old-fashioned oats
¾ cup apple butter

In a large bowl, mix the flour and sugar. Cut in the butter until the mixture resembles coarse crumbs. Stir in the oats until well blended. Press half the mixture (about 2¼ cups) firmly into a greased 8-inch-square pan to form a compact layer. Spread the apple butter to within ½ inch of the edges. Sprinkle the remaining oats mixture over the apple butter and press down carefully but firmly. Bake at 350° F. about 40 minutes, until lightly browned. Cool in the pan on a rack. Cut into 1 × 4-inch bars or 2-inch squares. Yield: 16 bars.

OATMEAL-RAISIN COOKIES

1 cup butter, softened
1 cup packed light brown sugar
2 teaspoons vanilla extract
⅔ cup raisins
2½ cups old-fashioned oats
1¼ cups whole wheat flour
1 teaspoon baking soda
¼ teaspoon salt

In a large bowl, cream the butter, sugar, and vanilla until fluffy. Stir in the raisins and then the oats until well blended. Gradually stir in the flour mixed with the baking soda and salt. Blend well, using your hands if necessary. Immediately press dough into a ¼-cup measure and unmold 3 inches apart onto ungreased baking sheets. Press and shape each mound into a firm 3-inch cookie. Bake at 325° F. 15 to 17 minutes, until light brown. Cool on the sheet 10 minutes before removing to a rack to cool completely. Yield: 16 cookies.

DOUBLE-PEANUT COOKIES

1 cup flour
½ teaspoon baking soda
½ cup shortening
½ cup smooth peanut butter
½ cup white sugar
½ cup packed light brown sugar
1 egg
½ cup salted peanuts

Sift together the flour and baking soda and set aside. In a medium bowl, cream the shortening and peanut butter until well blended. Add the sugars and beat until fluffy. Beat in the egg. Stir in the flour mixture until well blended, then stir in the peanuts. Drop by rounded table-spoonfuls 3 inches apart onto an ungreased cookie sheet. Bake at 350° F. about 10 minutes, until lightly browned. Cool on the cookie sheet about 5 minutes before removing to a rack to cool completely. Yield: 16 cookies.

THUMBKINS

1 (17-ounce) roll refrigerated slice-and-bake sugar cookie dough
¼ cup sesame seeds or shredded coconut
2 tablespoons preserves, jam, marmalade, or peanut butter

Cut the cold dough in 12 slices. Cut each slice in half and roll into a ball. Immediately roll in the sesame seeds. Place 2 inches apart on ungreased cookie sheets. Make a deep depression in each with your thumb and fill with about ¼ teaspoon preserves. Bake at 350° F. 10 to 12 minutes, until golden. Cool on the sheets about 5 minutes before removing to a rack to cool completely. Yield: 24 cookies.

Beverages

WINE is becoming increasingly popular as an accompaniment to meals; it makes a luncheon or dinner into a party. A chilled white wine with fish or chicken or a room-temperature red wine with meat is enjoyed by many. Cold white wine or vermouth can be served as an aperitif before meals, and wine forms an essential part of a number of beverages, especially at receptions. What would a bridal party be without a festive bowl? Here you will find not only traditional alcoholic and nonalcoholic fruit punches, but combinations you will wish you had thought of long ago.

Sangria is a Spanish concoction of red wine and citrus fruits; white wine with strawberries and soda is a German contribution. Both are most refreshing in midafternoon. Of course, iced tea and iced coffee are still popular, but there are new ways to add a zesty fillip to these standbys.

Here you will find low-calorie recipes, but also recipes for those who are fortunate enough not to have to count calories, or reckless enough not to care. These include eggnogs galore—and not only for New Year's Day. There are also beverages to serve at breakfast. In fact, if it's anything you'd like to drink, you'll find it here.

Alcoholic Drinks

APERITIF

Ice
2 ounces Dubonnet, Lillet, Pernod, vermouth, or Campari bitters
Club soda
Lemon peel (optional)

Fill a tall glass with pieces of ice; add the aperitif of your choice, and fill with cold club soda. Serves 1.

SCREWDRIVER

½ blender cracked ice
4 ounces orange juice
4 ounces vodka

Purée all the ingredients in a blender and strain into 2 chilled cocktail glasses. Serves 2.

BLOODY MARY

2 ounces vodka
½ cup tomato juice
1 teaspoon lemon juice
Pinch salt
Pinch sugar
Dash Worcestershire sauce
Cracked ice

Shake all the ingredients with the ice and serve in a tall glass with an ice cube or two. Serves 1.

VIRGIN MARY

This drink may be made without the alcohol, in which case it is called a Virgin Mary.

DRY MARTINI

2 ounces gin
1 ounce dry vermouth
Ice
Lemon peel or green olive (optional)

Pour the gin and vermouth into a glass or pitcher of ice and stir (*never* shake). Serve in a stemmed glass or on ice in an old-fashioned glass. Add the garnish, if desired. These proportions vary, and the drink is frequently made with 4 or 5 parts gin or more to 1 part vermouth. Serves 1.

VODKA MARTINI

This is made in the same way and in the same proportions as the Dry Martini*, with vodka in place of the gin. Usually served with a twist of lemon peel. Serves 1.

WHISKEY SOUR

1–1½ ounces lemon juice
1 ounce sugar
4 ounces bourbon or rye whiskey
Cracked ice

Pour the lemon juice, sugar, and bourbon or rye on cracked ice and purée in a blender until the ice is melted. Pour into chilled cocktail glasses. Serves 2.

SCOTCH SOUR

Proceed as for Whiskey Sour*, substituting scotch whiskey for bourbon and using ½ ounce lemon juice only. Serve in tall cold glasses. Serves 2.

MANHATTAN

2 ounces rye whiskey or bourbon
1 ounce sweet vermouth
Dash Angostura bitters (optional)
Ice
Maraschino cherry (optional)

Pour the rye, vermouth, and bitters into a glass or pitcher of ice and stir. Serve in a stemmed glass or in an old-fashioned glass. Garnish with the cherry, if you wish. Now frequently made with 3 parts whiskey to 1 part vermouth. When made with 3 parts whiskey to 1 part vermouth (half dry and half sweet), it is called a Perfect Manhattan. Serves 1.

Incidentally, my father, Charles H. Truax, invented the Manhattan in 1890, the year he founded and became president of the Manhattan Club in New York City.

MARGARITA

1½ ounces tequila
1 ounce Triple Sec
½ ounce lemon juice
Lemon wedge
Salt
Piece of lime

Shake the tequila, Triple Sec, and lemon juice and strain into a salt-rimmed cocktail glass. To salt the glass, rub the edge of the glass with a lemon wedge and dip the rim firmly into a saucer of salt. Decorate with a piece of lime. Serves 1.

TEQUILA SUNRISE

Ice cubes
1 ounce tequila
Orange juice
1 teaspoon grenadine

Fill a highball glass with ice cubes, the tequila, and orange juice. Stir. Add the grenadine. It will sink to the bottom of the glass and permeate the orange juice as you drink it—giving a "sunrise" effect. Serves 1.

SANGRIA

1 (750 ml) bottle red Spanish wine
Juice of 1 orange
Juice of 1 lemon
2 cups club soda
Cracked ice or ice cubes
Peel of 1 orange cut in a long spiral
Sugar to taste

Pour the wine, juices, and club soda into a pitcher of ice; put in the orange peel. Let each person add sugar to taste to the individual glasses. A lovely cool summer drink. Serves 6 to 8.

CITRUS PUNCH

1 (6-ounce) can frozen orange juice concentrate
1 (6-ounce) can frozen lemonade concentrate
1 tablespoon lemon juice
½ (28-ounce) bottle ginger ale
½ bottle dry white wine
Ice cubes

Add 4 cups cold water to the concentrates and put in a punch bowl. Just before serving, add the lemon juice, ginger ale, wine, and ice. Serves 10.

GERMAN BOWL

1 (750 ml) bottle white wine (German wine may be used)
1 pint club soda
Ice
½ (10-ounce) package sliced frozen strawberries, partially thawed
Sugar to taste

In a bowl, mix the wine and club soda over a large lump of ice. Stir in the berries. Sweeten to taste. Serves 6.

BACARDI

1 ounce lemon juice
¼ teaspoon sugar
2 ounces Bacardi rum
Crushed ice

Combine the ingredients in a blender or processor and purée. Pour into a tall cocktail glass with more cracked ice. Serves 1.

KIR

Put 2 ice cubes in a large white-wine glass; add 1 ounce crème de cassis. Do not add more or the drink is likely to be too sweet. Fill the glass with good dry white wine and chill. You can make a larger drink using twice as much wine and more cassis. This is a most refreshing summer drink. Serves 1.

Eggnogs

EGGNOG

12 eggs, separated, at room temperature
1 cup sugar
2 cups Jamaican rum
2 cups French brandy
1 quart heavy cream

Beat the egg yolks with the sugar until the sugar is dissolved. Slowly add the liquors and cream. Pour into a large bowl. Beat the egg whites until stiff and fold into the egg yolk mixture. Serves 12 to 16.

NOTE: You may whip part or all of the cream, if you wish, and stir in just before serving. The eggnog may be made the day before, and whipped cream added at the last minute.

FESTIVE MILK PUNCH

1 cup sherry
½ cup brandy
1 quart milk
Sugar to taste
1 cup heavy cream
Nutmeg (for garnish)

Mix the sherry, brandy, milk, sugar, and cream. Chill. Sprinkle with the nutmeg. Serve chilled. Serves 8 to 10.

COFFEE EGGNOG

4 eggs, separated, at room temperature
½–¾ cup sugar
5 tablespoons instant coffee
3 cups milk
½ cup heavy cream
1½ teaspoon vanilla extract
Nutmeg (for garnish)

Beat the egg yolks. Gradually add the sugar, beating until fluffy. Dissolve the coffee in 5 tablespoons hot water; stir in the milk, cream, and vanilla. Add to the egg yolk mixture. Chill. Beat the egg whites until stiff; fold into the egg yolk mixture. Pour into a punch bowl. Mix well before serving. Sprinkle with nutmeg. Serves 6 to 8.

ORANGE EGGNOG

4 eggs, separated, at room temperature
½ cup sugar
¼ teaspoon salt
1 (6-ounce) can frozen orange juice concentrate, partially thawed
3 orange juice cans milk
½ cup heavy cream
1 teaspoon vanilla extract

Beat the egg yolks; gradually add ¼ cup sugar and the salt and beat until fluffy. Combine the orange juice concentrate, milk, cream, and vanilla, and stir into the egg yolk mixture. Beat the egg whites until stiff. Gradually beat in the remaining ¼ cup sugar and fold into the egg yolk mixture. Pour into a punch bowl and chill. Serves 6 to 8.

Fruit Drinks

BANANA FRUIT DRINK

1 cup sugar
1 (8-ounce) can crushed pineapple in its own juice
2 bananas, cut up
½ cup orange juice
¼ cup lemon juice
1 (28-ounce) bottle club soda

In a saucepan, simmer the sugar and 1 cup water until the sugar is dissolved. Whirl the pineapple, bananas, and juices in a blender until smooth. Stir in the sugar syrup. Pour into an 8-inch-square cake pan and freeze until almost firm. Let stand at room temperature 15 minutes, cut in pieces, and pour into tall glasses. Fill with soda, stirring slightly. Serves 6 to 8.

CRANBERRY PUNCH

4 cups cranberry juice cocktail
½ cup sugar
¼ cup lemon juice
2 cups chilled club soda
Crushed ice
Mint sprigs (for garnish)

Combine the cranberry juice cocktail, sugar, and lemon juice; chill. To serve, add the club soda, pour over ice, and garnish with the mint sprigs. Serves 6 to 8.

LEMONADE CONCENTRATE

1¼ cups sugar
½ tablespoon grated lemon peel
1½ cups lemon juice
Ice
Club soda (optional)

Put the sugar and lemon peel in a jar with a tight-fitting lid. Stir in 1½ cups boiling water until the sugar is dissolved. Stir in the lemon juice, cover, and refrigerate. For each serving, pour ¼ cup concentrate over ice in tall glass and fill with cold club soda or water. Chill. Serves 8 to 10.

ORANGE BUTTERMILK DRINK

1 cup buttermilk
1 cup orange juice
¼ teaspoon sugar
½ teaspoon vanilla extract
4 ice cubes, crushed

Whirl all the ingredients in a blender until well mixed and chilled. Serves 2 to 3.

ORANGEADE CONCENTRATE

4 cups fresh-squeezed orange juice
2 tablespoons grated orange peel
½ cup sugar, or to taste
Ice
Orange slices (for garnish)
Mint sprigs (for garnish)

Mix the orange juice, peel, and sugar and store in a covered container in the refrigerator. For each serving, pour ⅓ cup concentrate over ice in tall glass, fill with cold water, and stir. Garnish with an orange slice and mint sprig if you wish. Serves 12.

STRAWBERRY BOWL

1 (6-ounce) can frozen grapefruit juice concentrate, reconstituted
1 (10-ounce) package frozen sliced strawberries, partially thawed
1 (28-ounce) bottle carbonated water, chilled

Whirl the grapefruit juice and strawberries in a blender. Pour into a punch bowl or pitcher of ice and add the carbonated water. Serves 6 to 8.

STRAWBERRY LEMONADE

1 cup hulled strawberries
2 tablespoons sugar
Ice
1 cup Lemonade Concentrate*
Ice, ice water
2 lemon slices, halved (optional, for garnish)

Reserve 4 whole strawberries for garnish; with a fork, crush the remaining strawberries with the sugar and let stand ½ hour or longer. Divide among 4 tall glasses and fill with ice. Pour ¼ cup Lemonade Concentrate into each glass, add ice water to fill, and stir. Garnish each with a strawberry, and a lemon piece if you wish. Serves 4.

WATERMELON COOLER

3 cups diced, seeded watermelon
2 teaspoons lemon juice
Dash salt
Ice cubes

In a blender, whirl the watermelon, lemon juice, and salt until smooth.
Pour over ice in 4 tall glasses. Serves 4.

Tomato Drinks

CHILI TOMATO JUICE

4 cups (1 quart) tomato juice
1 (2-ounce) can green chilies, drained
Grated peel of 1 lemon
½ teaspoon salt

Whirl all the ingredients in a blender. Chill. Serves 4 to 6.

NOTE: For a milder chili flavor, add 1 chili to 1 quart tomato juice.
Stir in the lemon peel and salt. Chill overnight.

ORANGE-TOMATO DRINK

1 cup orange juice, chilled
1 cup tomato juice, chilled
¼ teaspoon salt
2 drops hot pepper sauce, or to taste
Crushed ice
Orange peel (optional)

Mix together the juices, salt, and hot pepper sauce. Pour over chopped
ice in wide glasses. Add a twist of orange peel to each if you wish. Stir
and chill. Serves 3 to 4.

TOMATO BUTTERMILK DRINK

1 cup tomato juice
1 cup buttermilk
1 teaspoon lemon juice
8 drops hot pepper sauce (optional)
4 ice cubes

Whirl all the ingredients in a blender at high speed until the ice has melted. Pour at once into old-fashioned glasses. Serves 4.

Iced Tea, Iced Coffee

CLOUDLESS ICED TEA

8–10 tea bags, tags removed
Ice
2 ounces orange juice
Lemon wedges
Sugar

Measure 4 cups cold water into a pitcher, add the tea bags, cover, and let stand for 6 hours or overnight in refrigerator. Remove the tea bags, squeezing out the liquid. Add the orange juice. Stir well. To serve, pour into ice-filled tall glasses. Serve with lemon wedges and sugar. Serves 6.

FRUITED ICED TEA

6 tea bags, tags removed
¾ cup sugar (optional, or to taste)
5 cups ice water
½ (6-ounce) can frozen orange juice concentrate, thawed
Juice of 1 lemon
Ice

Pour 2 cups boiling water over the tea bags and steep 5 minutes. Remove the tea bags; squeeze. Stir in the sugar until dissolved, if desired. Stir in the ice water, orange juice concentrate, and lemon juice. Pour over ice in tall glasses or into a pitcher of ice. Serves 8.

SPICED TEA WITH CRANBERRY JUICE

6 tea bags, tags removed
¼ teaspoon nutmeg
¼ teaspoon cinnamon
½ cup sugar (optional, or to taste)
2 cups cranberry juice cocktail
½ cup orange juice
¼ cup lemon juice
Ice

Pour 3 cups boiling water over the tea bags and add the spices; steep 5 minutes. Remove the tea bags; squeeze. Stir in the sugar to taste, if desired, and cool. Add the juices and 1½ cups cold water; chill. Pour into ice-filled tall glasses or an ice-filled pitcher. Serves 4 to 6.

SPICED ICED COFFEE

1 cinnamon stick
4 cloves
4 cups hot strong coffee
Ice
Light cream (optional)
Sugar

Add the cinnamon, cloves, and sugar to the coffee; chill. Remove the spices and pour the coffee into ice-filled tall glasses. Serve with cream, if you wish, and sugar on the side. Serves 4.

Menus

Dinner Menus

TO SERVE 4

Melon and Prosciutto
Pasta with Yogurt-Anchovy Sauce
Green Beans
Berry Pie

Marinated Steak and Vegetables
Pasta-Olive Salad
Melon with Berries

Orange-Grapefruit-Avocado Salad
Chicken with Yogurt
Curried Lentils with Vegetables
Cheese Pie with Rhubarb Glaze

Peach-Plum-Cranberry Soup
Marinated Fish, Spanish Style
Green and Red Pepper Salad
Orange Raisin Nut Cake

Tomato Soup with Dill
Avocado-Seafood Platter
Barley Salad with Vegetables
Crème Fraîche with Strawberries

Blueberry-Orange Soup
Scandinavian Fish Mousse
Dilled Cucumber-Pasta Salad
Strawberry Tart

Stuffed Chicken Rolls
Pesto Primavera Salad
Marinated Tomatoes, Italian Style
Chilled Lemon Soufflé

Salmon Pâté Loaf
French bread
Blueberry-Radish Salad
Almond Cake with Peaches and
    Cream

Onion-Anchovy Pie
Herbed Pork Chops
Summer Squash with Sour Cream
Tomato Halves Stuffed with
    Marinated Cherry Tomatoes
Devil's Food Cake

Grapefruit-Avocado Appetizer
Soy-Sesame Chicken with Pineapple
Rice Salad
Coffee Cheesecake

Crudités
Yogurt Dip
Chicken with Walnut Sauce
Stuffed Lettuce Leaves
Sponge Cake with Strawberries

Walnut-Buttermilk Soup
Turkey-Pineapple Kebabs
Beet Salad with Egg
Sherbet (Lemon or Cranberry)
Nut Crisps

TO SERVE 6

Apple Soup
Braised Pork Shoulder
Peach-Rice Salad (doubled)
Grand Marnier Orange Parfaits

Green Vichyssoise
Pollo Tonnato
Asparagus Vinaigrette
Mocha Mousse with Coffee Sauce

Jellied Chicken Consommé
Turkey Tonnato
Green and Red Pepper Salad
Ambrosia
Date-Nut Bars

Vichyssoise
Chicken Breasts in Aspic
Green Beans and Shallots, Garni
Glazed Peaches with
    Strawberry Cream

Cucumber-Yogurt Soup (doubled)
Chicken-Mushroom-Rice Salad
Tomatoes with Basil
Nectarine Mousse Parfaits (doubled)

Beets Stuffed with Horseradish
Chicken with Apricot Mayonnaise
Green Beans (doubled)
Coconut Cake

TO SERVE 6 TO 8

Chicken Soup with Avocado and
    Lime
Salmon-Shrimp Mold
Green Beans (doubled)
Ladyfinger Ice Cream Cake

Spinach Soup
Duck and Onion Salad
Marinated Zucchini (doubled)
Apple Flan

Tuna Pâté (doubled)
Beef Salad
Rice Pilaf with Vegetables
Apple Flan

Boiled Artichokes—with White Wine–
    Lemon Mayonnaise (doubled)
Salmon-Pasta Salad
Tomato Halves Stuffed with
    Marinated Cherry Tomatoes
Macédoine of Fruits with Madeira

Green Vichyssoise
Brook Trout in Aspic
Cucumbers Stuffed with Peas and
    Beans
Strawberry Tart

Apple Soup
Whole Wheat Pasta with Ham
Tomatoes with Basil
Mocha Parfaits

TO SERVE 8

Grapefruit-Shrimp Appetizer
    (doubled)
Chicken Mousse
Lentil Salad
Summer Fruits with Lime Cream
    Dressing

Asparagus Vinaigrette
Duck and Onion Salad
Brown Rice Salad with Watercress
Pineapple Buttermilk Sherbet

Antipasto Platter (doubled)
Tortellini-Mushroom Salad
Zabaglione

Celery Victor
Salmon-Shrimp Mold
Rice Pilaf with Vegetables
Ambrosia (doubled)

Grapefruit-Avocado Appetizer
    (doubled)
Chicken Curry Mold
Minted Green Pea Salad (doubled)
Vienna Café Cake

Mussel Cocktail
Baked Ham with Cloves
Carrot Salad with Orange
Spanish Cream

Cucumber-Yogurt Soup (doubled)
Roast Beef with Green Sauce
Lentil-Stuffed Tomatoes
Vienna Café Cake

Scandinavian Cherry Soup (doubled)
Ratatouille
Tomato Aspic with Herbs
Devil's Food Cake

Boiled Artichokes—with Green
    French Dressing (doubled)
Chicken Mousse Loaf
Strawberries with Raspberry Sauce

Mussel Cocktail
Cornish Game Hens
Cucumber-Potato Salad (doubled)
Melon with Berries (doubled)

Boiled Artichokes—with Vinaigrette
    with Herbs (doubled)
Pasta with Chicken
Mocha Mousse with Coffee Sauce

Cucumbers Stuffed with Peas
    and Beans
Chicken and Ham with Tarragon
Avocado-Mushroom Pasta (doubled)
Vienna Café Cake

Beet Soup
French Beef Salad
Cucumber in Mustard-Yogurt Sauce
    (doubled)
Coffee Cheesecake

Iced Clam-Tomato Soup
Brown Rice Salad with Chicken
Greek Cheese Pie with Prunes

Watercress-Yogurt Soup
Chinese Pork Roast
Chinese Noodles
Glazed Oranges

TO SERVE 10 TO 12

Cucumbers Stuffed with Peas
    and Beans (doubled)
Ham with Honey-Mustard Glaze
Coleslaw with Parsley (doubled)
Peaches in Raspberry Sauce
    (doubled)

Melon and Prosciutto (doubled)
Ham with Honey-Mustard Glaze
Brown Rice Salad with Watercress
Grand Marnier Orange Parfaits
    (doubled)

Luncheon Menus

Served with appropriate bread, toast, or crackers.

TO SERVE 4

Ham-and-Herb-Stuffed Artichokes
Avocado-Mushroom Pasta
Ambrosia

Salade Niçoise
Pumpkin Pie

Chicken with Vegetables Vinaigrette
Baked Custard
Lace Cookies

Fresh Dilled Carrot Soup
Fish-Potato Salad
Cucumber in Mustard-Yogurt Sauce
Ladyfingers with Pineapple-Lemon
   Cream

Grapefruit-Shrimp Appetizer
Ham Salad with Hazelnuts
Rhubarb Whip
Lace Cookies

Asparagus Vinaigrette
Crab Salad
Raspberry-Nut Roll

Gazpacho from Madrid
Creamy Chicken Salad with
   Nectarines
Brownies

Chicken-Pineapple Rolls
Grapefruit-Banana-Celery Salad
Oatmeal and Apple Butter Bars

Stuffed Mushrooms
Sunset Salad with Lorenzo Dressing
Baked Custard
Thumbkins

Salmon-Pasta Salad
Macédoine of Fruits with Madeira
Meringue Kisses

Asparagus Vinaigrette
Roast Beef Salad Plate
Chilled Lemon Soufflé

Ham-and-Herb-Stuffed Artichokes
Pasta with Yogurt-Anchovy Sauce
Pecan Tart

Cream of Cucumber Soup
Turkey-Pineapple Kebabs
Green salad
Butterscotch Brownies

TO SERVE 6

Chicken Liver Mousse Pâté
Tomato Aspic Ring with
   Chicken Salad
Berry Pie

Tomato and Green Pepper Soup
Ecuadorian Stuffed Avocados
Cinnamon Cheesecake

Cottage Cheese–Spinach Pie
Mushroom-Endive Salad
Orange Yogurt Sherbet
Lace Cookies

Melon and Prosciutto
Italian Tuna Pie
Jellied Zabaglione

Crudités
Yogurt Dip
Brown Rice Salad with Watercress
Baked Apples with Maple Syrup

Gazpacho from Madrid
Cold cuts (sliced roast beef, ham,
    etc.)
Chive Sauce and/or Avocado Dressing
Lemon Sherbet
Banana-Pecan Squares

Cucumber-Yogurt Soup (doubled)
Chef's Salad II
Glazed Oranges
Meringue Kisses

Jellied Tomato-Chicken Consommé
Shrimp-Fruit Salad in Cantaloupe
Ladyfinger Ice Cream Cake

Heros
Mixed Greens Salad Bowl with Beets
Cranberry-Pear Crisp

Cream of Mushroom Soup I
Shrimp Salad
Peach-Blueberry Shortcake

Celery Stuffed with Olives and Nuts
Spinach Quiche
Rhubarb Whip
Nut Crisps

Zucchini-Pepper Pie
Brussels Sprouts Salad (doubled)
Chocolate Whole Wheat Brownies

Tomato Soup with Dill
Shrimp-Fruit Salad in Cantaloupe
Brownies

Curry Lamb Loaf
Armenian Green Beans (doubled)
Herbed New Potato Salad
Cranberry Sherbet

Curried Chicken-Rice Salad
Orange-Grapefruit-Avocado Salad
Thumbkins

Tomato Soup with Shrimp
Onion-Cheese Quiche
Marinated Vegetable Salad
Baked Apples with Maple Syrup

Ham-Chutney-Rice Salad with
    Plums
Tomatoes in Curry Marinade
    (doubled)
Orange Slices with Cranberry Sauce

Jellied Chicken Consommé
Turkey Club Sandwiches
Ambrosia

Fish Salad Lorenzo
Broccoli and Bermuda Onion Salad
Orange-Raisin-Nut Cake

Chick-Pea Dip
Whole wheat pita bread
Spinach Salad with Sesame Seeds
Orange Yogurt Sherbet

TO SERVE 8

Cream of Mushroom Soup II
Chef's Salad I
Poached Pears (doubled)
Lace Cookies

Lentil-Stuffed Tomatoes
Sausage Rolls
Fresh fruit

Cornish Game Hens
Greek Salad (doubled)
Ladyfinger Ice Cream Cake

Spicy Cauliflower
Mediterranean Fish-Rice Salad
Jellied Orange-Cheese Pie with
    Strawberries

Curried Cream of Corn Soup
    (doubled)
Fish Salad in Tomato Aspic
Mocha Parfaits

Luncheon Platter
Okra with Lemon (doubled)
Nesselrode Pie

Gazpacho from Madrid
Chicken Curry Mold
Almond Cake with Peaches
    and Cream

Picnic Basket

Crudités, with Yogurt Dip:
    Green peppers
    Radishes
    Carrots
    Celery
    Turnips or kohlrabi
    Fennel
    Cherry tomatoes
    Cauliflowerets
    Thin green asparagus
Celery Stuffed with Olives and Nuts
Boiled Artichokes
Asparagus Vinaigrette
Finger sandwiches
Deviled Eggs
Cornish Game Hens

Buttered French bread
Beef Salad (any)
Salads (choose any two):
    Green Beans
    Coleslaw with Parsley
    Marinated Vegetable Salad
    Brown Rice Salad with
        Watercress
    Herbed New Potato Salad
        (or other)
    Cracked Wheat Salad I
Melon and Prosciutto
Fruit Salad
Fruits and cheeses (arranged)
Cookies
Devil's Food Cake

Putting It All Together

Delicious, well-balanced meals are a result of planning and skillful shopping. Some hints and suggestions follow on how to take advantage of what's in season. Be venturesome—try a new herb or spice, try an unfamiliar vegetable or fruit, and your favorite dish may surprise you with a new texture or flavor.

On Using Herbs and Spices

When trying a new herb, crush some in the palm of your hand, let it warm a moment or two, then sniff and taste it, to get an idea of how it will taste when used in cooking.

Start with a light touch—more can be added, but it's very difficult to correct overseasoning. Use only a few herbs or spices in each dish—too many will fight or cancel each other out. Also, do not use the same flavor in several dishes at one meal. If you have no recipe, use about ¼ teaspoon dried herb or spice per pound of meat or pint of liquid. When dried herbs are used, allow about one quarter the amount you would usually need of fresh herbs, since the flavor in dried herbs is more concentrated. Many fresh herbs are easy to grow in a kitchen window, for instance, chives, thyme, rosemary, dill, and tarragon (be sure to get the French tarragon, as the Russian tarragon is less flavorful and tends to be bitter). Fresh herbs are much better than dried.

It's generally best to add crushed or ground herbs and spices to long-cooking foods near the end of cooking, but to add whole spices or seeds, such as peppercorns and cloves, at the beginning to fully flavor the dish. When adding herbs and spices to foods that will not be cooked, it's usually better to add them a few hours before serving so flavors have time to release and blend.

To store, place herbs and spices in airtight containers (preferably glass) in a cool, dark, dry place. Try to buy them while they still have their full flavor and aroma. It's best to buy from a store that has a rapid turnover, since flavors gradually deteriorate during long storage. Whole spices and seeds keep the longest, followed by ground spices. Leaf herbs are the most fragile; they deteriorate after a year of storage.

When freezing dishes with herbs and/or spices, remember that freezing destroys much of the flavor, so taste after removing from the freezer and add more seasoning if necessary. (A few seasonings increase in flavor strength when frozen, among them garlic, green pepper, cloves, and black pepper.)

HERBS AND SPICES

NAME	FORM	FLAVOR	USE
Allspice	Whole or ground	Blend (in flavor) of cloves, nutmeg, cinnamon	Fruits, baked desserts, cold meats, potatoes, eggplant
Anise	Whole seed or ground	Licorice	Coffee cakes, rolls, cookies, salads, vegetables, stews, sauces
Basil (sweet)	Leaf, fresh or dried	Sweet, with pungent spicy tang	Soups, vegetables (especially tomatoes, eggplant, zucchini), salads, pasta, poultry, cold meats, eggs
Bay leaves (Mediterranean bay leaf is more flavorful than Californian)	Dried whole leaf	Aromatic, pungent	Marinades, pickling, meat, fish, soups, stews, vegetables, bouquet garni, cooked salads
Caraway seed	Whole	Pungent, intense	Rye bread, cabbage (sauerkraut), soups, meats, vegetables (especially carrots), cheese, fish
Cardamom	Pod containing seeds or ground seeds	Pungent, aromatic, a bit peppery (belongs to the ginger family)	Baked desserts, Middle Eastern salads, cold meats, chicken, curries
Cayenne pepper (hot red pepper)	Ground	Very hot, peppery	Meats, fish, sauces, vegetables, cheese dishes
Chervil	Leaf, fresh or dried (feathery leaf)	Warm, dry, spicy (for an herb), slightly anise-flavored	Eggs, winter squash, soups, salads, dried beans, fish and shellfish, chicken, vegetables (especially carrots, potatoes, green beans), salad dressings

NAME	FORM	FLAVOR	USE
Chives	Leaf, fresh or frozen	Fresh and delicate onion flavor	Soups, dips, salads, vegetables (especially cucumbers, peas, squash, tomatoes)
Cinnamon	Stick or ground	Pungent, warm, and sweet	Cookies, cakes, puddings (especially good with chocolate desserts), fruit, iced tea and coffee
Cloves	Whole or ground	Strong, pungent, and sweet	Ham, tongue, meats, pickled vegetables such as beets, fruits, desserts
Coriander	Seed, whole or ground	Fragrant, peppery	Vegetables (especially beets), curries, salads, chicken, pork, lamb, stewed fruits
	Leaf, fresh (cilantro)	Cool green taste, slightly spicy	Salads, vegetables, soups, meats, chicken, sauces (added at last minute); may be used in place of parsley (has stronger flavor)
Cumin seed	Whole or ground	Strong, hot taste, slightly sharp	Meats, vegetables (especially eggplant, tomatoes, green beans), poultry, cheese, seafood, curries
Dillseed	Whole	Dry, aromatic, with faint tinge of caraway	Salads (especially potato), vegetables (including beets, avocados, cucumbers), sauces, meats, poultry, fish, shellfish
Dillweed	Whole leaf, fresh or dried	Cool, sharp taste, slightly sweet, with faint caraway taste	Salads (especially cucumber, seafood, potato), soups, vegetables, dips, fish, poultry, pickles
Fennel (for leaf, fresh, *see under* Dillweed—similar taste)	Seed, whole	Sweet, aromatic taste, slightly resembling anise	Soups, apples, fish, pork, salads, cabbage, peas, beans

NAME	FORM	FLAVOR	USE
Ginger	Dried, whole or ground; fresh whole root	Spicy, slightly hot, pungent	Baked desserts, poultry, fruits, vegetables (especially beans), salad dressings, fish and shellfish
Mace	Ground	Intense, similar to nutmeg (outer shell of nutmeg) —use sparingly	Soups, baked desserts, seafood, vegetables (especially green beans), fruit, salads
Marjoram	Leaf, fresh or dried	Aromatic, slightly bitter undertone	Egg dishes, soups, pâtés, vegetables (especially spinach, carrots, corn, eggplant), lamb
Mint	Leaf, fresh or dried	Fresh, clean, cool, sweet taste	Fish, lamb, soups, vegetables (especially cucumbers, peas, potatoes, carrots, mushrooms), salads, ices, fruits, cold beverages
Mustard	Seed, dried, whole or ground; prepared	Hot, dry, and pungent	Chicken, meats, fish, sauces, salad dressings, cheese, vegetables, dried beans, marinades, pickling
(Dijon style: use three times as much as dried)			
Nutmeg	Whole or ground	Warm, sweet, and spicy	Baked desserts, sauces, soups, vegetables (especially spinach, cauliflower, green beans), winter squash, meats
Oregano (wild marjoram)	Leaf, fresh or dried	Strong, slightly bitter	Italian food, meat, vegetables (especially tomatoes, zucchini), marinades, salads, eggs, fish
Paprika (Hungarian is best)	Ground	Dry, slightly spicy, with peppery, bitter undertones	Soups, chicken, meats, eggs, vegetables, salads, salad dressings, garnish

NAME	FORM	FLAVOR	USE
Parsley	Leaf, fresh (preferably) or dried (Italian broadleaf has a slightly stronger flavor)	Green, pleasant taste	Garnish, soups, salads, fish, shellfish, vegetables, bouquet garni (practically everything savory)
Pepper (black, white, or green)	Whole or ground	Hot, biting, pungent	Soups, vegetables, meats, salads, salad dressings, marinades
Poppy seed	Whole	Nutlike flavor	Salad dressings, breads, baked desserts
Rosemary	Leaf, fresh or dry	Fragrant, slightly sweet, slightly bitter, reminiscent of pine needles—do not overuse	Soups, fish and seafood, sausage, game, salads, meats (particularly good with lamb), vegetables (especially peas, corn, zucchini, spinach), egg dishes, chicken
Saffron	Threads, whole or ground	Sweet, aromatic (if overused, will become too pungent)	Soups, rice, fish, curries, poultry
Sage	Leaf, fresh or dried whole or ground	Aromatic, slightly bitter —do not overuse	Pork, pea soups, chicken, fish, sausage, salad dressings, cheese
Savory (summer or winter)	Leaf, fresh or dried whole or ground	Aromatic, peppery	Meats, poultry, soups, stews, salads, vegetables (especially beans, tomatoes, zucchini, cucumbers), sauces
Tarragon	Leaf, fresh or dried	Sweet, slightly anise flavor	Salads, salad dressings, meats, poultry, fish, seafood, mayonnaise, vegetables (especially tomatoes, avocados, broccoli, summer and winter squash), egg dishes

NAME	FORM	FLAVOR	USE
Thyme	Leaf, fresh or dried whole or ground	Aromatic, pungent, strong flavor—use rather sparingly	Soups, meats, poultry, fish, vegetables (especially carrots, eggplant, tomatoes, dried beans, green beans), salads, aspics, bouquet garni
Turmeric	Ground	Sweet, delicately spicy	Curries, rice, fish, poultry, vegetables (especially green beans)

SOME SPICE AND HERB COMBINATIONS:

Apple pie spice: mostly cinnamon, with some cloves, allspice, ginger, and nutmeg or mace

Bouquet garni: parsley, bay leaf, and thyme, sometimes celery leaves or garlic

Chili powder: chili peppers, cumin, oregano, garlic powder, and salt; sometimes allspice and cloves added

Curry powder: blend of up to 16 or 20 spices, usually including turmeric, coriander seed, cloves, black and red peppers, cumin, mace, ginger

Fines herbes: chervil, parsley, marjoram, savory, thyme; sometimes include oregano, sage, basil, or rosemary

Poultry seasoning: sage, thyme, marjoram, savory, tarragon or chervil, sometimes rosemary

Pumpkin pie seasoning: cinnamon, cloves, ginger, and nutmeg (also good sprinkled on vanilla ice cream)

Shrimp spice: usually includes peppercorns, red peppers, bay leaf, allspice, mustard, dillseed, cloves, and ginger

Cheese

Cheeses should be individually wrapped in plastic or foil and stored in the refrigerator. For best flavor, take cheese out of the refrigerator several hours before serving. If hard cheese begins to get too dry, wrap it in a cloth dampened with vinegar, wine, or water, and cover with plastic wrap.

Cheese may be frozen for up to eight weeks. Thaw the cheese overnight in the refrigerator and use within a day or two.

Cheese has a particular affinity with fresh fruit—some examples:

> Pont l'Évêque with pears
> Bel Paese with fresh figs
> Blue or Roquefort with pears
> Port Salut with apples
> Stilton with plums
> Edam with honeydew
> Swiss with oranges or tangerines
> Camembert with plums or grapes
> Brie with pears or apples

CHEESE TYPES

ALOUETTE—Whole milk with cream. An American version of Boursin (and cheaper). Creamy, soft, and white, flavored with herbs or pepper.

ASIAGO—Whole milk; imported Italian asiago made from partly skimmed milk. Dark rind, creamy inside, with a hard, granular texture and tart flavor.

BEL PAESE—Whole milk. A semisoft cheese with a grayish brown rind and light yellow interior. The Italian cheese has a more robust flavor than the American, which is fairly mild.

BLUE—Whole milk. A semisoft, crumbly cheese with a tangy, piquant flavor; white interior with blue veins of mold, which give the characteristic flavor. The flavor gets stronger with age—the more blue, the stronger the taste. The American, Canadian, or Danish version of Roquefort.

BRIE—Whole milk. A French cheese with an edible tan crust and a creamy yellow inside. When ripe, the cheese is soft, with a fine, delicate flavor, which becomes more pungent with age. COULOM-MIERS is a smaller, nuttier Brie. Serve at room temperature.

CACCIOCAVALLO—Whole milk. An Italian cheese with a light brown, glossy surface and yellowish white interior. A firm cheese, slightly salty, with a smoky overtaste. May be grated when old and dry. (An Eastern European version, called KASHKAVAL, is made with part sheep's milk and comes from Bulgaria or Romania.)

CAMEMBERT—Whole milk. A French cheese with an edible gray-white crust and a soft, creamy interior that becomes slightly softer when ripe. Do not refrigerate until the cheese ripens to its proper con-sistency. Its flavor is full but mild, changing to pungency as it becomes older. Serve at room temperature.

CHANTELLE—Whole milk. Red, waxed surface with a yellow interior; a firm, mild-flavored cheese.

CHEDDAR—Whole milk. Black, red, or yellow-brown surface, with a white to deep orange interior. A firm cheese, mild-flavored when young, sharper the longer it is cured and aged. English Cheddar is usually a little drier and can be milder than the American. Keeps well.

CHESHIRE—Whole milk. Yellow rind, creamy to deep yellow interior. This is a firm English cheese, but more crumbly than Cheddar. The flavor becomes sharper with age.

COLBY—Whole milk. A mild English cheese, with a deep yellow color. Softer than a Cheddar because it contains more moisture.

COTTAGE CHEESE—Skim milk with cream and salt added. A soft, white cheese with a pleasant tart flavor. Skim-milk cottage cheese has no cream added. POT cheese is a form with a larger, drier curd. RICOTTA is a sweeter cottage cheese, soft and runny, with a light, fresh taste.

CREAM CHEESE—Whole milk and cream. A soft, white, smooth cheese with a delicate taste. Try to find fresh cream cheese without vegetable gum added, but if this is unavailable, mixing a little sour cream in with the cream cheese improves the flavor.

EDAM—Partly skim milk. Red waxy surface with a semisoft to hard yellowish interior, sometimes with small holes. A mellow-flavored cheese from the Netherlands with a nutlike flavor.

FETA—Sheep's milk. White, soft, salty cheese with a sharp, tangy flavor. Originally from Greece.

FONTINA—Whole milk; may be part sheep's milk. A slightly yellow cheese with an oiled surface; semisoft to hard in consistency. The

Italian cheese is much superior to the Danish or American and has a delicate, almost nutty flavor.

GAMMELÖST—Skim milk, soured. A golden brown Norwegian cheese, firm to hard, with a tart flavor.

GORGONZOLA—Whole milk. This Italian cheese has a clay-colored surface and a creamy white interior with blue veins, and a semisoft texture. Its distinctive flavor is tangy, almost peppery, and strong, although not as strong as it smells. It is likely to become crumbly when imported.

GOUDA—Whole or partly skimmed milk. Gouda is made in the Netherlands and in the United States; it has a red or yellow rind, a semisoft to hard yellow interior, and a mellow, full flavor. Similar to Edam.

GRUYÈRE—Whole milk. A light yellow, fine-grained cheese with small holes and a mellow, nutty flavor. It is made in Switzerland, Austria, and France. The American version is a bland, processed cheese.

LIEDERKRANZ—Whole milk. A pale orange surface, creamy inside, with a soft, robust flavor. A great American cheese.

LIMBURGER—Whole milk. A reddish or grayish brown surface, depending on whether it comes from Belgium or the United States, with a creamy white interior. Semisoft, with a full, strong, aromatic taste.

MONTEREY JACK—Whole or partly skimmed milk. A mild, semisoft cheese, excellent for melting.

MORBIER—Whole milk. A French cheese with a light brown, mottled rind, and a pale yellowish white interior, streaked with gray from the soot used in the processing. It is semisoft, and the full, smoky flavor gets stronger with age.

MOZZARELLA—Whole or partly skimmed milk. A firm, elastic white cheese, made in Italy and the United States, with a mild, milky flavor. Also comes with a smoked, edible surface. This cheese gets harder with age.

MUENSTER—Whole milk. A yellowish tan surface with a pale yellow interior and many small holes. A mild, semisoft cheese, which sometimes comes with caraway or anise seeds.

PARMESAN—Partly skimmed milk. Black or dark green rind, whitish interior, with a hard, granular texture. The flavor is pungent and slightly salty and gets stronger with age. Imported Italian Parmesan is superior to American. Keep well wrapped to avoid drying. Aged Parmesan is usually grated; often served with pasta.

PETIT SUISSE—Whole milk with cream. A soft, rich French cream cheese with a slight tartness.

PONT L'ÉVÊQUE—Whole or slightly skimmed milk. A French cheese, yellow, semisoft, and medium strong, with a slightly sweet taste.

PORT SALUT—Whole or partly skimmed milk. A French cheese with a russet surface with a creamy yellow interior, smooth and elastic. When properly aged, it is mild, but with an interesting flavor.

PROVOLONE—Whole milk. A brown, hard rind, with a yellowish hard interior, and a salty, smoky flavor. Originally from Italy; also made in the United States.

REGGIANO—Whole milk. An Italian cheese, very hard and granular, similar to Parmesan.

RICOTTA—Whey. A soft, creamy cheese with a fresh, sweet flavor. Made in Italy and the United States.

ROMANO—Partly skimmed cow's, goat's, or sheep's milk. A firm Italian or American cheese similar to Parmesan.

ROQUEFORT—Sheep's milk. A French cheese with a semisoft white interior with bluish green veins; tangy, with a slightly sweet undertone, this cheese becomes stronger with age. When imported it becomes crumbly.

SAGE—Whole or partly skimmed milk. A firm to hard cheese, with a pale yellow interior with green flecks (of sage or sage extract). An English or American cheese with a mellow flavor.

SAINT-ANDRÉ—Whole milk with cream. A French triple-cream cheese, very soft, with a full, rich flavor and a delicate tanginess.

SAMSÖE—Whole milk. A semihard Danish cheese with a mild, nutty flavor, slightly sweet.

SAPSAGO—Skim milk, slightly soured. A small, light green, hard cheese with a pungent flavor. Powdered clover leaves give it its flavor. Originally from Switzerland.

STILTON—Whole milk. A crumbly English cheese, creamy-colored, with blue-green veins and a wrinkled surface. This is a milder cheese than the French Roquefort, with a rich, sharp flavor.

SWISS—Whole milk. A firm, pale yellow cheese with holes that vary in size, developing as the cheese ripens. It has a delicate, sweet, nutty flavor and is much used in salads and sandwiches. Swiss cheese from Switzerland is also called Emmental; Swiss cheese is made as well in Austria, Finland, and the United States. The Norwegian Jarlsberg looks like Swiss cheese but tastes quite different—bland and buttery.

TILSIT—Whole or skim milk. A medium-firm cheese, creamy yellow, with a medium-sharp taste. Originally from Germany, it is also made in the United States.

VACHERIN—Whole milk. This aromatic French cheese has a firm rind and a soft interior. Like many cheeses, it becomes softer and tangier with age.

Fruits and Vegetables

When buying fruits, select firm, brightly colored fruits with a fresh appearance. Carefully examine prepackaged fruits to make sure that each piece is of good quality. Before you store fruit, it's a good idea to throw out or separate any that are badly bruised or moldy.

Do not wash fruits before refrigerating, since this increases the chance of spoilage. Fruits are better kept at room temperature (ripening fruits should be kept out of direct sunlight).

Fruits will ripen quickly in a paper bag, twisted shut, at room temperature. Don't store fruit too close together. Fruit will last a few days at room temperature and up to two weeks in the refrigerator, and may be frozen up to three months.

FRUITS

FRUIT	PEAK AVAILABILITY	SHOPPING HINTS
Apples	Year round; at their best in fall and winter	Look for firm, well-colored apples; avoid overripe or mealy fruit, or ones with brown, bruised areas.
Apricots	May–September	Look for uniform color; should be slightly soft—avoid both the underripe firm pale yellow or green ones and the overly ripe, mushy ones.
Avocados	Year round	Ripen at room temperature 2 to 3 days; should yield to pressure; avoid ones with large mushy dents or large black spots or bruises.
Bananas	Year round	Avoid bruised bananas. Let ripen at room temperature; bananas will last longer in the refrigerator; the peel will blacken, but the interior will stay fresh.
Berries:		
Blackberries	July–August	(same as raspberries)
Blueberries	Summer months; peak in July–August	Plump berries with full skin; avoid shriveled, leaking, or moldy berries or too many green berries.
Cranberries	Year round frozen; fresh: peak in fall	Plump berries—avoid shriveled ones.
Raspberries	Summer and early fall	If possible, check bottom of boxes for mold, green berries, or crushed, leaky berries. Unwrap and sort before storing.

FRUIT	PEAK AVAILABILITY	SHOPPING HINTS
Strawberries	Year round; peak: May–June	Berries should have rich red color, firm flesh, with stem attached. Avoid berries with light, discolored areas or large soft spots. If possible, check the bottom of the box for moldy or green berries. Wash under cold running water before hulling, but do not soak in water.
Cherries	May–September	Choose dark, glossy cherries with firm flesh—avoid both pale, unripe cherries and shriveled, overripe ones.
Figs	Summer	Choose soft (but not overly), slightly purplish fruits with no bruises.
Grapefruit	Year round; peak: January–May	Look for firm, heavy fruit with thin skin. Grapefruit is ready to eat when it's picked, so it doesn't usually arrive in markets unripe.
Grapes	Year round	Choose well-colored, plump grapes. Avoid soft, wrinkled, or discolored ones. Rinse just before serving; do not wash before storing in refrigerator.
Kiwis	Year round	Choose firm fruit without bruises, soft spots, or fermenting odor; let ripen a few days at room temperature.
Lemons	Year round	Choose smooth, glossy, thin-skinned lemons; avoid too soft or dried, shriveled ones, and ones with thick, hard skin.
Limes	Year round	Look for shiny, glossy fruit; avoid ones with hard, dry skin, mold, or punctures.

FRUIT	PEAK AVAILABILITY	SHOPPING HINTS
Mangoes	May–August	Should be soft, without black spots. Keep at room temperature until ripe, then refrigerate until ready to use.
Melons:		
Cantaloupe	Year round; peak: May–September	Skin color should be pale yellow, not green; the stem end should yield to pressure in a ripe melon, and the melon should have a full, fragrant aroma; avoid melons with large bruised areas. Ripen, if necessary, at room temperature a few days before serving. Chill only 3 to 4 hours before serving, if at all.
Casaba	July–November	Pumpkin-shaped, golden-yellow rind with shallow furrows; a slight softening at stem end (but no smell) indicates a ripe fruit.
Cranshaw	August–September	Rounded at both ends, with shallow furrows in the rind; the rind is a deep golden yellow, smooth. Surface yields slightly to pressure; has a pleasant aroma.
Honeydew	Year round; peak: July–October	White to creamy yellow smooth rind; ripe honeydew has a slightly sticky surface and full, translucent green flesh.
Persian	August–September	Similar to cantaloupe, but larger, with a finer rind.
Watermelon	May–September	Look for halves with a deep red color; avoid those with pale, dry, or mealy flesh.

FRUIT	PEAK AVAILABILITY	SHOPPING HINTS
Nectarines	June–September	Look for brightly colored fruit with a slight softening at the "seam"; avoid those with soft spots and ones that are shriveled or overripe; allow two to three days at room temperature for full ripening.
Oranges	Year round	Look for heavy, thin-skinned fruit; avoid thick-skinned oranges, and ones with soft spots, dents, or punctures.
Papayas	May–June and October–December	Green papayas will not ripen unless they have a yellow tinge at the larger end; avoid those with black spots.
Peaches	June–September	Firm but should yield to pressure, with yellow or creamy color and red markings; avoid really green ones—they won't ripen; avoid any that are overripe or have big bruises or the tan spot that marks decay. Ripe peaches have a strong fragrance.
Pears	A number of varieties at different times of the year	Avoid firm fruit with a softening near the stem—these will not ripen; avoid mushy, discolored fruit.
Persimmons	October–February	Buy firm fruit, orange in color with stem still attached; ripen at room temperature.
Pineapples	Year round; peak: April–May	Choose fruit that is pale yellow, with strong, characteristic aroma; a leaf from the top should pull away easily; avoid bruised fruit, as the decay will spread rapidly.

FRUIT	PEAK AVAILABILITY	SHOPPING HINTS
Plums	June–October	Choose plump, deep-colored fruit (except the greengage plum, which is a greenish yellow); ripen at room temperature a few days. Avoid oversoft or bruised fruit, or fruit with broken skin.
Tangerines	November–March	Choose fruit with a deep color and a glossy pebbly or smooth skin.

VEGETABLES

VEGETABLE	PEAK AVAILABILITY	SHOPPING HINTS
Artichokes	Year round	Check base for worm injury; inner part should be green and fresh, though the outer leaves may have brownish streaks; artichokes should have compact, tight leaves.
Asparagus	Year round; peak: April–June	Choose bright green stalks with tightly closed tips; avoid dry or wilted-looking stalks; best to store in refrigerator upright in water; try to buy stalks of uniform size.
Beans, green	Year round	Look for clean, crisp, bright green beans—they should snap when bent. Wash beans before refrigerating, which will help keep them moist and fresh.

VEGETABLE	PEAK AVAILABILITY	SHOPPING HINTS
Bean sprouts	Year round	Look for crisp, white sprouts, without brown; store in water in refrigerator.
Beets	Year round; peak: June–July	Choose small to medium beets (large tend to be woody), firm, and with a deep red color; avoid flabby, shriveled ones. Store in a plastic bag in refrigerator.
Broccoli	Year round	Choose firm, compact clusters of small flower buds, evenly colored and dark green or green with a purplish tinge; avoid dried stems and large, open heads of flowerets. Store in refrigerator.
Brussels sprouts	August–May	Look for bright green sprouts, closed, free of brown spots and bruises and of wilted, loose leaves; store in refrigerator.
Cabbages	Year round	Choose fresh, firm heavy heads without too many loose outer leaves. Wrap in plastic bag and refrigerate.
Carrots	Year round	Choose smooth, firm, well-colored carrots; refrigerate in plastic bag.
Cauliflowers	Year round; peak: September–June	Choose smaller head, white, compact, and clean-looking; avoid any clusters with brown spots or discoloring. Wrap in plastic and refrigerate.
Celeriac (knob celery)	October–April	Choose firm, brown, apple-sized knobs.
Celery	Year round	Choose fresh, crisp, smooth stalks; avoid wilted or limp celery with brown spots. Refrigerate in plastic bag.

VEGETABLE	PEAK AVAILABILITY	SHOPPING HINTS
Corn	May–October	Husks should be fresh green and not dried and withered; check for worms and insect damage and be sure the kernels are plump and medium yellow; refrigerate.
Cucumbers	Year round	Look for cucumbers with a good green color, firm, and without dried furrows or softening; avoid ones with shriveled ends; refrigerate.
Eggplants	Year round	Choose eggplants with a shiny deep purple skin, firm and without soft spots or discolorations; refrigerate.
Endive	October–May	Choose firm, medium-sized endive, well bleached. Do not wash, as water soaking makes them very bitter—just wipe with damp paper towels; refrigerate in plastic bag.
Fennel	October–March	Choose crisp, fresh bulbs; avoid limp stalks; refrigerate.
Garlic	Year round	Choose large, firm white heads; avoid those with soft or shriveled cloves. Store in a cool, dry place.
Kohlrabi	May–December; peak: June–July	Choose small to medium bulbs with fresh tops and rind that gives to pressure of nail; avoid large, woody bulbs; refrigerate in plastic bag.
Leeks and Scallions	Year round	Look for bulbs of the same size, with bright green tops; avoid yellowed, withered, or discolored ones; refrigerate in plastic bag.

VEGETABLE	PEAK AVAILABILITY	SHOPPING HINTS
Lettuces	Year round (various types)	Choose fresh, bright greens; avoid wilted, limp, or brown-spotted lettuce; refrigerate in plastic bag.
Mushrooms	Year round	Choose small, plump mushrooms, closed or only moderately opened; avoid large, woody, wide-open ones with dark gills. Wipe with damp paper towels—do not soak in water. Do not wash before refrigerating. Mushrooms may be refrigerated 1–2 days.
Onions	Year round	Choose firm, dry onions without soft spots; store in cool, dry place.
Parsnips	Year round	Avoid wilted, soft ones, and those with large, coarse roots; store in refrigerator.
Peas	Year round; peak March–August	Look for small glossy pods with a fresh green color; refrigerate.
Peppers, Bell, green and red	Year round	Choose well-colored, firm, glossy peppers; avoid those with punctures and ones that are flabby or wilted or have a pronounced rotten odor; refrigerate.
Potatoes	Year round	Choose firm, dry potatoes, without sprouted eyes or soft spots; store in cool, dry, well-aerated place.
Pumpkin	Fall	Choose small, eating pumpkins for best flavor; avoid pumpkins with soft or blackened patches or with rotten smell.

VEGETABLE	PEAK AVAILABILITY	SHOPPING HINTS
Radishes	Year round	Choose small radishes with tops attached; they should look fresh, not limp; refrigerate in plastic bag.
Rhubarb	March–June	Choose firm, shiny stems with plenty of pink to red color; avoid large, thick, pale green stems; refrigerate in plastic bag.
Snow Peas	Year round	Look for fresh, bright green pods with small bumps (peas).
Spinach	Year round	Choose young tender leaves with an even dark green color and no blemishes; refrigerate in plastic bag.
Sugar Peas	June-July	Crisp, bright green.
Squash:		
Summer	Year round	Choose firm, bright yellow squash; avoid ones that have become slightly limp or ones with too many spots or cuts; refrigerate.
Winter	Year round; peak: August–March	These are harvested when ripe, so just choose ones without large blemishes; keep in a cool, dry place.
Zucchini	Year round	Choose firm, deep green zucchini, small to medium-sized; avoid ones that are limp or have soft spots; refrigerate.
Sweet Potatoes/ Yams	Year round	Look for firm potatoes, with unshriveled skins.
Tomatoes	Year round; peak: July–October	Choose tomatoes with an overall rich color and slight softness; may be ripened in a warm, dark place; refrigerate when ripe.

VEGETABLE	PEAK AVAILABILITY	SHOPPING HINTS
Turnips	October–March	Choose small to medium-sized smooth, firm turnips; refrigerate.
Watercress	Year round	Choose very crisp bright to deep green bunches; avoid wilted or tired-looking bunches; store with stems in water in refrigerator.

Index